Spanish in the United States: Sociolinguistic Issues

John J. Bergen
Editor

T0346347

Georgetown University Press, Washington, D.C.

Library of Congress Cataloging-in-Publication Data

Spanish in the United States : sociolinguistic issues / John J.
  Bergen, editor.
        p.   cm.
      Papers from the Seventh Conference on el Español en los Estados
  Unidos, held Oct. 24-25, 1986 at the University of New Mexico.
      ISBN 0-87840-232-2
      1. Spanish language--Dialects--United States--Congresses.
  2. Spanish language--Social aspects--United States--Congresses.
  3. Spanish language--Study and teaching--United States--Congresses.
  I. Bergen, John J.   II. Conference on el Español en los Estados
  Unidos (7th : 1986 : University of New Mexico)
  PC4826.S65 1990
306.4'4'08968073--dc20   90-32166
                                                             CIP

To Karen

Contents

3. Language pedagogy

4. Language policy

Introduction

The Seventh Conference on *El español en los Estados Unidos* was held at the University of New Mexico in Albuquerque, October 24-25, 1986. That conference was a continuation within a series initiated in 1980 by Professors Lucía Elías-Olivares and David Nasjleti, the aim being to provide an annual forum for discussion on research on the varieties of Spanish spoken in the United States.

Twenty-four papers were presented at the conference. Given the unique site in which the conference was held, it is not surprising that the majority of the studies focused upon the Spanish of the Southwest. Nevertheless, there were also presentations dealing with the use of Spanish in other regions of the country--New York, New Jersey, Florida, Louisiana, Iowa, and Indiana. From those many excellent papers I have selected fifteen for inclusion in this volume.

Each presents an informative aspect of a variety of Spanish spoken in this country or of a social issue related to such a variety. The issues examined cover a broad perspective within the theme suggested by the title of this book. That is, among the studies are those which have a more general linguistic and sociolinguistic orientation (such as language maintenance, syntactic variation, and lexicography), others which deal with the sociology of language (namely, language use and language teaching), and still others which are concerned with purely humanitarian issues (specifically, the socioeconomic, political, and cultural aspects related to the use of Spanish in our society).

The book begins with John Lipski's survey of the survival of the rather unknown archaic and almost obsolete variety of Mexican Spanish called Sabine River Spanish, which is spoken in eastern Texas and adjacent areas in Louisiana. The next paper discusses the syntax of better known home varieties. June Jaramillo describes the use of *tú* and *usted* among Spanish-speakers in Tomé, New Mexico, in respect to two contextual factors--domain of interaction and domain relationship. Two studies derive from the ongoing research program directed by Silva-Corvalán on the Spanish spoken in East Los Angeles, California. In one of these, Francisco Ocampo documents the progressive loss of the subjunctive mode through three generations of speakers of this dialect. In the other, Manuel Gutiérrez reveals the changes which occur in the use of the various types of subordinate clauses within these same three generations of such Spanish-speakers. Turning attention from syntax to the lexicon, Halvor Clegg and Rob Smead use a type of computer analysis to identify those lexical items in Chicano Spanish which are of Aztec origin.

Among the studies dealing with language use, Nora González and Irene Wherritt point out language use and attitudes within the recently arrived Mexican-American community of food-processing workers and their families in West Liberty, Iowa. Two papers examine code-switching. In the first, Rosa Fernández discusses the psychological, social, and pragmatic reasons which account for code-switching in the speech of an educated speaker of northern New Mexican Spanish and, in doing so, points out that there is often a discrepancy between speakers' professed attitudes toward and reasons for code-switching on one hand, and their actual practice of this linguistic phenomenon on the other. In the other study, Rodolfo Jacobson explains the speaker's preference for one of five possible code-switching strategies as correlated with his or her socioeconomic and personal background. The section on language use concludes with Rosa H. Yáñez's discussion of the syntactic structures, the culturally recognized values, and the language choice(s) in compliments used among Chicano women in the Mesilla Valley of southern New Mexico.

Four papers deal with language pedagogy. In the first, René Cisneros and Elizabeth Leone discuss ways to improve instruction in literacy in English as suggested by their analysis of the motivations of adult Mexicans in San Antonio, Texas, for acquiring such literacy and the strategies which they use to do so. The next two papers deal with the teaching of Spanish to Spanish-speaking students in colleges and universities in the United States. In one of these, Margarita Hidalgo makes recommendations on the methodology and content of such instruction on the basis of an identification of the salient linguistic differences between standard Spanish on one hand, and southwestern and Caribbean varieties spoken in the United States on the other. In the other study, Ana Roca gives methodological and curricular suggestions emanating from her survey on teaching practices used by universities in the Greater Miami area. The final study in this section on language teaching is that by Teresa González-Lee. She describes an innovative program for teaching Spanish to health professionals within the geographically, linguistically, and culturally unique setting at the School of Medicine of the University of California at San Diego.

The final section of the volume presents two papers dealing with language policy in our country. Lourdes Torres refutes the rationales and strategies for the eradication of the use of Spanish in the United States, professed by reactionary groups, through an examination of opposing rationales and strategies for its preservation. The book concludes with a discussion by sociolinguist Ana Celia Zentella on the research role which Spanish linguistics should play in American universities, given the socioeconomic reality of the Spanish-speaking community in the United States.

I wish to extend my gratitude to the twenty-seven scholars whose research efforts made the conference such a success, to the many friends and colleagues at the University of New Mexico whose efforts in organizing and conducting the conference made it such an amicable event, and to the editorial staff of Georgetown University Press for their help in making this volume on *Spanish in the United States* available to the members of our profession.

JOHN J. BERGEN

Albuquerque, New Mexico

Sabine River Spanish: A neglected chapter in Mexican-American dialectology

John M. Lipski
University of Florida

1 The external history of Sabine River Spanish. In addition to the major Spanish-speaking groups in the United States, there exists a number of isolated groups whose use of the Spanish language has virtually no interaction with the remainder of the country's Spanish speakers. One tiny group, whose use of Spanish is now nearing extinction, is found on either side of the Sabine River, in northwestern Louisiana (Sabine and Natchitoches Parishes) and in northeastern Texas (Nacogdoches County), and their Spanish dialect stands in contrast both to the *isleño* dialect of St. Bernard Parish,[1] and to those now current in other parts of Texas, although it is related typologically to the latter.[2] This paper describes the salient characteristics of the Sabine River Spanish dialect, and attempts to situate this speech community in a wider dialectological perspective.[3]

The majority of the Spanish speakers in question are found in northwestern Louisiana, in and around the towns of Zwolle and Noble (Sabine Parish) and in the Spanish Lake community near Robeline (Natchitoches Parish), and in Texas, in the Moral community just to the west of Nacogdoches. Even more so than with the *isleños*, the Spanish language has nearly died out along the Sabine River; the total number of individuals with significant active competence in Spanish is probably no greater than fifty on each side of the state border, with perhaps only half being truly fluent. Apparently, a larger number have some passive competence in Spanish, recognizing words and phrases, but are neither able to sustain a conversation nor even grasp the entirety of spoken Spanish sentences, thus placing them below the level of the 'semispeaker.'[4] All Spanish speakers are among the oldest community residents; the youngest are in their sixties, although a few younger individuals have some Spanish language abilities, while the oldest are over the age of one hundred. As with the *isleños,* the Spanish language died out along the Sabine River in the course of little more than a single generation, largely for the same reasons.

Racially, the Sabine River Spanish speakers present a varied panorama, but, particularly in Louisiana, a significant number are of native-American extraction. The Ebarb residents have largely identified with the Choctaw nation, but historical and linguistic evidence suggests that many descend from natives of Mexican territory. For example, the Aguayo expedition which founded the mission at Los Adaes in 1721 consisted of 117 conscripts, of whom only 44 were Spaniards, the rest being of mixed race.[5] In the Moral community, there is less evidence of racial mixture, and while residents freely acknowledge that many are *trigueños* ('having a dark complexion'), there is no identification with or even awareness of native-American culture.

Curiously, the Sabine River Spanish communities have no lexical items (such as, for example, the term *isleño* as used in St. Bernard Parish) which identify the ethnic Spanish-speaking group, although the term *adaeseño* (a derivative of the traditional *adaesano* 'resident of Los Adaes') has been applied by some investigators[6] to the Spanish Lake dialect, derived from the Spanish settlement of Los Adaes, which was located nearby. Despite incontrovertible linguistic and ethnographic evidence to the contrary, Louisiana residents reject the designation *Mexican/mexicano* and do not identify themselves as descendants of arrivals from Mexican territory. In Moral, on the other hand, the term *mexicano* is freely used, and even the local Spanish dialect is frequently referred to as *mexicano* rather than *español*.

Little accurate information is available to trace the formation of the Sabine River Spanish communities, but such evidence as exists indicates that immigration occurred in several stages for more than half a century.[7] Spain made several attempts to settle eastern Texas and adjoining areas of Louisiana, but it was not until 1716 that missions and then permanent communities were established at Los Aes (San Agustine), Nacogdoches, and subsequently at Los Adaes, near present-day Robeline, Louisiana. These communities prospered, despite general disinterest by the Spanish government and occasional raids by hostile Indians, and by the second half of the eighteenth century the settlements were well established and were indisputably home to all residents. Spain had intended to settle eastern Texas to create a buffer zone against incursions from French Louisiana, particularly the outpost at Natchitoches, but when the Louisiana territory was ceded to Spain in 1762, such a front line was no longer needed, and the Spanish government decided to withdraw all settlers from the troublesome border region. In 1773 the order arrived in eastern Texas to abandon the settlements at Nacogdoches, Los Aes, and Los Adaes within five days, for immediate resettlement in Béxar (San Antonio); despite bitter protests most residents were forced to abandon their homes and crops and make an onerous journey of more than three months to the principal Spanish settlement in Texas. Upon arrival the newcomers were treated poorly, given inferior land, and left to languish; immediately they began planning for a return to the only place they knew as home. Finally, in 1779 and with only reluctant approval by the Spanish authorities, many settlers moved back to eastern Texas, led by Antonio Gil Ybarbo, who founded the town of Nacogdoches in 1779 at the site of the old mission of Nuestra Señora de Guadalupe. It appears, in fact, that many of the original residents, including members of Ybarbo's immediate family (his brother, mother, and sister-in-law), did not leave the region under the 1773 evacuation order, remaining instead in the area surrounding Los Adaes, at Ybarbo's ranch near Los Aes, and in other outlying regions; thus, some sort of continuous Spanish occupation can be postulated for this region. When the Louisiana Territory once again came under French sovereignty in 1800, the Spanish settlers remained, and with the Louisiana Purchase by the United States government in 1808, immigration of English-speaking Americans became a significant factor.

The foregoing brief historical sketch gives some idea as to the origins of the Sabine River Spanish community, but does not entirely answer the question of the linguistic sources of the local Spanish dialect. Linguistically, Sabine River Spanish shares no similarities with the *isleño* dialect, but is an offspring of rural Mexican Spanish. The number of subsequent direct arrivals from Spain among the Sabine River Spanish communities was evidently minimal, if any such immigration occurred at all, and such dialect mixing as did occur consisted of successive overlays of Mexican Spanish, from a variety of regions, social strata, and time periods. If this historical reconstruction is accurate, then the vestigial Spanish found among the Louisiana Sabine River Spanish speakers is a direct continuation of eighteenth century Mexican vernacular, while the dialect spoken in the Moral community may reflect some aspects of Mexican Spanish from the first decades of the nineteenth century. Both speech communities, then, represent the survival of some of the earliest varieties of Spanish still found in the United States.

By all indications, the settlers at Los Aes, Nacogdoches, and Los Adaes, both at the time of the first founding and following the reoccupation led by Ybarbo, came from the lowest socioeconomic classes of Spanish Mexico, being largely conscripts and poor farmers. Even relatively prosperous landowners like Ybarbo were several rungs below the Spanish intellectual class in terms of literacy and formal education; the majority of the settlers were totally illiterate and, judging by contemporary accounts and historical reconstructions, entirely ignorant of the world outside of their own communities. One would naturally expect that the linguistic characteristics of the Spanish dialects derived from these settlements would reflect not only archaic elements, but also a rural, uneducated background; this, in fact, is manifest upon considering Sabine River Spanish.

2 Phonological characteristics. Being a derivative of central and particularly northern Mexican Spanish (since the original settlers came from Coahuila and west/central Texas, with a few perhaps being from as far away as Mexico City), Sabine River Spanish is phonologically rather conservative.[8] This is apparent in the general retention of consonants and the lack of wholesale neutralizations found in other dialects. At the same time, the rural/ popular origins of Sabine River Spanish result in numerous phonological misidentifications and analogical creations. Detailed features include:

(1) Syllable- and word-final /s/ is normally retained as [s], with a much lower proportion of cases of aspirate [h]. Certain cases of the change /s/ > [h] are pan-Hispanic, such as the popular pronunciation of *nosotros* as *nojotros* (or *lojotros*, more common in Sabine River Spanish).

(2) Phrase-final and word-final prevocalic /n/ is uniformly alveolar [n].

(3) The opposition between the single flap /r/ and the multiple trill /r̃/ is partially neutralized, with the majority of cases of the latter phoneme realized as flap [r]. This neutralization is frequent in other vestigial Spanish dialects but also occurs sporadically in other Spanish-speaking regions (Lipski 1985 and Germán de Granada 1969:111); the widespread nature of the change /r̃/ > [r] in both Sabine River Spanish communities suggests an early date of inception. Syllable- and word-final /r/ is normally realized as [r], but in phrase-final position elision of /r/ is relatively frequent, particularly in verbal infinitives.

(4) The phoneme /y/ is weak, and frequently falls in contact with /i/ (*gallina* > [gaína], *silla* > [sía]) and after /e/ (*sello* > [seo]). This feature is shared with most contemporary dialects of Central American, Mexican, and Mexican-American Spanish, and probably dates from the formative period of Sabine River Spanish (Canfield 1981:15 and Ross 1980:552-54).

(5) The opposition between intervocalic /d/ and /r/ is partially neutralized in favor of [r] (e.g., *cada* > [kara]); this pronunciation is not consistent among Sabine River Spanish speakers, and probably results from interference, since the same variation is found among other vestigial Spanish-English bilinguals.

(6) The phoneme /t/ is occasionally given an alveolar realization, and may emerge as a voiceless flap [ɾ̯]; as in the preceding case, this is evidently a transfer from English.

(7) Sabine River Spanish speakers normally reduce unstressed vowels, giving them a centralized realization [ə] or [ɐ]. Many Mexican speakers devoice and elide unstressed vowels,[9] but the high rate of centralization rather than simple elision in the Sabine River area is most probably a consequence of the prolonged isolation of this dialect.

(8) As in *isleño* and other vestigial or isolated Spanish dialects, Sabine River Spanish exhibits many cases of phonological misidentification, both sporadic and unstable variations, and total relexification. Common examples include: *buja* < *aguja*; *rabilán* < *gavilán*; *bujero* < *agujero*; *jolote/jalote* < *guajolote*; *murcégalo* < *murciélago*; *los/losotros/lojotros* < *nos/nosotros*; *azúc(a)ra* < *azúcar*; *amaricano* < *americano*, etc.

3 Morphosyntactic features.[10] Sabine River Spanish is characterized by a high concentration of archaisms, forms typical of rural and popular Spanish, and analogical formations, not to mention syntactic transference from English among the last generation of semispeakers. Among the salient morphosyntactic peculiarities are:

(1) Archaic forms, including *trujo/truje, vido/vide, mesmo, muncho,* and *asina/ansina*.

(2) Numerous analogical verb forms, largely resulting in verbal paradigms with a single canonical root: *cierramos < cerramos, dijieron < dijieron, cocinear < cocinar, tenimos < tuvimos,* etc.

(3) Use of *mero* instead of general Spanish *mismo* in the sense of 'same, one and only': *aquí mero* 'right here', and *éste mero* 'this very one'; *mero* also appears in the expression *ya mero* 'almost'.

(4) Expressions with *no más* 'only, precisely' are used as in Mexican Spanish, to the complete exclusion of *sólo/solamente*.

(5) Among Sabine River Spanish speakers there is consistent use of *estar* in cases where other Spanish dialects, including those of Mexico, employ *ser*, particularly with predicate nouns. This may be a function of vestigial usage among semispeakers, but nearly all Spanish speakers interviewed in both communities exhibit some nonstandard use of *estar*, leading to the supposition that this verb gradually evolved away from general and Mexican Spanish patterns at an earlier date. Examples include:

> *Toa la gente que tá aquí tá blanco.*[11] 'All the people around here are white.'
> *Los Peñas están trigueños.* 'The Peñas are dark-skinned.'
> *El tacuache no tá malo.* 'Possums aren't bad.'
> *Una coquena tá medio amarillo.* 'A guinea hen is sort of yellow.'
> *Si 'taban novios por mucho tiempo.* 'If they were engaged for a long time.'

(6) As in Mexican Spanish, the Sabine River dialects use questions with *¿qué tanto?/¿qué tan?* nearly exclusively, instead of *¿cuánto?*; thus: *¿Qué tanto ganas?* 'How much do you earn?' and *¿Qué tan vieja es esta casa?* 'How old is this house?'

(7) Curious and significant in Sabine River Spanish is the use of expressions with *para atrás (patrás)* in combinations where English uses the verbal particle *back: Venga patrás* 'Come back', *Vamos patrás* 'Let's go back', and *Te pago patrás* 'I'll pay you back'. That this expression is a syntactic calque from English is beyond doubt, since the combination is only attested in areas of Spanish-English bilingualism. At the same time, expressions with *patrás* are found in such unrelated Spanish dialects as those spoken in Gibraltar, Belize,

Trinidad, and *isleño* Spanish, in addition to being characteristic of Mexican-American, Puerto Rican (particularly within the United States), and most recently, Cuban-American Spanish.[12] The existence of identical combinations in isolated bilingual areas suggests the possibility for independent development in several areas, and the presence of *patrás* calques in the Sabine River area adds substance to this hypothesis. Examples from the Sabine River dialect include:

Habla patrás en español. 'Answer in Spanish.'
Venga patrás mañana. 'Come back tomorrow.'
Unos vinieron patrás con él. 'Some came back with him.'

4 Lexical characteristics.[13]   The Sabine River Spanish lexicon is a combination of Mexican, archaic, and rural/popular Spanish items, with an admixture of French loans in the Louisiana community, and a handful of indigenous elements.

(1) Mexicanisms. These are most abundant in Sabine River Spanish, and definitively prove the Mexican provenance of this dialect. Common items include: *atole* 'thin sweet gruel', *guajolote* 'turkey', *tecolote* 'owl', *zopilote* 'buzzard', *cacahuate* 'peanut', *zacate* 'grass, weed', *camote* 'sweet potato, yam', *tamal* 'hot tamale', *tortilla* 'Mexican corn tortilla', *comal* 'griddle for cooking tortillas', *nixtamal* 'hominy', *metate* 'grinding stone', *molcajete* 'mortar for grinding herbs and chiles', *petate* 'mat', *mecate* 'rope', *cuate* 'twin', *tacuache* 'possum', *tejón* 'raccoon', *güero* 'blond, light-complexioned', *elote* 'tender cob of corn', *ejote* 'snap bean', *charola* 'tray', *labor* 'division of land (approximately 177 acres)', *blanquillo* 'egg', *tuza* 'mole (rodent)', *tapanco* 'roof beam', *coquena* 'guinea hen', *ándale* 'let's go, OK', *pinche* 'damned, cursed', and the universal Mexican expletive *chingar* and its derivatives, originally referring to the sexual act, but now merely vulgar expressions.

(2) Archaic/rustic items. These include *mercar/marcar* 'to buy', *calzón/calzones* 'pants', *túnico* 'lady's dress', *calesa* 'horse-drawn buggy', *la provisión* 'supplies, provisions', *noria* 'water well', *truja/troja* 'barn', *peje* 'fish', *fierro* 'iron, tool', *lumbre* 'fire', and *prieto* 'black'.

(3) Other items. Among the miscellaneous words of possible Latin-American Spanish, French, English, and Amerindian origin, only a few are found among Sabine River Spanish speakers. These include: *huaguín (waguín)* 'farm wagon', *payaso* 'bat' (alternating with the popular *murcégalo < murciélago*), the Caribbean *maní* 'peanut', which alternates (in Louisiana) with English *goober* and the normal Mexican *cacahuate*, *ojo negro* 'black-eyed pea', *pan de molino* 'corn bread', and the most curious form *cusca/cushca* 'buzzard', which

alternates with the Mexican *zopilote*. No convincing etymology has been offered for *cusca/cushca*, but in Mexico and other Latin American areas, the word *cusca/chusca* often means 'dissimulated prostitute, slovenly woman' and this designation may have been applied metaphorically to the ill-omened bird; the use of *payaso* 'clown' to refer to the common bat supports the possibility of a metaphorical extension of *cusca*.[14]

Equally telling in the Sabine River Spanish dialect is the absence of currently popular Mexicanisms, such as *chamaco* and *huerco* 'small child', *chavalo/chavala* 'boy/girl', and *gabacho* 'Anglo-American'. The absence of the latter designation may be explained by the origins of the dialect in the pre-Anglo-American period of Texas and Louisiana, when national and racial conflict had not yet emerged. The term *gabacho*, originally applied by Spaniards to the French, apparently arose in Mexico following independence from Spain and probably after the Mexican-American War and succeeding events, when racial and cultural differences between Mexicans and Anglo-Americans became the object of constant discord. It is interesting to note the existence among the Sabine River speakers of *bolillo*, which is still a common designation among Mexicans and Mexican-Americans; for Sabine River speakers, the term refers generically to 'anyone from outside the ethnic Spanish community, who by extension does not speak Spanish'. In support of the preceding hypothesis, the word *gachupín*, a derogatory epithet for Spaniards in Mexico, does not appear in Sabine River Spanish.

5 Conclusions. It is not possible to give a total reconstruction of the original Sabine River Spanish dialect, given the small number of remaining speakers, but the general nature of this early Texas dialect does emerge from the preceding considerations. It is clear that, at least from the beginning of the eighteenth century, the Spanish language brought to the Texas frontier was more Mexican than peninsular, and that the Mexicanisms had penetrated the speech of Spanish citizens with no demonstrable indigenous background. At the same time, the low sociocultural level of the Spanish/Mexican frontiersmen is also reflected in the features of Sabine River Spanish, which contains a high proportion of rustic and popular elements. Further research is called for on this significant Spanish-speaking group, which is on the verge of extinction, in order to close some of the gaps in our knowledge of the growth and spread of the Spanish language in North America.

Notes

1. The standard work on *isleño* Spanish is MacCurdy (1950); cf. also MacCurdy (1959, 1975), Armistead (1978, 1981b, 1983a, 1983b, 1986), Varela (1979), Guillote (1982), and Lipski (1986b, 1987).

2. The only linguistic references to these groups are by Stark (1980:163-76) and Armistead (1982:379-87, 1983a:41-42, 1985:251-62). Cf. also Armistead and Gregory (1986:21-30). The contemporary existence of Spanish speakers along the Sabine River has occasionally been commented on; cf., for example, Sepulvedo (1977), Montero de Pedro (1979:120-21), Fernández Shaw (1972:344-46), Abernathy (1976:21-33), Smith and Hitt (1952:47), and Gregory and McCorkle (1981).

3. My ongoing research program on Sabine River Spanish was begun in late 1985. Special thanks are due to the following individuals without whose help no material progress could have been made: Prof. Hiram Gregory of Northwest State University in Natchitoches, Louisiana; Prof. James Corbin of Stephen F. Austin State University in Nacogdoches, Texas; Prof. Samuel Armistead of the University of California, Davis; Ms. Mary Van Rheenen of Louisiana State University, Baton Rouge; and Mr. Sam Montes of the Moral community in Nacogdoches, Texas.

4. The linguistic notion of the 'semispeaker' has been most carefully developed by Dorian (1977, 1980). For a survey of phenomena common to vestigial Spanish dialects, including Louisiana *isleño* Spanish, cf. Lipski (1986a).

5. Abernathy (1976:25) and Tjarks (1974:326), who indicates that Ybarbo himself was a 'mulatto,' although it is known that at least one of his parents came from Andalusia.

6. E.g., Armistead (1983a, 1985). The term *adaesaños* was used by Bolton (1915:394), but there is no evidence of this designation being used by residents of the area at any time period. Armistead (1985:251, fn. 2) points out that he has used the term *adaeseño,* a designation not used by community members themselves.

7. The most comprehensive study is that of Bolton (1905). Cf. also Bolton (1915:375-476; 1921:227-51). Other useful information is provided by Carlos E. Castañeda in the series *Our Catholic Heritage in Texas,* published by the Knights of Columbus (1936:144-45; 1938:passim; 1939:chaps. 7 and 8, especially 298-302; and 1950: chap. 8). Other important sources for a composite history of Spanish colonization along the Sabine River include Crockett (1932:19-58); Nardini (1963:55-88); John (1975); Carruth (1970:passim); McReynolds (1976a:2-5, 1976b:77-84, 1978, 1980a:19-25, 1980b:26-32); Stewart (1976:34-38); McDonald (1980:11-18); Robinson (1943:41-47); Bridges and Deville (1936); Acosta Rodríguez (1979:19-33); Hatcher (1917); Faulk (1964:14-15, 97-102; 1965:127); the collection *Documentos para la historia eclesiástica y civil de la provincia de Texas o Nuevas Philipinas 1720-1779* (1961), especially the 'Carta del señor Barón de Ripperdá al Caballero de Croix,' 335-42; Dunn (1917:110-45); and Belisle (1912:39-60).

8. Sources for rural Mexican Spanish pronunciation (and grammar) include Matluck (1951), Boyd-Bowman (1960), Cárdenas (1967), Marden (1896), Perissinotto (1975), and Canfield (1981:60-64).

9. Lope Blanch (1966:119), Matluck (1963:534), Boyd-Bowman (1952:138-40), and Canellada and Zamora Vicente (1960:221-24).

10. Sources of information on rural/popular Mexican Spanish characteristics, in addition to those in note 13, include Espinosa (1911, 1930), Ornstein (1951), Espinosa, Jr. (1957), Post (1933), Rael (1939), and Hensey (1973).

11. This study is based on exact transcriptions of utterances of speakers of Sabine River Spanish. 'Errors,' such as lack of gender agreement with a distant subject, occur consistently in the dialect. Another example is *Una coquena tá medio amarillo*.

12. Lipski (1989), Sánchez (1972), Pérez Sala (1971), García (1979, 1982), and Varela (1974).

13. Lexical sources for Mexican Spanish include Santamaría, (1942, 1959), Islas Escacega (1945), Prieto Mejía (1981), Galván and Teschner (1977), Bayo (1931), and Cerda, Cabaza, and Farías (1953).

14. Santamaría (1942:1.445, 552) and Prieto Mejía (1981:38), who explains that *cusca* comes from *cuscuta*, a parasitic sucking plant. The term is not used in the sense of 'buzzard' in contemporary educated Mexican Spanish; cf. *Léxico del habla culta de México* (1978:558).

References

Abernathy, F. 1976. The Spanish on the Moral. In: *The bicentennial commemorative history of Nacogdoches*. Nacogdoches, Tex.: Nacogdoches Jaycees. 21-33.

Acosta Rodríguez, A. 1979. *La población de Luisiana española (1763-1803)*. Madrid: Ministerio de Asuntos Exteriores.

Alessio Robles, V. 1945. *Coahuila y Texas desde la consumación de la independencia hasta el tratado de paz de Guadalupe Hidalgo*, I. Mexico City: n.p.

Armistead, S. 1978. Romances tradicionales entre los hispanohablantes del estado de Luisiana. *Nueva Revista de Filología Hispánica* 27.39-56.

_____. 1979. Hispanic traditional poetry in Louisiana. In: *El romancero hoy: Nuevas fronteras*. A. Sánchez Romeralo, ed. Madrid: Cátedra Seminario Menéndez Pidal. 147-58.

_____. 1981a. Hispanic folk literature among the isleños. In: *Perspectives on ethnicity in New Orleans*. J. Cooke and M. Blanton, eds. New Orleans: University of New Orleans. 21-31.

_____. 1981b. Spanish language and folklore in Louisiana. *La Corónica* 9:2.187-89.

_____. 1982. Un corrido de la muerte de Madero cantado en Luisiana. *Anuario de Letras* 20.379-87.

_____. 1983a. Más romances de Luisiana. *Nueva Revista de Filología Hispánica* 32.41-54.

_____. 1983b. Spanish riddles from St. Bernard Parish. *Louisiana Folklore Miscellany* 5:3.1-8.

_____. 1985. Adivinanzas españolas de Luisiana. In: *Homenaje a Alvaro Galmés de Fuentes*, 2. D. Alonso, D. García, and R. Lapesa, eds. Madrid: Gredos. 251-62.

_____. 1986. Three Spanish dialects in Louisiana. Unpublished MS, University of California, Davis.

_____, and H. Gregory. 1986. French loan words in the Spanish dialect of Sabine and Natchitoches Parishes. *Louisiana Folklife* 10.21-30.

Atwood, E.B. 1962. *The regional vocabulary of Texas*. Austin: University of Texas.

Barker, E. 1923. Notes on the colonization of Texas. *Southwestern Historical Quarterly* 27.108-19.

Bayo, C. 1931. *Manual del lenguaje criollo de Centro y Sudamérica*. Madrid: Rafael Scaro Raggio, Editor.

Beardsley, T., Jr. 1972. Influencias angloamericanas en el español de Cayo Hueso. *Exilio* 6:4-7.87-100.

Belisle, J. 1912. *History of Sabine Parish, Louisiana.* Many, La.: Sabine Banner Press.

Bolton, H. 1905. The Spanish abandonment and re-occupation of East Texas, 1773-1779. *Quarterly of the Texas State Historical Association* 9:2.67-137.

———. 1915. *Texas in the middle eighteenth century.* Berkeley: University of California.

———. 1921. *The Spanish borderlands.* New Haven, Conn.: Yale University.

Boyd-Bowman, P. 1952. La pérdida de vocales átonas en la planicie mexicana. *Nueva Revista de Filología Hispánica* 6.138-40.

———. 1960. *El habla de Guanajuato.* Mexico City: Universidad Nacional Autónoma de México.

Bridges, K., and W. Deville. 1936. Natchitoches in 1776. *Louisiana History* 4.145-59.

Canellada, M., and A. Zamora Vicente. 1960. Vocales caducas en el español mexicano. *Nueva Revista de Filología Hispánica* 14.221-24.

Canfield, D.L. 1951. Tampa Spanish: Three characters in search of a pronunciation. *Modern Language Journal* 35.42-44.

———. 1981. *Spanish pronunciation in the Americas.* Chicago: University of Chicago.

Cárdenas, D. 1967. *El español de Jalisco.* Madrid: Consejo Superior de Investigación Científica.

Carruth, V. 1970. *Caddo: 1,000. A history of the Shreveport area from the time of the Caddo Indians to the 1970's.* Shreveport, La.: Shreveport Magazine.

Castañeda, C. 1936. *The winning of Texas 1693-1731.* Austin: Knights of Columbus at the Von Boeckmann-Jones Co. Vol. 2 of the series *Our Catholic Heritage in Texas.*

———. 1938. *The mission era: The missions at work 1731-1761.* Austin: Knights of Columbus at the Von Boeckmann-Jones Co. Vol. 3 of the series *Our Catholic Heritage in Texas.*

———. 1939. *The mission era: The passing of the missions 1762-1782.* Austin: Knights of Columbus at the Von Boeckmann-Jones Co. Vol. 4 of the series *Our Catholic Heritage in Texas.*

———. 1950. *The transition period: The fight for freedom 1810-1836.* Austin: Knights of Columbus at the Von Boeckmann-Jones Co. Vol. 6 of the series *Our Catholic Heritage in Texas.*

Centro de Lingüística Hispánica. 1978. *Léxico del habla culta de México.* Mexico City: Universidad Nacional Autónoma de México, Centro de Lingüística Hispánica.

Cerda, G., B. Cabaza, and J. Farías. 1953. *Vocabulario español de Texas.* Austin: University of Texas.

Cobos, R. 1983. *A dictionary of New Mexico and southern Colorado Spanish.* Santa Fe: Museum of New Mexico Press.

Crockett, G. 1932. *Two centuries in East Texas: A history of San Agustine county and surrounding territory from 1685 to the present time.* Dallas: Southwest Press.

Documentos para la historia eclesiástica y civil de la provincia de Texas o Nuevas Philipinas 1720-1779. 1961. Madrid: Ediciones José Porrúa Turanzas.

Dorian, N. 1977. The problem of the semi-speaker in language death. *International Journal of the Sociology of Language* 12.23-32.

———. 1980. Language shift in community and individual: The phenomenon of the laggard semi-speaker. *International Journal of the Sociology of Language* 25.85-94.

Dunn, W. 1917. *Spanish and French rivalry in the Gulf region of the United States, 1678-1702.* Austin: University of Texas.

Ericson, C. R. 1974. *Nacogdoches: Gateway to Texas.* Fort Worth: Arrow/Curtis Printing.

Espinosa, A. 1911. *The Spanish language: New Mexico and Southern Colorado.* Santa Fe: Historical Society of New Mexico.

———. 1917. Speech mixture in New Mexico: The influence of the English language on New Mexican Spanish. In: *The Pacific Ocean in history.* H. Stephens and H. Bolton, eds. New York: Macmillan. 408-28.

_____. 1930. *Estudios sobre el español de Nuevo México.* A. Alonso and A. Rosenblat, trans. Buenos Aires: Biblioteca de Dialectología Hispanoamericana.

Espinosa, A., Jr. 1957. Problemas lexiocográficos del español del sudoeste. *Hispania* 40.139-43.

Faulk, O. 1964. *The last years of Spanish Texas 1778-1821.* The Hague: Mouton.

_____. 1965. *A successful failure: The saga of Texas 1519-1810.* Austin: Steck-Vaughn Co.

Fernández Shaw, C. 1972. *Presencia española en los Estados Unidos.* Madrid: Ediciones Cultura Hispánica.

Galván, R., and R. Teschner. 1977. *El diccionario del español chicano.* 2nd ed. Silver Spring, Md.: Institute of Modern Languages.

García, M.E. 1979. *Pa(ra)* usage in United States Spanish. *Hispania* 62.106-14.

_____. 1982. Syntactic variation in verb phrases of motion in United States-Mexican Spanish. In: *Spanish in the United States: Sociolinguistic aspects.* J. Amastae and L. Elías-Olivares, eds. New York: Cambridge University Press. 82-92.

Granada, G., de. 1969. La desfonologización de /r/-/r̄/ en el dominio lingüístico hispano. *Boletín del Instituto Caro y Cuervo* 24.1-11.

Gregory, H., and J. McCorkle. 1981. *Los Adaes: Historical and archaeological survey.* Natchitoches, La.: Northwestern State University.

Guillotte, J. 1982. *Masters of the marsh: An introduction to the ethnography of lower St. Bernard Parish.* New Orleans: University of New Orleans, Dept. of Anthropology and Geology.

Hatcher, M.A. 1917. *The opening of Texas to foreign settlement 1801-1821.* Austin: University of Texas.

Hensey, F. 1973. Grammatical variation in Southwest American Spanish. *Linguistics* 108.5-26.

Islas Escacega, L. 1945. *Vocabulario campesino nacional.* Mexico City: Secretaría de Agricultura y Fomento.

John, E. 1975. *Storms brewed in other men's worlds: The confrontation of Indians, Spanish and French in the Southwest, 1540-1795,* College Station: Texas A&M University.

Jones, O., Jr. 1979. *Los paisanos: Spanish settlers on the northern frontier of New Spain.* Norman: University of Oklahoma.

Kany, C. 1960. *American Spanish euphemisms.* Berkeley: University of California.

Lathrop, B. 1949. *Migration into east Texas 1835-1860.* Austin: Texas State Historical Association.

Lerner, I. 1974. *Arcaísmos léxicos del español de América.* Madrid: Insula.

Lipski, J. 1975. The language battle in Puerto Rico. *Revista/Review Interamericana* 5.347-54.

_____. 1976. Structural linguistics and bilingual interference. *Bilingual Review/Revista Bilingüe* 3.229-37.

_____. 1985. Creole Spanish and vestigial Spanish: Evolutionary parallels. *Linguistics* 23.963-84.

_____. 1986a. The importance of Louisiana isleño Spanish for Hispanic dialectology. *Southwest Journal of Linguistics* 7.102-15.

_____. 1986b. La reducción de /s/ y /n/ en el español isleño de Luisiana: Vestigios del español canario en América. *Revista de Filología de La Laguna* 2.

_____. 1987. Language contact phenomena in Louisiana isleño Spanish. *American Speech* 62:4.320-31.

_____. 1989. On the construction *pa(ra) atrás* among Spanish-English bilinguals: Common tendencies and universal features. *Revista/Review Interamericana* 15.91-102.

Lope Blanch, J. 1966. En torno a las vocales caedizas del español mexicano. *Nueva Revista de Filología Hispánica* 17.1-19.

MacCurdy, R. 1950. *The Spanish dialect of St. Bernard Parish, Louisiana.* Albuquerque: University of New Mexico.

_____. 1959. A Spanish word-list of the 'brulis' dwellers of Louisiana. *Hispania* 42.547-54.

_____. 1975. Los isleños de Luisiana: Supervivencia de la lengua y folklore canarios. *Anuario de Estudios Atlánticos* 21.471-591.

Marden, C. 1896. *The phonology of the Spanish dialect of Mexico City*. Baltimore: Johns Hopkins University.

Matluck, J. 1951. *La pronunciación del español en el Valle de México*. Mexico City: Universidad Nacional Autónoma de México.

_____. 1963. La *e* trabada en la ciudad de México. *Anuario de Letras* 3.5-34.

McDonald, A. 1980. *Early Spanish settlement in Nacogdoches: Missions*. In: *Nacogdoches: Wilderness outpost to modern city 1779-1979*. A. McDonald, ed. Burnet, Tex.: Eakin Press. 11-18.

McReynolds, J. 1976a. *An historical survey of Nacogdoches 1690-1779*. Nacogdoches, Tex.: Nacogdoches Jaycees. 2-5.

_____. 1976b. *Survival in East Texas: Food, clothing, shelter, 1779-1860*. Nacogdoches, Tex.: Nacogdoches Jaycees. 77-84.

_____. 1978. Family life in a borderland community: Nacogdoches, Texas 1779-1860. Ph. D. dissertation, Texas Tech University.

_____. 1980a. *Spanish Nacogdoches 1779-1821*. A. McDonald, ed. Burnet, Tex.: Eakin Press. 19-25.

_____. 1980b. *Mexican Nacogdoches 1812-1836*. A. McDonald, ed. Burnet, Tex.: Eakin Press. 26-32.

Montero de Pedro, J. 1979. *Españoles en Nueva Orleáns y Luisiana*. Madrid: Ediciones Cultura Hispánica.

Nacogdoches Jaycees. 1976. *The bicentennial commemorative history of Nacogdoches*. Nacogdoches, Tex.: Nacogdoches Jaycees.

Nardini, L. 1963. *My historic Natchitoches, Louisiana, and its environment*. Natchitoches, La.: Nardini Publishing Co.

Ornstein, J. 1951. The archaic and the modern in the Spanish of New Mexico. *Hispania* 34.137-42.

_____. 1972. Toward a classification of Southwest Spanish non-standard variants. *Linguistics* 93.70-87.

Perissinotto, G. 1975. *Fonología del español hablado en la Ciudad de México*. Mexico City: Colegio de México.

Pérez Sala, P. 1971. *Interferencia lingüística del inglés en el español hablado en Puerto Rico*. Hato Rey: Inter American University.

Post, A. 1933. Some aspects of Arizona Spanish. *Hispania* 16.35-42.

Prieto Mejía, J. 1981. *Así habla el mexicano*. Mexico City: Editorial Panorama.

Rael, J. 1939. Associative interference in New Mexican Spanish. *Hispanic Review* 7.324-36.

Robinson, R. 1943. *Texas: The Lone Star State*. New York: Prentice-Hall.

Ross, J. R. 1980. La supresión de /y/ en el español chicano. *Hispania* 63.552-54.

Sánchez, J. M. 1926. A trip to Texas in 1828. C. Castañeda, trans. *Southwestern Historical Quarterly* 29:4.249-88.

Sánchez, R. 1972. Nuestra circunstancia lingüística. *El Grito* 6.45-74.

Santamaría, F. 1942. *Diccionario general de americanismos*. 3 vols. Mexico City: Editorial Pedro Robredo.

_____. 1959. *Diccionario de mejicanismos*. Mexico City: Editorial Porrúa.

Sepulvedo, D. 1977. Folk curing in a Spanish community. *Lousiana Folklife Newsletter* 2:1.

Smith, T.L., and H. Hitt. 1952. *The people of Louisiana*. Baton Rouge: Louisiana State University.

Solé, J.V. 1956. *Diccionario de regionalismos de Salta*. Buenos Aires: Talleres Gráficos de Sebastián de Amorrorta e Hijos.

Sopena. 1982. *Americanismos: Diccionario ilustrado Sopena*. Barcelona: Editorial Ramón Sopena.

Stark, L. 1980. Notes on a dialect of Spanish spoken in northern Louisiana. *Anthropological Linguistics* 22:4.163-76.

Stewart, B. 1976. *The founding of Nacogdoches by Antonio Gil Y'Barbo*. Nacogdoches, Tex.: Nacogdoches Jaycees. 34-38.

Tarpley, F. 1964. Historical aspects of linguistic research in East Texas. *East Texas Historical Journal* 2.1:18-25.

Tjarks, A. 1974. Comparative demographic analysis of Texas 1777-1793. *Southwestern Historical Quarterly* 77:3.291-333.

Varela, B. 1974. La influencia del inglés en los cubanos de Miami y Nueva Orleáns. *Español Actual,* abril 1974.16-25.

_____. 1978. Observaciones sobre los isleños, los cubanos y la importancia del bilingüismo. *New Orleans Ethnic Cultures* 1.63-68.

_____. 1979. Isleño and Cuban Spanish. *Perspectives on Ethnicity in New Orleans* 2.42-47.

Domain constraints on the use of TÚ and USTED

June A. Jaramillo
Albuquerque Public Schools

While scholars in general have expressed theoretical interest concerning the nature and use of address forms (e.g., Hockett 1958; Brown and Gilman 1960; Friedrich 1972; Ervin-Tripp 1972; Head 1978), it is surprising that the variants TÚ/USTED[1] themselves have received so little in-depth scholarly attention. Available research on TÚ/USTED is unsystematic, often impressionistic (e.g., Espinosa 1946; Rael 1937; Sánchez 1982), and speaks to varied linguistic methodologies and approaches. A scattering of studies addresses the topic of TÚ/USTED with regard to such issues as semantic feature analysis (Hadlich 1971), stylistic function based on the presence or absence of the subject pronominal forms in discourse (Rosengren 1974), and grammatical features in terms of typologies of pronominal and address systems (Head 1978).

Most descriptions of TÚ/USTED, however, attempt to delineate the elements that either elicit or constrain the choice of one address form over the other. For instance, grammatical explanations of TÚ and USTED, such as those exemplified by Ramsey (1894) and others, allude to extralinguistic constraints which seem to be operative in the selection of the two address forms. Traditional grammarians have associated the differentiated use of TÚ and USTED with role-relationships, attitudinal or affective postures, and stylistic considerations. Nonetheless, traditional descriptions fall short of explaining explicitly and adequately present-day use, diversity, and social meaning of TÚ/USTED. Sociolinguistic inquiry attempts to address these issues.

The past few decades have seen an increase, though rather limited, in sociolinguistic research which aims to elucidate the covariation between address form choice and extralinguistic criteria. Various studies have shown that the use of TÚ/USTED is closely related to such contextual features as domain of interaction, role-relationship, and transient moods and attitudes. My purpose here is to explore the use of TÚ and USTED solely with respect to two contextual factors--domain of interaction and role-relationship.

Data for this study are derived from the reported use of TÚ and USTED by a sample population of 50 adult Spanish-speaking residents of Tomé, New

Mexico, a small rural community in the Río Grande Valley of central New Mexico. The criteria for selecting consultants were the following:

(1) Consultants between the ages of 17 and 50 must have been born and raised in the community.
(2) Consultants over 50 years old who were not natives of Tomé must have moved to Tomé from another rural area in the vicinity by the ages of 15 to 20.
(3) Parents of the individual consultant must have been born and raised in the area of the Río Grande Valley of central New Mexico. For this investigation, each consultant claimed, to the best of his or her knowledge, to be a descendant of one of the founding families that settled this area.

The selection of the 50 Spanish-speaking residents who served as consultants for the present investigation was based on availability sampling techniques. Residents from throughout the community were approached in a door-to-door survey. The 50 consultants were preselected to provide equal representation by sex, 25 males and 25 females. Three groupings by age were also preselected with a balanced representation by sex in each group: ages 17-30 (16 consultants), ages 31 to 50 (18 consultants), ages 51 and above (16 consultants). These age groups were arbitrarily set at ages 17 to 30, 31 to 50, and 51 and above in order to sample broadly the speech of three generations of adult speakers. The data on the use of TÚ and USTED with respect to the sociological factors, age and sex, are not explored in this paper.

An adaptation of a questionnaire on personal address use designed by Lambert and Tucker (1976) was administered to the 50 consultants on an individual basis. Specifically modified to include interactional situations likely to be encountered in the Tomé social network, the questionnaire probes the use of TÚ/USTED in role-relationships such as the following:

(a) Nuclear and extended family members
(b) Friends, acquaintances, and strangers
(c) Employment personnel
(d) Professionals and service-oriented personnel
(e) Other, e.g., clergy, nuns, situations of transient anger or disgust

The questionnaire, incorporated into a general interview session on the Hispanic culture of Tomé, was administered by the author in the presence of a secondary interviewer. As with the remainder of the interview, the question and answer session on TÚ/USTED use was tape-recorded and afterwards transcribed.

The Statistical Package for the Social Sciences (SPSS-X) was employed in the statistical analysis of the data. Percentages of frequencies were calculated for each address form, TÚ and USTED, by domain of interaction and role-relationship for both given and received address.

Domain of interaction has been identified as an important contextual factor related to the use of TÚ/USTED. Fishman (1972:22) defines domain as

> a higher order generalization from congruent situations (i.e., from situations in which individuals interacting in appropriate role-relationships with each other, in the appropriate locales for these role-relationships, and discussing topics appropriate to their role-relationships...).

In order to examine the relationship between the domain variable and the TÚ variable, six domains of interaction were identified to be of potential relevance in Tomé society: (1) nuclear family, (2) friendship, (3) ceremonial family, (4) employment, (5) low status professional, and (6) high status professional.

Data on the use of the TÚ variant by domain of interaction are included in Table 1. Overall results yield two domain 'clusters'--an 'informal' one with TÚ predominant and a 'formal' one with USTED predominant. The informal domain cluster is comprised of the nuclear family and friendship domains, whereas the formal domain cluster consists of the ceremonial family, employment, low status professional, and high status professional domains.

Table 1. The use of TÚ by domain.

Domain	Given % (TÚ/N)	Received % (TÚ/N)
Nuclear family	63.7 (223/350)	64.9 (227/350)
Friendship	73.3 (220/300)	74.7 (224/300)
Ceremonial family	38.3 (115/300)	37.3 (112/300)
Employment	32.0 (96/300)	41.7 (125/300)
Low status professionals	31.1 (140/450)	28.9 (130/450)
High status professionals	5.4 (38/700)	32.4 (227/700)

With regard to the informal domain cluster, the prevailing use of TÚ in the nuclear family and friendship domains is consistent with the standard or prescriptive view of the address form. This use of TÚ with friends and certain family members reflects, on the one hand, intimate or informal interpersonal relations and equality of social status on the other. Within this informal domain cluster, Tomé consultants report considerably less use of TÚ, and hence more use of USTED, with members of their immediate family than with friends. A possible explanation is that relationships within the nuclear family domain include hierarchical differences such as those generally found between parents and children.

The predominant use of USTED in the formal domain cluster also is in agreement with standard norms of usage. In this case, the use of USTED may well be a reflection of the community's awareness of power and status differences affecting social relationships and of social interactions which tend to be more formalized and impersonal in nature. Even so, differentials in the use of USTED are found, as one might expect, among the diverse domains. For instance, regarding given address, speakers tend to use USTED relatively less often in the ceremonial family domain than in the other formal domains. The ceremonial family domain is comprised of role-relationships which are, in general, assumed by means of religious ceremony. These special role-relationships include godparenthood and *compadrazgo* relationships. The higher frequencies of TÚ could indicate that relationships within this domain represent somewhat of a social quandary for Tomé speakers. That is, while participants in this domain assume special formalized ties and social obligations, they are, at the same time, considered 'family' in Tomé society. An examination of given address with regard to the low status and high status professional domains reveals other striking results. Speakers report using TÚ six times more often in talking to low status professionals than to high status professionals. It may well be that Tomé speakers are aware of status differences among the various professionals and, therefore, behave accordingly, using TÚ substantially more often in addressing socially less prominent professionals.

Differences are also observed with regard to given and received address in the formal domain cluster. For example, in the employment domain, speakers report giving USTED two-thirds of the time, but receiving it in return comparatively less often, the lowest use found in the formal domain cluster. Perhaps the frequency discrepancy between given and received address indicates that hierarchical differences often come into play in work-related encounters. Curiously, the highest report of USTED usage in terms of received address is encountered in the low status professional domain. One may speculate that consultants expect more courteous and deferential treatment from persons occupying less prestigious service-oriented positions.

Role-relationship has also been considered an exceedingly important contextual variable in the study of TÚ/USTED. Role-relationship has been defined as 'implicitly recognized and accepted sets of mutual rights and obligations between members of the same sociocultural system' (Fishman 1971:45). A consideration of individual role-relationships may be expected to reveal new perspectives on constraining elements influencing the use of TÚ and USTED within the diverse domains. Variability in the use of TÚ/USTED according to role-relationship is illustrated in Table 2.

In the nuclear family domain, Tomé speakers report addressing their parents only as USTED, but receiving only TÚ from them in return. Conversely, the consultants report that they address their own sons and daughters more frequently as TÚ and in turn are most often addressed by them as USTED. The nonreciprocal use of TÚ/USTED between parents and children signals hierarchical differences within the nuclear family structure. It seems that in the community of Tomé rules of personal address etiquette require the individual to 'respect' or defer to the authority figure of the parent, thereby entailing the use of USTED.

Table 2. The use of TÚ by role-relationship.

Received	Given %	Received %		Given %	%
Nuclear family:			**Low status professionals:**		
Father	0	100	Male store		
Mother	0	100	employee	38	30
Husband	100	100	Female store		
Wife	96	96	employee	36	28
Son	98	2	Female		
Daughter	98	2	secretary	28	34
Brother	76	76	Male office		
Sister	76	76	employee	30	34
			Female office		
			employee	28	34
Friendship:			Male nurse	26	26
Younger male			Female nurse	24	24
friend	84	64	Male dental		
Same age male			hygienist	36	26
friend	76	76	Female dental		
Older male			hygienist	34	24
friend	62	84			
Younger female			**High status professionals:**		
friend	84	64	Male teacher	2	44
Same age			Female teacher	2	44
female friend	74	76	Male professor	2	44
Older female			Female professor	2	44
friend	60	84	Male principal	2	42
			Female principal	2	42
Ceremonial family:			Male attorney	16	24
Godfather	4	100	Female attorney	10	22
Godmother	2	100	Male judge	2	26
Godson	100	0	Female judge	2	24
Goddaughter	100	0	Male physician	6	24
Compadre	12	12	Female physician	6	24
Comadre	12	12	Male dentist	12	26
			Female dentist	10	24
Employment:					
Male boss	4	66			
Female boss	4	64			
Speaker's employee,					
male	40	6			
Speaker's employee,					
female	38	6			
Male co-worker	54	56			
Female co-worker	52	52			

Note: N = 50 in all cases.

Nevertheless, many Tomé speakers, particularly the older ones, report that younger family members are increasingly using TÚ with parents. Protests one

57-year-old female: '*No hay respeto. Más antes había muncho amor en la familia.*' When examining the same phenomenon, other scholars have reported diverse findings that no doubt reveal dialect variation in TÚ/USTED use with regard to parents. Brown (1975:127), for instance, finds that the majority of the Mexican-American students in her survey use USTED in addressing their parents. Other studies, in contrast, document a tendency for younger speakers in various Spanish-speaking societies to use predominantly TÚ with parents. Parents are addressed primarily as TÚ among Spaniards (Fox 1969:690; Marín 1972:908) and Latin Americans from various regions (Marín 1972:908; Solé 1970:177-78, 182-83).

Regarding spouses and siblings in the nuclear family domain, the predominant address form in given and received address is TÚ. Because of the intimate and informal nature of the relationships involved, personal interactions among spouses and siblings, as well might be expected, deemphasize status or hierarchical differences.

In the friendship domain, social encounters appear to be guided by a somewhat simplified rule system: friends tend to address each other with TÚ. The prevalent use of TÚ among friends has been observed by Solé (1970:177-78, 182) for Puerto Rico and Peru, by Keller (1974:85) for various Latin American regions, and by Fox (1969:691) for Spain.

In the ceremonial domain, while typified by the use of USTED, Tomé speakers do make important distinctions among the various role-relationships that comprise the domain. For example, consultants report a high use (88%) of USTED in both given and received address in *compadrazgo* relationships. This compares with only a two-thirds use of USTED among Latin American speakers as reported by Keller (1974:93). As one may predict, consultants further report giving USTED overwhelmingly to godparents (at least 96% of the time) and receiving a full 100% use of TÚ in return. In the same vein, consultants give 100% TÚ usage to their godchildren, at the same time receiving 100% USTED usage in return.

The exceedingly high use of USTED with *compadres* and godparents is not at all surprising in this speech community. In Tomé society the Catholic religion and its associated institutions and activities are important focal points in the daily life of the community. Brought into existence through religious ceremony, *compadrazgo* relationships and godparenthood create special religious, moral, and social responsibilities. Though *compadres* and godparents are either close friends or relatives, the predominant use of USTED may reflect the importance placed on respect and formalized social interaction among *compadres* and godparents. Perceptive observations expressed by several community members seem to bear out this interpretation of the data. For instance, the *compadrazgo* relationships are '*relaciones sagradas y especiales*' in the words of a 61-year-old female. Moreover, friends who become *compadres* adjust their address form from TÚ to USTED in making the transition to a new relationship now laden with formality and mutual respect. One 61-year-old male remarks that once he and his best friend became *compadres, 'ya nos tratamos de USTED porque semos compadres... por el puro respeto de ser compadres.'* Indeed, both *compadrazgo* and godparenthood relationships appear to transcend other considerations that enter into the structuring of a relationship:

> *Si es compadre o comadre, es usted. Como tengo un compadre que es diez años menor que yo, le digo usted por respeto. No le digo tú. A un padrino o una madrina le digo usted anque sean menores o lo que sean* (41-year-old male).

The employment domain, as it may be remembered, is characterized by the predominant use of USTED. A closer examination of the individual role-relationships included in the domain, however, reveals interesting contrasts in TÚ/USTED usage. Tomé speakers report using USTED an overwhelming 96% of the time in addressing their employers or supervisors, while receiving it only one-third of the time in return. The clearly differential use of TÚ/USTED--more use of USTED in employees addressing bosses, more use of TÚ in bosses addressing employees--appears to signal interpersonal associations which are defined by hierarchical or power distinctions. Such status or hierarchical differences in the employment domain are duly recognized by the community, as revealed in the following comments. A boss receives USTED treatment: *'mas que fuéramos amigos y fuera menor él. El respeto de su título que tiene... su título que tiene lo trata uno con más respeto'* (61-year-old male). A younger respondent (a 28-year-old male) expresses still another sentiment: *'Con relaciones en el trabajo, con el patrón, quiero mantenerlas de una manera profesional.'* In contrast, when in the position of employer or supervisor themselves, Tomé consultants report addressing their employees as USTED over half of the time (60%) and, in turn, receiving it from them 94% of the time. The jump in USTED use with employees leaves the impression that community members perceive themselves to interact with their employees in a more respectful and professional manner than the typical boss. In effect, as one 23-year-old male respondent points out: *'Si va a trabajar por mí, debe 'garrar USTED.'*

In addition, coworkers show a slight preference for TÚ in addressing each other. The almost equal split between TÚ and USTED suggests that work-related encounters are characterized by vacillating social behavior. Tomé speakers may find themselves in a dilemma. On the one hand, they are involved in encounters or activities of a more impersonal or formal nature, thus requiring the use of USTED. On the other hand, they may perceive co-workers as members of an ingroup, which would necessitate the use of TÚ.

As noted earlier, overall our data show that USTED is given and received most frequently in the low status professional and high status professional domains. An inspection of the data in Table 2 reveals that USTED is the favored address form for all role-relationships comprising the two domains. The use of USTED with service-oriented working professionals may well be an index of a high value placed on status derived from achievement, prestige, and authority in the outside world. It is worthy of note that the majority of consultants expect to receive USTED in return. Presumably, professionals occupying status-laden positions may be expected to demonstrate the dignity of their profession or position by being courteous or formal in their contact with the community. That professionals are highly esteemed and respected for their authority and achievement is evidenced by the following remarks.

Regarding working professionals:
Respeta una a la gente que trabaja (36-year-old female).
Regarding a judge:
Tiene mucha autoridad (38-year-old female).
Pus, por el puro respeto y el calibre, tendría que ser usted por las calificaciones (45-year-old female).
Regarding a school principal:
Tiene autoridad (19-year-old male).
Regarding professors:
Les hablo de usted porque están muy altos ellos pa' uno--en su educación--tenemos que tener respeto, usted (50-year-old male).
Regarding secretaries:
Digo usted para enseñar respeto (24-year-old female).
Regarding dental hygienists and office employees:
Uso usted para enseñarles respeto (28-year-old male).

In conclusion, our investigation reveals that the use of both second person address forms, TÚ and USTED, constitutes an integral part of the personal address system in Tomé. That is, Tomé speakers prefer using predominantly TÚ for informal domains and favor using predominantly USTED for formal domains. In this connection, personal address in Tomé is generally consistent with norms of standard usage. Finally, while the use of TÚ and USTED by Tomé speakers tends to be in agreement with usage in other Spanish-speaking societies, personal address etiquette in Tomé appears to be more conservative than what has been reported by various other scholars, particularly with regard to parent/child and *compadrazgo* interactions.

Note

1. The terms TÚ and USTED refer to the ideological notions of '*tratar de TÚ*' (*tuteo*) and '*tratar de USTED*' (*ustedeo*) in everyday social interactions. *Tuteo* and *ustedeo* imply the manifestation of the subject pronouns TÚ and USTED as well as any number of cooccurring linguistic elements such as oblique pronouns as well as possessive and verbal forms. Other cooccurring linguistic items may include nominal forms such as titles, titles plus names, and common nouns. For this reason, the present study hereafter employs the

subject pronouns TÚ and USTED in small capitals in order to refer to the use of *tuteo* and *ustedeo* in social encounters.

References

Brown, D. 1975. The use of 'TÚ' and 'USTED' with parents by some Mexican American students. *Hispania* 58:1.126-27.

Brown, R., and A. Gilman. 1960. The pronouns of power and solidarity. In: *Style in language.* T.A. Sebeok, ed. Cambridge, Mass.: MIT Press. 253-76.

Ervin-Tripp, S. 1972. On sociolinguistic rules: Alternation and co-occurrence. In: *Directions in sociolinguistics: The ethnography of communication.* J.J. Gumperz and D. Hymes, eds. New York: Holt, Rinehart, and Winston. 213-50.

Espinosa, A.M. 1946. *Estudios sobre el español de Nuevo Méjico. Segunda Parte: La morfología.* A. Rosenblat, trans. Buenos Aires: Biblioteca de Dialectología Hispanoamericana.

Fishman, J.A. 1971. *Sociolinguistics: A brief introduction.* Rowley, Mass.: Newbury House.

_____. 1972. The relationship between micro- and macro-sociolinguistics in the study of who speaks what language to whom and when. In: *Sociolinguistics: Selected readings.* J.B. Pride and J. Holmes, eds. New York: Penguin Books. 15-32.

Fox, J. 1969. The pronouns of address in Spanish. In: *Actes de Xe Congrès International de Linguistes.* Bucharest: Academie de la République Socialiste de Roumanie. 685-93.

Friedrich, P. 1972. Structural implications of Russian pronominal usage. In: *Directions in sociolinguistics.* J.J. Gumperz and D. Hymes, eds. New York: Holt, Rinehart, and Winston. 270-300.

Hadlich, R.L. 1971. *A transformational grammar of Spanish.* Englewood Cliffs, N.J.: Prentice-Hall.

Head, B.F. 1978. Respect degrees in pronominal reference. In: *Universals of human language.* J. Greenberg et al., eds. Stanford: Stanford University Press. 151-211.

Hockett, C.F. 1958. *A course in modern linguistics.* New York: Macmillan.

Keller, G.D. 1974. Spanish *tú* and *usted*: Patterns of interchange. In: *1974 Colloquium on Spanish and Portuguese Linguistics.* W.G. Milan et al., eds. Washington, D.C.: Georgetown University Press. 84-96.

Lambert, W.E., and G.R. Tucker. 1976. *Tú, vous, usted*: A social-psychological study of address patterns. Rowley, Mass.: Newbury House.

Marín, D. 1972. El uso de tú y usted en el español actual. *Hispania* 55.904-8.

Rael, J.B. 1937. A study of the phonology and morphology of New Mexican Spanish based on a collection of 410 folk-tales. Dissertation, Stanford University.

Ramsey, M.M. 1894. *A textbook of modern Spanish.* New York: Holt, Rinehart, and Winston.

Rosengren, P. 1974. *Presencia y ausencia de los pronombres personales sujetos en español moderno.* Stockholm: Almqvist and Wiksell.

Sánchez, R. 1982. Our linguistic and social context. In: *Spanish in the United States: Sociolinguistic aspects.* J. Amastae and L. Elías-Olivares, eds. New York: Cambridge University Press. 9-46.

Solé, Y.R. 1970. Correlaciones socio-culturales del uso de 'tú'/'vos' y 'usted' en la Argentina, Perú y Puerto Rico. *Thesaurus* 25:2.161-95.

Aztequismos en el español chicano

Robert N. Smead
University of Arizona
J. Halvor Clegg
Brigham Young University

1 Introducción. Existe la tendencia, en la actualidad, de criticar o aun denigrar los estudios léxicos calificándolos de poco valor. Como muchos de estos estudios suelen ser meramente descriptivos y a menudo se ocupan de ligeras variantes o curiosidades, pueden ser de poco interés general. Es más, se hacen empleando técnicas y metodologías que son reliquias del antaño ('del año del caldo' dirían los chicanos); usan técnicas y metodologías que hacen caso omiso de muchas de las realidades lingüísticas actuales que se han mostrado tan importantes para explicar y entender la realidad vivida del lenguaje.

Sin embargo, si se reconocen las limitaciones de tales estudios y no se utilizan para fines normativos, pueden ser valiosos. De hecho, paulatinamente van llenando los incontables huecos que permanecen en el conocimiento del español chicano. Pueden proveernos con los datos brutos que son tan necesarios en este caso para delimitar, en forma definitiva, lo que es el léxico chicano.

Desgraciadamente, se oyen voces, aun de nuestros colegas malinformados, que dan vida a un sinfín de mitos sobre el léxico chicano. Tal vez sea este dialecto el más evocador de todos los dialectos castellanos. ¿Será esto porque todavía queda 'por ai' escondido, cubierto de mitos donde, entre otras muchas, exageran las influencias anglizantes o niegan su hispanicidad? Si se hiciera un análisis frío, a la luz del día, los hechos arrojarían otra perspectiva de la que se presenta.

Entre los hechos imprescindibles hay que reconocer el fondo de abolengo castellano. En estudios hechos sobre la literatura chicana, Hinckley (1976) encontró que más de 90% del vocabulario se hallaba en el *Diccionario de la Real Academia Española*. Si insistimos en que la literatura no refleja la lengua hablada y bajamos la cifra, nunca se remontaría más allá del 70%. Así que no hay que dudar de su hispanicidad.

Segundo hecho imprescindible tiene que ser su mexicanidad. Este rasgo tan obvio tampoco debe prestarse a la discusión. Hasta los chicanos prefieren llamarse 'mexicanos.' El análisis del léxico chicano que llevamos a cabo comprueba su mexicanidad.

Tercer hecho imprescindible es su categoría de dialecto castellano hablado. Como tal, comparte docenas de rasgos del castellano hablado con los demás dialectos castellanos. Este hecho ya es incontrovertible; queda bien probado por varios estudiosos como Studerus (1980).

Partimos de la premisa que el español chicano es un fértil laboratorio de cambios lingüísticos. También reconocemos que la rama más creativa de la ciencia de la lengua es la de la semántica. El lenguaje de los chicanos ha sido muy activo en creaciones léxicas y en cambios semánticos. Su posición en la frontera entre dos grandes lenguas le ha prestado una fuerza alentadora a esa creatividad.

Cuando comenzamos el estudio del léxico chicano, esperamos encontrar ejemplos de las influencias aparentes como los anglicismos, los mexicanismos, los pachuquismos, etc. De hecho, llegamos a distinguir entre diecinueve diferentes fuentes léxicas distintas de las históricas del castellano. Lo que no esperábamos encontrar fue la cantidad, la variedad, la extensión, y la actualidad de aztequismos en el español chicano.

2 Los aztequismos. El aztequismo se define como locución, giro o vocablo prestado del náhuatl--el idioma de los aztecas. El náhuatl desempeñó un papel importante en la historia de México. Según Hasler (1964:123), cuando los españoles comenzaron la conquista de las Américas, '[el náhuatl] era el idioma hablado por distantes etnías esparcidas desde la Huasteca hasta Guerrero y desde la Huasteca hasta El Salvador.' Más tarde, en manera *de facto*, los conquistadores emplearon el náhuatl como una especie de *lingua franca*, o lengua general como lo denomina Zamora (1970), para facilitar la conquista misma de gentes de distintas regiones y hablas. Por casi tres cuartos de siglo (de 1521 hasta 1590 cuando se decretó una Real Orden imponiendo el español como lengua oficial), el náhuatl gozó de mucho prestigio y un 'estatus' elevado a pesar de ser lengua de los conquistados y no de los conquistadores. Sirvió aún de medio de cristianización de la población indígena mexicana y fue estudiado por los frailes y misioneros católicos, quienes, a su vez, escribieron catecismos, diccionarios y diversos tratados sobre el mexicano (como llegó a conocerse el náhuatl) u otros elementos relacionados con la vida y la cultura de Nueva España. Es más: en 1547--pocas décadas después de la publicación de la gramática de Nebrija--Olmos (1875) escribió la primera gramática náhuatl (siendo también la primera gramática de un idioma americano indígena).

Debido, entonces, a un largo período de bilingüismo y contacto interlingual que siguen hasta el momento, el español (tanto las variedades mexicanas como la variedad general o 'estándar') ha tomado prestada mucha materia lingüística del náhuatl. Como se ha comprobado, la materia lingüística que más fácilmente se transmite de un idioma a otro es la materia léxica--y en este caso parece ser la única materia que el náhuatl ha contribuido en forma significativa y perdurable al español.

Los aztequismos forman una parte significativa del español mexicano. Un análisis preliminar del *Diccionario de mejicanismos* (Santamaría 1959) revela que aproximadamente 11,5% de sus vocablos son de origen náhuatl. Esta cifra equivale a unos 3,360 artículos de un total de unos 28,950 vocablos. Como veremos en seguida se han categorizado estos aztequismos de diversos modos.

En el prólogo del *Diccionario de aztequismos* de Cabrera (1974:12) Federico Robinson A. describe la tarea que emprendió de clasificar los préstamos del náhuatl al español mexicano. Para facilitar su encuesta estudió los primeros 120 vocablos tomados de 10 secciones alfabéticas de los materiales de Cabrera, los cuales constituyen un 30% de los 4,100 artículos totales. Su esquema incluye seis categorías y puede resumirse de la siguiente forma:

(1) plantas y árboles (38%: 1560 vocablos)
(2) animales (10%: 410 vocablos)
(3) gentes y grupos sociales (12%: 492 vocablos)
(4) nombres de lugar (7%: 300 vocablos)
(5) enfermedades, remedios y alimentos (10%: 410 vocablos)
(6) vocablos no clasificados (23%: 943 vocablos).

De esa forma responde por el 77% de los vocablos contenidos en el diccionario. Como ya hemos mencionado no clasifica los artículos restantes, pero sí indica, que en su mayoría, son variantes ortográficas. Esto, según Robinson, 'refleja el interés del autor por regularizar o tipificar la ortografía al deletrear los "aztequismos"' (Cabrera 1974:10).

3 Aztequismos en el español chicano. Con eso ya en mente, pasemos al análisis del papel de los aztequismos en el español chicano. A fin de realizar este análisis hemos catalogado, a base de computadora, los primeros 8,544 artículos que aparecen en el *Diccionario del español chicano (DEC)* (Galván y Teschner 1975). Hemos referenciado cada artículo con posibles fuentes léxicas (como son los anglicismos, americanismos, mexicanismos, pachuquismos, etc.), representadas ellas mismas (es decir, las fuentes léxicas) por unos 15 diccionarios, vocabularios y refraneros, por supuesto, dentro del español chicano. Puesto que el dialecto es hablado, verificamos las formas con informantes del norte de México.

Descubrimos que el 3,14% de estos artículos (o sea 268 vocablos) podría clasificarse como aztequismo o locución que contiene el mismo. Consideramos que 15 de estos 268 vocablos son de etimología dudosa, así que 253 fueron comprobados como aztequismos (2,96% del corpus). Esta cifra es baja y se debe, en parte, a la omisión de muchos aztequismos de alta frecuencia. Los vocablos *camote, chocolate, tomate* y *tequila,* por ejemplo, no figuran en el diccionario. Agregando los otros muchos vocablos derivados del náhuatl que se oyen en el español chicano, uno calcularía un porcentaje de 4 o 5, por lo menos.

Estos 268 aztequismos caen en 5 subcategorías geográficas más la categoría de 'etimología dudosa.' Hay aztequismos generalizados, es decir, que ocurren en otras lenguas. Los hay también que ocurren en Centro y Sudamérica. Se espera que hubiera aztequismos exclusivos al mexicano, pero dentro de esta división se puede distinguir entre los que se usan por toda la república y los mayormente norteños. Así que la cuarta subcategoría es la de aztequismos norteños. Ultima subcategoría geográfica es la del aztequismo chicano que se hallan usados entre los chicanos. A continuación se presentan las subcategorías, incluyendo los aztequismos clasificados como de 'etimología dudosa.'

Aztequismos generalizados. El criterio para los aztequismos generalizados es que se hallen documentados en otros idiomas (inglés, francés, catalán, sueco, italiano, etc.) o en el español peninsular. Ejemplos son:

En otros idiomas (incluyendo vocablos no encontrados en el *DEC*):

aguacate (avocado)
chicle
chocolate
enchilada
guacamole
tamal (tamale)
tequila
tomate (jitomate)

Peninsulares (incluyendo vocablos no encontrados en el *DEC*): (2 artículos; 0,7%)

apachurrar 'to smash, crush, squash'
coco 'boogie man'
cacahuate (cacahuete) 'peanut'
gachupín 'Spaniard'
tiza 'chalk'

Aztequismos americanos. El criterio para los aztequismos americanos es que se hallen documentados en las Américas en general, en Centroamérica (incluyendo el Caribe), o en Sudamérica. Ejemplos son:

Americanos (centro [incluye el caribe] y sudamericanos): (19 artículos; 7,1% del corpus; 42% de los aztequismos americanos)

chamaco 'boy'
chiche 'breast, sinecure'
chueco 'twisted, crooked, dishonest'
mitote 'uproar, disturbance, loud party'
tololoche 'string bass'

Centroamericanos (incluye el caribe): (19 artículos; 7,1% del corpus; 42% de los aztequismos americanos)

chapulín 'grasshopper'
ejote 'green bean'
esquite 'popcorn'
tepalcates 'odds and ends of little value'
tepocate 'runt, squirt'

Sudamericanos: (2 artículos; 0,7% del corpus; 4,4% de los aztequismos americanos)

chicoteada 'whipping, lashing'
petacona 'large and shapely woman'

Variantes: (5 artículos; 2% del corpus; 11% de los aztequismos americanos)

cenzontle 'mocking bird'
cenzoncle 'mocking bird'
sinsonte 'mocking bird'

Los aztequismos americanos forman un total de 45 aztequismos, es decir, un 16,8% del corpus de aztequismos.

Aztequismos mexicanos. El criterio para los aztequismos mexicanos es que se hallen documentados en México en general. Tenemos también ejemplos de dichos entre los aztequismos mexicanos. Ejemplos son:
Vocablos: (87 artículos; 32,5% del corpus)

apapachar 'to spoil, pamper'
cochino 'nasty, indecent'
cuate 'twin, pal, peer'
chi(s)pear 'to drizzle'
pizca 'harvest'

Frases y dichos: (11 artículos; 4,1% del corpus)

*hacerse *atole* 'to become watery, overdilute'
*no valer un *cacahuate* 'not to be worth a damn'
*andar como burro sin *mecate* 'to run wild and free'
*el mero *petatero* 'the head honcho, the genuine article'
**papalotearle para* + infinitivo 'to excel at doing something'

Los aztequismos mexicanos contribuyen un total de 98 entradas, es decir, un 36,6% del corpus de aztequismos.

Aztequismos norteños. Los criterios para los aztequismos norteños son que se hallen documentados en el norte de México o reconocidos como usual en el norte por nuestra informante. Ejemplos son:
Vocablos: (38 artículos; 14,2% del corpus)

coyote 'youngest member of a family'
chante 'house, home'
mayate 'black person'
moyote 'mosquito'
papalote 'windmill; propeller'

Frases y dichos: (9 artículos; 3,4% del corpus)

*hacer *atole* 'to flatten; to break every bone in one's body'
*andar *canicas* 'to be passionately in love'
*marrana *cuina* 'fat and ugly old bitch'
*sepa el burro de los *mecates* 'Who can say?; Who knows?'
*cara de *molcajete* 'ugly face'

Los aztequismos norteños son un total de 47, es decir, un 17,5% del corpus de aztequismos.

Aztequismos chicanos. Los criterios para los aztequismos chicanos son que se hallen documentados en Coltharp (1965) (sin contradicciones) o no documentados en publicaciones mexicanas ni reconocidos por nuestra informante norteña. Ejemplos son:

Vocablos: (50 artículos; 18,7% del corpus)

ahuichote 'pimp, whoremaster'
asquela 'mosquito'
cizote/sisote 'boil; sore; ringworm'
chayote 'tom-boy; dollar, greenback'
mezquite 'month'

---

* Aztequismo

Frases y dichos: (12 artículos; 4,5% del corpus)

apachurrar la oreja 'to sleep'
chicotearle el aparato 'to excel at doing something'
*ir hecho *chile* 'to run rapidly, to go like a bat out of hell'
*ciertos *elotes y cañas heladas* 'certain so-and-sos'
*tirar *zoquete* 'to defecate'

Hay un total de 62 aztequismos chicanos, es decir, un 23,1% del corpus de aztequismos.

Etimología dudosa. Las palabras de etimología dudosa son palabras no comprobadas como procedentes del náhuatl. Es posible que sean aztequismos, pero falta una comprobación a manos de una autoridad lingüística. Ejemplos son:
Vocablos: (15 artículos; 5,6% del corpus)

chancaquía 'thistle; burr'
chapul 'child'
chongo 'knot of hair tied up in the back of the head'
pilingo 'small child; child small for his age'
tacuache 'drunk, inebriated'

Referencias

Alcalá Venceslada, A. 1951. *Vocabulario andaluz.* Madrid: Real Academia Española.
Alex, S. 1980. *The informer: An apple data base manager.* Vacaville, Calif.: Apple Orchard.
Alfaro, R. J. 1964. *Diccionario de anglicismos.* 2a ed. Madrid: Gredos.
Cabrera, L. 1974. *Diccionario de aztequismos.* 1974. México, D. F.: Editorial Oasis.
Coltharp, L. 1965. *The tongue of the Tirilones: A linguistic study of a criminal argot.* Tuscaloosa: University of Alabama Press.
Espinosa, A.M. 1930. *Estudios sobre el español en Nuevo México. Parte I: Fonética.* Biblioteca de Dialectología Hispanoamericana. Buenos Aires.
_____. 1946. *Estudios sobre el español en Nuevo México. Parte II: Morfología.* Biblioteca de Dialectología Hispanoamericana. Buenos Aires.
Galván, R.A., y R.V. Teschner. 1975. *El diccionario del español de Tejas.* Silver Spring, Md.: Institute of Modern Languages.
_____. 1977. *El diccionario del español chicano.* Silver Spring, Md.: Institute of Modern Languages.
Hasler, J.A. 1964. *Etimos latinos, griegos y nahuas.* 1964. Xalapa, México: Universidad de Veracruz.
Hills, E. C. 1906. New Mexico Spanish. *PMLA* 21.706-53.
Hinckley, G. 1976. Chicano Spanish vocabulary. Trabajo no publicado. Brigham Young University.
Juilland, A., y E. Chang-Rodríguez. 1964. *Frequency dictionary of Spanish words.* La Haya: Mouton.

---

* Aztequismo

Kercheville, F.M. 1934. A preliminary glossary of New Mexican Spanish. En: *University of New Mexico Bulletin*. Albuquerque. 9-69.

Malaret, A. 1946. *Diccionario de americanismos*. 3a ed. Buenos Aires: Emecé Editores.

Manuel, H. T. 1965. *Spanish-speaking children of the Southwest: Their education and the public welfare*. Austin: University of Texas Press.

McWilliams, C. 1968. *North from Mexico: The Spanish-speaking people of the United States*. Nueva York: Greenwood Press.

Morínigo, M.A. 1966. *Diccionario manual de americanismos*. Buenos Aires: Muchnik Editores.

Olmos, A. 1875. *Grammaire de la langue Nahuatl ou Mexicaine, composée en 1547 par le franciscain André de Olmos et publiée avec notes, éclaircissements, etc. par Rémi Siméon*. París: Imprimerie Nationale.

Real Academia Española. 1970. *Diccionario de la lengua española*. Madrid: Espasa-Calpe.

Santamaría, F.J. 1942. *Diccionario general de americanismos*. 3 vols. México, D.F.: Editorial Pedro Robredo.

_____. 1959. *Diccionario de mejicanismos*. México, D. F.: Editorial Porrúa.

Studerus, L. H. 1980. Regional, universal, and popular aspects of Chicano Spanish grammar. *Bilingual Review/Revista Bilingüe* 7:2.249-54.

Teschner, R.V. 1972. Anglicisms in Spanish: A cross-referenced guide to previous findings, together with English lexical influence on Chicago Mexican Spanish. Tesis doctoral no publicada. University of Wisconsin, Madison.

Velasco Valdés, M. 1967. *Repertorio de voces populares en México*. México, D.F.: B. Costa-Amic.

Zamora Vicente, A. 1970. *Dialectología española*. 2a ed. Madrid: Gredos.

Sobre el mantenimiento de las cláusulas subordinadas en el español de Los Angeles

Manuel Gutiérrez
University of Southern California

Múltiples son los factores que afectan los cambios y el mantenimiento de una lengua al encontrarse ésta en una situación de contacto con otra. Los primeros que habría que mencionar son los de naturaleza social: el tamaño del grupo de hablantes, la tasa de nacimiento, el tiempo de inmigración de sus integrantes, etc. Otro factor que afecta el fenómeno que aquí discutimos es el de las actitudes, es decir, la relación entre el grupo y su lengua, la lengua mayoritaria, el grupo mayoritario, etc. El uso de las lenguas es también importante, pues el dónde, para qué y con quién se usa determinan el mantenimiento de una lengua en ciertos contextos. Hay factores más generales y ajenos a los grupos minoritarios propiamente dichos. Sin lugar a dudas, el más importante de éstos es relacionado con el gobierno. A veces, el gobierno elimina por decreto el uso de determinada lengua en favor del uso de la llamada lengua oficial; ello obliga a que el grupo minoritario se asimile lingüísticamente a la comunidad general. Por el contrario, a veces sucede que ciertos gobiernos promueven el uso de las lenguas de las minorías; esta situación permite el desarrollo 'natural' de estas lenguas, de tal modo que los posibles cambios que en ellas ocurran se deberán fundamentalmente a factores derivados de su situación de contacto. Todo esto nos permite dejar en claro lo siguiente: no es sólo un factor el que influye en el mantenimiento de una lengua; son múltiples y varían de comunidad a comunidad.

¿Qué aspectos de la lengua son más susceptibles al cambio, qué aspectos se mantienen y por qué?

Considerando la situación general de las lenguas que se van simplificando debido a su situación de contacto con la lengua de la mayoría, podríamos señalar tres razones lingüísticas que parecen determinar qué aspectos de la lengua van simplificándose: oposición difusa, redundancia y complejidad. La primera alude a aquellos sectores de la lengua en los cuales el uso de una u otra forma es difícil de explicitar por el hablante común (y a veces incluso por el profesor de lengua). En español, por ejemplo, estaría el caso de las oposiciones *ser/estar*, subjuntivo/indicativo, imperfecto/pretérito, etc. La segunda tiene que ver con los aspectos de la lengua que manifiestan mayor redundancia. Correspondería señalar aquí las categorías de género y número del español, las cuales deben ser marcadas por el hablante en cada uno de los elementos que conforman el sintagma (artículo, adjetivo y verbo, en el caso del número; artículo y adjetivo, en el caso del género). La tercera razón dice relación con los distintos niveles de complejidad de las estructuras de la lengua. De este modo se podría decir que la yuxtaposición, por ejemplo, es una operación más sencilla que la subordinación, puesto que en aquélla el hablante relaciona cláusulas que como una totalidad tienen un mismo nivel jerárquico; en esta última, en cambio, necesita incrustar una totalidad (la oración subordinada) para relacionarla con un elemento determinado de la unidad mayor sin que la relación entre los elementos de esta unidad mayor se vea alterada.

De acuerdo a los tres puntos discutidos más arriba, es posible establecer, de manera general, ciertas tendencias en el proceso de simplificación. Así, sería esperable en la primera situación, la ampliación del espacio semántico de una de las forma y la disminución del mismo en la otra, con la desaparición de esta última. Sería esperable también una simplificación en la marcación de ciertas categorías, de tal modo que no sea necesario marcarlas en todos los elementos de un sintagma. Finalmente, esperaríamos asimismo que en una situación de contacto lingüístico los representantes de generaciones nuevas utilizaran algunos tipos de estructuras con menor frecuencia que los representantes de generaciones anteriores.

Este trabajo se propone como estudio preliminar para determinar en qué medida van desapareciendo o manteniéndose en las narrativas orales las diferentes estructuras subordinadas del español en el continuo generacional bilingüe de la ciudad de Los Angeles.

Tomamos el concepto de narrativa de acuerdo a la definición entregada por Labov, según la cual ésta está constituida por una serie de oraciones ligadas unas a otras por una relación de causa-efecto, conformando de este modo acciones que se desarrollan en el tiempo.

El material utilizado consiste en diez narrativas orales de tres generaciones sucesivas, la mayor parte de éstas pertenecientes al proyecto sobre el español del Este de Los Angeles dirigido por Silva-Corvalán. La primera generación comprende a los hablantes nacidos fuera de Estados Unidos y que han emigrado a este país después de los once años de edad. La segunda generación consta de los hablantes de español que han nacido en los Estados Unidos o que han emigrado a este país antes de los once años; además, uno de sus padres pertenece a la primera generación. La tercera generación incluye a los hablantes que han nacido en los Estados Unidos; además sus padres han nacido en este país o han emigrado a él antes de los once años de edad.

Para la clasificación de las estructuras subordinadas estudiadas hemos seguido lo propuesto por el *Esbozo de una nueva gramática de la lengua española* (1975:504), la cual aparece en el Cuadro 1.

Al considerar la distribución de las estructuras subordinadas a través de las generaciones se aprecia una significativa disminución a medida que el continuo generacional avanza. Algunos ejemplos que ilustran la situación de las estructuras presentadas en el Cuadro 2 son los siguientes:

(1) ... diles *que nosotros estamos tranquilos.*
(2) Y siempre tenían botellas en la mano, de cerveza, o qué sé yo, *que se quebraron.*
(3) Pos ya *cuando terminé de hablar con él* le salió las lágrimas.

Cuadro 1. Clasificación de cláusulas subordinadas.

Sustantivas	oraciones de sujeto oraciones complementarias directas oraciones complmentarias de un sustantivo o adjetivo
Adjetivas	especificativas explicativas
Circunstanciales	de tiempo de lugar de modo comparativas finales causales consecutivas condicionales concesivas

Cuadro 2. Totales.

	Gen. 1	Gen. 2	Gen. 3
Sustantivas	46.7% (50)	39.7% (27)	55.4% (31)
Adjetivas	14.0% (15)	16.2% (11)	10.7% (6)
Circunstanciales	39.3% (42)	44.1% (30)	33.9% (19)
	46.3% (107)	29.4% (68)	24.2% (56) (231)

En este cuadro de resumen general se aprecia que el 46.3% de uso de cláusulas subordinadas de la primera generación disminuye a un 29.4% en la segunda y éste a un 24.2% en la tercera.

Consideramos que la oración es una secuencia que contiene distintos niveles de relación. En un primer nivel se encuentra la relación entre las unidades mayores de la oración; corresponde a la relación entre sujeto y predicado. En un segundo nivel están las relaciones entre el elemento principal del sujeto y del predicado con los elementos que los determinan. Así sucesivamente habrá tantos niveles de relación según la complejidad que tenga la secuencia oracional en cuestión.

Las cláusulas subordinadas sirven para expresar relaciones dentro de los componentes de una oración, ya sea dentro de una frase nominal ya sea dentro de una frase verbal; por lo tanto, las relaciones de la cláusula subordinada con su elemento determinado nunca aparecen en un primer nivel, sino incrustadas de tal modo que surgen al explicitar las relaciones que se encuentran en un segundo o tercer nivel.

Llevando esta situación al problema que nos interesa se podría predecir que las relaciones más susceptibles a la desaparición son aquéllas que se encuentran en los niveles inferiores de la estructura relacional; las relaciones que aparecen en los primeros niveles, por el contrario, se mantendrán con insistencia. Evidencia de esto sería la disminución progresiva de las cláusulas subordinadas a través del continuo generacional bilingüe.

En relación a la subordinación sustantiva se puede decir que es una estructura que se mantiene con una alta frecuencia de uso a través de todas las generaciones. Es más: mientras aparece cierta disminución de uso en la segunda generación, esta estructura alcanza su porcentaje mayor en la tercera generación.

Las adjetivas y circunstanciales muestran un comportamiento relativamente diferente. En ambas se observa un leve aumento de su frecuencia por parte de la segunda generación; sin embargo, hay una disminución de su uso en la tercera generación.

En las cláusulas sustantivas hemos hecho una diferenciación de acuerdo a la función que cumple la cláusula subordinada, ya sea ésta sujeto de oración, en oraciones del tipo:

(4) Es importante *que lo hagan.*

ya sea complemento sujetivo, por ejemplo:

(5) ... pero lo que hicieron fue *que quitaron los asientos.*

ya se complemento directo de un verbo, en oraciones del tipo:

(6) ... sabe *que me robaron las llaves del carro.*

Cuadro 3. Cláusulas sustantivas según su función en la oración.

	Gen. 1	Gen. 2	Gen. 3
Sujeto	4% (2)	0%	0%
Complemento sujetivo	2% (1)	0%	0%
Complemento directo	94% (47)	100% (27)	100% (31)
	50	27	31

Sólo encontramos dos cláusulas sustantivas en función de sujeto y una en la de complemento sujetivo en las narrativas estudiadas; todas ellas pertenecen a la primera generación. La segunda y la tercera generación no muestran ningún uso de estas estructuras. Sin embargo, cuando la oración sustantiva funciona como objeto directo se aprecia un uso frecuente de ésta en todas las generaciones. En este punto hicimos una subclasificación de acuerdo a la presencia o ausencia de la conjunción subordinante. Se ejemplifican los dos casos en las siguientes oraciones:

(7)   ... le dije *que* corriera porque le iba a dar (un balazo) a él también.

(8)   ... le dije: córrale porque le va a dar a usted también.

Aquellas construcciones que no usan la conjunción corresponden al estilo narrativo directo, en el cual, el hablante asume dos puntos de vista diferentes--el propio y el de la persona citada. En esta situación se observan ciertas tendencias, como se aprecia en el Cuadro 4.

Cuadro 4. Complemento directo: Estilo directo vs. estilo indirecto.

	Gen. 1	Gen. 2	Gen. 3
Estilo indirecto (con conjunción)	51.1% (24)	48.1% (13)	41.9% (13)
Estilo directo (sin conjunción)	48.9% (23)	51.9% (14)	58.1% (18)
	47	27	31

El uso del estilo indirecto disminuye a medida que avanza el continuo generacional; el estilo directo, en cambio, aumenta. Es decir, la tendencia va dirigida a adoptar la doble perspectiva discursiva y a evitar el uso de la conjunción subordinante, con lo cual se evita el problema de la forma que tiene que adquirir el verbo de la cláusula subordinada.

En la subordinación adjetiva hemos determinado la situación que se presenta al considerar la función que desempeña el pronombre relativo. Tal como se aprecia en el Cuadro 5, la función sujeto del pronombre relativo muestra una tendencia decreciente. Esta función la ejemplifica la siguiente oración:

(9)   Sí, porque han estudiado también de mucha gente *que se muere por unos segundos.*

La función complemento directo se mantiene con cierta estabilidad. Estas son oraciones del tipo:

(10)   ... aquí en el brazo tenía, tenía algunas municiones en el brazo, *que todavía tengo aquí.*

Cuadro 5. Función del pronombre relativo.

	Gen. 1	Gen. 2	Gen. 3
Sujeto	53.3% (8)	36.4% (4)	16.7% (1)
Complemento directo	40.0% (6)	63.7% (7)	50.0% (3)
Complemento circunstancial	6.7% (1)	0.0%	33.3% (2)
	46.9% (15)	34.4% (11)	18.8% (6) (32)

Considerando, sin embargo, el conjunto de las cláusulas adjetivas se observa claramente una tendencia decreciente de su uso. Por su naturaleza adjetiva, las cláusulas relativas son las que se encuentran más cohesionadas con el sustantivo al cual determinan. Con éste conforman una unidad difícil de concebir separadamente. Por ello, cuando el proceso de relativización ha sido incorporado por un hablante, éste lo mantendrá y perfeccionará; por el contrario, el hablante que no lo ha incorporado y se encuentra más distanciado generacionalmente del sistema lingüístico del español tendrá más dificultad para mantenerlo y perfeccionarlo.

Dentro de las cláusulas subordinadas que expresan una circunstancia hay algunas que manifiestan una situación bastante interesante. Esto se puede apreciar en el Cuadro 6.

Cuadro 6. Cláusulas circunstanciales.

	Gen. 1	Gen. 2	Gen. 3
Tiempo	19.0% (8)	30.0% (9)	31.6% (6)
Modo	4.8% (2)	0.0%	0.0%
Lugar	0.0%	3.3% (1)	0.0%
Finales	45.2% (19)	40.0% (12)	26.3% (5)
Causales	21.4% (9)	13.3% (4)	42.1% (8)
Consecutivas	7.1% (3)	0.0%	0.0%
Condicionales	2.4% (1)	3.3% (1)	0.0%
Comparativas	0.0%	10.0% (3)	0.0%
	42	30	19

Sólo aparecen en el habla de los de la primera generación las cláusulas de modo (11) y las consecutivas (12):

(11) Entonces, él se devolvió, *como es natural, verdad.*
(12) ... la muchacha es bien bonita, mano ..., está bonita, bonita *así es que a mí me parece justo el precio.*

Entre los hablantes de la segunda y tercera generaciones no hay ninguna manifestación de estas construcciones.

La tercera generación tampoco muestra manifestación alguna de circunstanciales de lugar, condicionales y comparativas; sólo se observan algunas de estas últimas en la segunda generación.

Muestran cierta estabilidad a través de las tres generaciones las circunstanciales de tiempo, como:

(13) ¿Y estaba sabroso *cuando te los comistes?*

y las causales, como:

(14) Ni se nota, *porque mi carro está chocado.*

Las finales del tipo:

(15) Bueno, pues a ... ese día fui *a pelear* y peleamos.

manifiestan una tendencia descendente de uso, pues mientras en la primera y segunda generaciones evidencian una frecuencia bastante similar, ésta cae bruscamente en la tercera generación.

Dado el tipo de discurso con el que trabajamos (el narrativo) sólo es posible la aparición significativa de ciertos tipos de oraciones circunstanciales. De este modo se explica la escasez de oraciones condicionales, por ejemplo, cuya aparición es esperable en un discurso de carácter hipotético. Ello explica también la recurrente aparición de las cláusulas temporales, finales y causales. Es interesante destacar, sin embargo, que tanto la primera como la segunda generación hacen uso de una variedad más amplia de cláusulas circunstanciales. Por el contrario, la tercera generación sólo utiliza aquéllas que le sirven para cumplir las necesidades básicas de un discurso de tipo narrativo, ya que más de la mitad de las oraciones circunstanciales son utilizadas por este grupo en la parte de la narrativa que corresponde a la acción concreta, mientras el resto de estas cláusulas se divide, por una parte, para cumplir con la función de orientar al oyente y, por otra, para cumplir con la función de evaluar la historia narrada.

Al parecer, el fenómeno de la subordinación está asociado con la exposición de los hablantes a los medios de erudición que una lengua estándar desarrolla con el propósito de que cumplan una función de acercamiento a la norma. Estos medios corresponden fundamentalmente a la práctica de la expresión escrita, a la práctica de la lectura y a cierta exposición a la enseñanza en la lengua respectiva. La primera generación de hablantes bilingües está más familiarizada con estos medios, pero esta situación va cambiando a medida que el continuo bilingüe también cambia.

Como se puede apreciar, las situaciones de contacto lingüístico conducen a que se produzcan cambios en las lenguas en cuestión. Estos cambios afectan fundamentalmente a aquella lengua que pertenece al grupo de minoría, el cual se ve obligado a generar estrategias que le permitan seguir manteniendo su lengua como parte fundamental de su identidad cultural.

Referencias

Andersen, R. W. 1983. The one principle of interlanguage construction. Trabajo presentado en el TESOL Convention, Toronto.

Bernárdez, E. 1982. *Introducción a la lingüística del texto.* Madrid: Espasa-Calpe.

Bronckart, J. P., y H. Sinclair. 1973. Time, tense and aspect. *Cognition* 2.107-30.

Cano Aguilar, R. 1981. *Estructuras sintácticas transitivas en el español actual.* Madrid: Gredos.

Corder, S. P. 1981. *Error analysis and interlanguage.* Oxford: Oxford University Press.

Chomsky, C. 1969. *The acquisition of syntax in children from 5 to 10.* Cambridge, Mass.: MIT Press.

Demonte, V. 1977. *La subordinación sustantiva.* Madrid: Cátedra.

Dorian, N. 1981. *Language death (The life cycle of a Scottish Gaelic dialect).* Filadelfia: University of Pennsylvania Press.

Echeverría, M. S. 1978. *Desarrollo de la comprensión infantil de la sintaxis española.* Serie lingüística 3. Universidad de Concepción, Chile.

Gili y Gaya, S. 1967. *Curso superior de sintaxis española.* 9a ed. Barcelona: Bibliograf.

Grosjean, F. 1982. *Life with two languages: An introduction to bilingualism.* Cambridge, Mass.: Harvard University Press.

Hayman, J., y S. A. Thompson. 1986. Subordination. En: *Universal grammar: Fifteen essays.* E.L. Keenan, ed. Nueva York: Methuen.

Klein, F. 1980. A quantitative study of syntactic and pragmatic indications of change in the Spanish of bilinguals in the U.S. En: *Locating language in time and space.* W. Labov, ed. Nueva York: Academic Press. 69-82.

Labov, W. 1981. Speech actions and reactions in personal narrative. En: *Georgetown University Round Table on Languages and Linguistics 1981.* D. Tannen, ed. Wáshington, D.C.: Georgetown University Press. 219-47.

_____, y I. Waletzky. 1967. Narrative analysis: Oral versions of personal experience. En: *Essays on the verbal and visual arts.* J. Helm, ed. Seattle: University of Washington Press. 12-44.

Pfaff, C.W. 1987. Functional approaches to interlanguage. En: *First and second language acquisition processes.* C.W. Pfaff, ed. Cambridge Mass.: Newbury House. 81-102.

Real Academia Española. 1976. *Esbozo de una nueva gramática de la lengua española.* 3a ed. Madrid: Espasa-Calpe.

Rozencvejg, V. 1976. *Linguistic interference and convergent change.* La Haya: Mouton.

Silva-Corvalán, C. 1983. Tense and aspect in oral Spanish narrative. *Language* 59.760-80.

_____. 1984. *Estar* en el español méxico-americano. Trabajo presentado en el VII Congreso de ALFAL, Santo Domingo.

Snow, M.A., A. Padilla y R. Campbell. 1984. Factors influencing language retention of graduates of a Spanish immersion program. National Center for Bilingual Research Report 19. Los Alamitos, Calif.

Tannen, D. 1982. Oral and literate strategies in spoken and written narratives. *Language* 58.1-21.

El subjuntivo en tres generaciones de hablantes bilingües

Francisco Ocampo
University of Southern California

Un rasgo en común que el español tiene con otras lenguas romances es la presencia del modo subjuntivo, junto al indicativo, en su sistema verbal. Es así que, en contextos que permiten la variación, el empleo de uno u otro modo transmite diferentes matices semánticos.

Es sabido que en una situación de dos lenguas en contacto se puede producir simplificaciones en la lengua del grupo minoritario. En el presente trabajo se intenta indagar qué cambios sufre el uso del subjuntivo a lo largo de tres generaciones de hablantes bilingües de inglés y español de la zona Este de Los Angeles. El punto de partida lo constituyen las siguientes preguntas:

(a) ¿Cuál es el resultado final del proceso: el mantenimiento o la pérdida del modo en cuestión?

(b) ¿Qué sucede con los matices que distinguen semánticamente al subjuntivo del indicativo?

(c) Si el subjuntivo se pierde es necesario saber de qué manera se realiza este proceso. Es decir, hay que averiguar qué contextos presentan una mayor tendencia a su desaparición, y cuál es la causa.

1 Corpus. Los datos para este trabajo fueron tomados del corpus obtenido por el proyecto East Los Angeles de Silva-Corvalán; este proyecto consiste en entrevistas grabadas y transcritas a hablantes bilingües de origen mexicano residentes en la zona Este de Los Angeles. En el corpus se les divide a los hablantes en tres generaciones. Se considera pertenecientes a la primera generación a los nacidos en México que emigraron a los Estados Unidos antes de los once años de edad. La segunda generación comprende a los que emigraron de México antes de los seis años y a los nacidos en los Estados Unidos, con un progenitor, por lo menos, de la primera generación. Son de la tercera generación los hablantes nacidos en los Estados Unidos que tienen por lo menos un progenitor de la segunda generación. Para la presente investigación se tomaron nueve hablantes, pertenecientes a la primera, segunda y tercera generaciones de bilingües. De esta manera se incluyeron tres representantes por generación.

2 Clasificación. Para clasificar los datos y comparar los resultados de las tres generaciones es necesario determinar qué construcciones en español utilizan el subjuntivo, y dentro de éstas, cuáles emplean este modo con exclusividad y cuáles permiten la variación. La base de los criterios utilizados la constituyen principalmente los trabajos de Terrell y Hooper (1974) y Bell (1980) para las proposiciones independientes y sustantivas, y el de Solé y Solé (1977) para las restantes construcciones en que aparece el subjuntivo. La clasificación resultante, que es nuestra, es la siguiente.

2.1 Proposiciones subordinadas sustantivas e independientes. Dentro de esta clase se incluyen también las cláusulas encabezadas por *ojalá, tal vez, acaso,* etc. Se sigue así el criterio de Terrell y Hooper (1974) que consideran dentro de la categoría 'construcciones calificadas' a las cláusulas subordinadas sustantivas y a las encabezadas por los términos arriba citados.

2.1.1 Comentario. Las oraciones de esta clase permiten al hablante hacer comentarios sobre las proposiciones. Son oraciones encabezadas por expresiones tales como *es una lástima que, es una pena que, me alegro de que, me extraña que, está bien que, sentir, gustar,* etc. Algunos ejemplos son:

(1) No está bien que *hagan* esas cosas.
(2) Nunca me ha gustado que *digan* que porque soy la menor que estoy chiquiada.

En tales oraciones en algunas variantes del español puede estar presente la variación subjuntivo/indicativo:

(3) Me da lástima que *estudia/estudie* tanto.

Pero en el corpus estudiado no se observó este fenómeno. Se considerará entonces que la presente variedad sólo utiliza el subjuntivo en esta clase.

2.1.2 Acto mental. La proposición principal describe un acto mental con respecto a, pero no causado por, la proposición subordinada. Son construcciones encabezadas por *darse cuenta, tomar en consideración, aprender,* etc. Se admite la variación entre los modos subjuntivo e indicativo:

(4) Voy a tomar en consideración que Pepe *es/sea* miope.

2.1.3 Volitivas. Tales oraciones permiten expresar órdenes o deseos. Esta categoría sólo emplea el subjuntivo. Comprende proposiciones independientes y construcciones subordinadas a una principal que contenga verbos como *ordenar, prohibir, suplicar, proponer, querer,* etc.:

(5)   No me *hagas* esos chistes.
(6)   Tú quieres que te lo *describa.*

2.1.4 Incertidumbre. Están encabezadas por expresiones como *quizás, acaso, tal vez,* etc., o proposiciones subordinadas a una proposición principal que contenga *dudar que, es posible que,* etc. También expresan incertidumbre construcciones aseveradas negativas. Son aseveradas aquellas construcciones que contienen verbos como *creer, pensar, afirmar, considerar, declarar,* o expresiones como *estar seguro que, es evidente que, está demostrado que, es cierto que,* etc.   La aseveración no está definida en base a condiciones necesarias y suficientes sino que es un concepto prototípico.   Por ejemplo, la negación del verbo principal en una construcción aseverada provoca una disminución de la aseverancia y un incremento de la incertidumbre, aumentando así las posibilidades del uso del subjuntivo; de la misma manera la negación de la duda aumenta la aseveración, facilitando el uso del indicativo.   Es posible, entonces, la variación subjuntivo/indicativo que puede obedecer a razones propias del hablante y reflejar procesos sicológicos internos.   Es decir, que muchas veces no se halla en el contexto del discurso la causa de esta variación que permite al hablante, por medio de los modos indicativo y subjuntivo, desplazarse en una escala que va de lo real a lo irreal:

(7)   No viene una cosa sola, parece que *vienen* todas juntas, ¿verdad?
(8)   Me parece que *hubiera sido* mejor allá.
(9)   No creo que nadie lo *pueda* hacer.

2.1.5 Imposibilidad. Estas construcciones expresan la imposibilidad de que lo contenido en la subordinada se cumpla.   Están encabezadas por expresiones como *es imposible que, no es probable que, no es posible que,* etc. Como esta clase está situada semánticamente en el extremo irreal de la escala, matiz este expresado por el subjuntivo, no es posible entonces la variación con el indicativo:

(10)   Es imposible que *lleguen* antes de las seis.
(11)   No es posible que Araceli *haya podido* hacerlo.

2.1.6 Causativas.   Estas construcciones están subordinadas a una proposición principal que contiene verbos como *hacer que, obligar a, causar que,* etc. Solamente emplean el subjuntivo:

(12)   ... me hacen que *sea* mala a veces.
(13)   Y empezó a salir un aroma muy penetrado a pescado que podía hacer que tú *vomitaras.*

2.2 Proposiciones subordinadas relativas. Cuando el antecedente del pronombre relativo es pensado con una existencia más real, el verbo está en modo indicativo; cuando el hablante no le otorga realidad concreta al antecedente, se emplea el modo subjuntivo. Es posible entonces la variación subjuntivo/indicativo:

(14) Va a ser una batalla, y especialmente para las personas que *vayan* allí.

(15) A veces no hay brazos donde *puedan* quedarse los carros que se *descomponen.*

2.3 Proposiciones subordinadas temporales. Son construcciones encabezadas por *cuando, mientras, hasta que, después que, a medida que,* etc. Cuando se expresa un hecho real, que acaece en el presente o pasado, el verbo de la subordinada temporal aparece en modo indicativo. Si se expresa un hecho posible, situado en el futuro, el verbo de la subordinada temporal está en modo subjuntivo:

(16) Cuando uno menos se lo *imagina,* cuando uno menos lo *piensa,* llegan las tragedias.

(17) Imagínate cuando se *case* uno de tus hermanos.

(18) Ahí en la Biblia dice que cuando *venga* el Anticristo van a venir bastantes falsos profetas.

2.4 Proposiciones subordinadas finales. Están encabezadas por *para que, a fin de que,* etc. Siempre llevan el modo subjuntivo:

(19) Van a curanderos para que le *den* consejos para que les *cambie* la suerte.

(20) Le pagamos para que la *dejara* entrar.

2.5 Proposiciones subordinadas condicionales. Las encabeza la conjunción *si.* Permiten la variación subjuntivo/indicativo. El modo transmite diferencias de hipoteticidad en una escala epistémica (Akatsuka 1985) que se extiende de hecho posible a hecho imposible:

(21) (Mi mujer) empezó a trabajar; es mejor para ella, porque si yo la *dejo,* al menos tiene con qué vivir.

(22) Si *necesitan* dinero se lo doy.

(23) Si lo *conociera* y de veras *necesitaba* el dinero, no se lo prestaría, se lo daría.

2.6 Proposiciones subordinadas concesivas. Están encabezadas por *aunque, aun cuando, siquiera,* etc. Permiten la variación subjuntivo/

indicativo. Como en la lengua estándar, el uso del modo depende de la mayor o menor dosis de realidad que el hablante otorga a la situación:

(24) Voy a salir aunque *llueve.*
(25) Se llevan todos muy bien aunque se *enojen* y todo.

Por ejemplo, en (25) el hablante quiere disminuir la oposición entre los conceptos 'llevarse bien' y 'enojarse,' minimizando la importancia que el segundo de ellos pueda tener. Con ese fin le otorga a este último menos realidad, colocando el verbo en modo subjuntivo.

2.7 Proposiciones subordinadas causales negadas. Están encabezadas por *porque, ya que, como, puesto que,* etc. En forma afirmativa siempre emplean indicativo. Este modo se usa, entonces, cuando la relación causa-efecto se cumple. Cuando están encabezadas por una negación, la relación causa-efecto no se cumple y se permite la variación subjuntivo/indicativo:

(26) No porque *es/sea* la mayor va a hacer lo que quiere.
(27) Pero hay una gente muy floja ... y no porque *estén* malos.

2.8 Proposiciones subordinadas locativas. Están encabezadas por *donde, dondequiera,* etc. Permiten la variación subjuntivo/indicativo. Cuando el hablante puede identificar de alguna manera el objeto localizado, emplea el indicativo; en caso contrario usa el modo subjuntivo:

(28) Llévame donde *está* tu casa.
(29) ¿Tú te imaginas corriendo donde no *estén* pasando los carros, al lado de la carretera, ahí a dejar a los niños?

2.9 Proposiciones subordinadas modales. Están encabezadas por *como, según,* etc. Es posible la variación subjuntivo/indicativo; otra vez como en la lengua estándar, permite expresar matices de mayor o menor realidad:

(30) No me gusta cuando lo haces como tú *quieres.*
(31) Me gusta tener la casa como yo *quiera.*

En las categorías anteriores se observa que la variación subjuntivo/indicativo permite expresar matices semánticos a lo largo de una escala epistémica que abarca los dominios--real (indicativo), probable (subjuntivo) e irreal (subjuntivo). En las categorías que sólo admiten subjuntivo, éste pierde su contenido semántico, ya que la elección del modo está condicionada gramaticalmente; al hablante le está vedada la opción. Podría afirmarse que al nivel semántico el subjuntivo sólo indica posibilidad o irrealidad, y que el resto de los matices que pueden expresarse con este modo son producto de interpretaciones a nivel pragmático.

3 Procedimientos y resultados. Después de identificar las varias categorías anteriores hemos considerado la totalidad de los verbos presentes en cada una de las entrevistas y los clasificamos de acuerdo a tales categorías, y a la presencia o ausencia del subjuntivo en contextos categóricos o variables.

El contexto se define aquí como la construcción oracional en la que ocurren las formas verbales que se estudian. Es decir, no se toma en consideración el contexto general del discurso en el que aparece el modo en cuestión. Contextos categóricos son las construcciones oracionales que no permiten la variación modal. Comprenden las siguientes categorías: comentario, volitivas, imposibilidad, finales y causativas. Contextos variables son las categorías en las que es posible la variación subjuntivo/indicativo: acto mental, incertidumbre, relativas, temporales, condicionales, concesivas, causales negadas, locativas y modales. Los siguientes son ejemplos de presencia y ausencia del subjuntivo en contextos categóricos y variables:

(32) Están buscando otro *work study* pa que yo le *pueda* enseñar todo lo que yo hago. (Presencia de subjuntivo en contexto categórico--finalidad.)

(33) Me están arreglando un carro, el carro chiquito que estaba atrás; lo están arreglando ya por fin y ojalá *puedo* registrarlo este fin de semana. (Ausencia de subjuntivo en contexto categórico--volitiva.)

(34) ¿Me podrías describir tu casa, todo, todas las cosas que *tengas?* (Presencia de subjuntivo en contexto variable--relativa.)

(35) Y entonces lo tuvimos que llevar a un lugar que tienen allí en la playa, como de emergencia, que están doctores, pues no son salvavidas, pero son como unos que te dan ayuda cuando la *necesitas.* (Ausencia de subjuntivo en contexto variable--temporal.)

La cantidad de verbos presentes para cada categoría y para cada una de las tres generaciones pueden observarse en los Cuadros 1, 2 y 3 en el Apéndice. Como paso siguiente se contaron los verbos presentes en las categorías que indican la presencia o la ausencia del subjuntivo en contextos categóricos y variables. Los resultados están presentes en el Cuadro 4. Luego, unas categorías fueron opuestas a otras. En la Figura 1 se compara la presencia y la ausencia del subjuntivo por generación. Aquí se observa qué sucede con la frecuencia general de uso del subjuntivo. En la Figura 2 se compara la presencia y la ausencia del subjuntivo en los contextos categóricos. Como en ellos no hay posibilidad de elección se observa la fuerza de las coerciones formales en el uso del subjuntivo para cada generación. En la Figura 3 se compara la presencia y la ausencia del subjuntivo en los contextos variables. Aquí es posible observar en qué medida cada generación es capaz de utilizar los matices semánticos que lleva consigo el uso del subjuntivo.

4 Interpretación de los resultados. Ya que sólo se han examinado nueve hablantes, los resultados no pueden considerarse conclusivos. Sin embargo, indican que en la presente situación de lenguas en contacto la tendencia apunta a la pérdida del subjuntivo. La ausencia del subjuntivo en los contextos variables muestra que este modo ya casi no constituye una opción para la tercera generación; ha perdido los matices semánticos que lo distinguían del indicativo. El hecho de que su mayor empleo se sitúe en los contextos categóricos es muestra de que su uso está regido solamente por restricciones formales; el aspecto semántico ya no juega ningún papel. Más aún, la disminución que se observa en la tercera generación en los contextos categóricos, sumada a una disminución del uso total, indica que también las restricciones formales se están perdiendo.

La disminución del uso del subjuntivo, que se muestra más marcada en los contextos variables, con la consiguiente pérdida de los matices semánticos, es reflejo de un fenómeno más amplio, ya señalado por Dorian (1980), Silva-Corvalán (1986) y Gal (a aparecer), quienes acotan que los procesos de simplificación se presentan en contextos donde es posible elegir entre dos formas semánticamente próximas. Silva-Corvalán (1986) especula que este hecho tiene por causa una mayor complejidad cognoscitiva asociada con la elección de formas de significados muy cercanos entre sí. Por el contrario, los contextos gramaticalizados, que no permiten la variación, favorecen el mantenimiento de la forma en cuestión. Esto podría ser una indicación que las asociaciones mecánicas son más simples de internalizar y producir que las semánticas.

En consecuencia, se observa que la situación de lenguas en contacto inicia un proceso que comienza con la disminución del subjuntivo en los contextos en los que es posible la variación, con la consiguiente pérdida de los matices semánticos, seguido de la eliminación de las restricciones formales y, por último, de la desaparición total de este modo.

Apéndice

Cuadro 1. Primera generación.

	Ausencia Contextos variables	Contextos categóricos	Presencia Contextos variables	Contextos categóricos
Comentario	-	-	-	7
Acto mental	-	-	-	-
Volitivas	-	-	-	41
Incertidumbre	3	-	12	-
Imposibilidad	-	-	-	2
Relativas	4	-	19	-
Temporales	3	-	5	-
Finales	-	-	-	18
Condicionales	5	-	8	-
Concesivas	-	-	5	-
Causales negadas	-	-	-	-
Locativas	-	-	2	-
Modales	1	-	9	-
Causativas	-	-	-	2

Cuadro 2. Segunda generación.

	Ausencia Contextos variables	Contextos categóricos	Presencia Contextos variables	Contextos categóricos
Comentario	-	-	-	2
Acto mental	2	-	2	-
Volitivas	-	5	-	45
Incertidumbre	8	-	26	-
Imposibilidad	-	-	-	-
Relativas	10	-	10	-
Temporales	13	-	19	-
Finales	-	1	-	19
Condicionales	11	-	2	-
Concesivas	-	-	3	-
Causales negadas	-	-	1	-
Locativas	-	-	1	-
Modales	-	-	2	-
Causativas	-	1	-	6

Cuadro 3. Tercera generación.

| | Ausencia | | Presencia | |
	Contextos variables	Contextos categóricos	Contextos variables	Contextos categóricos
Comentario	-	-	-	-
Acto mental	-	-	-	-
Volitivas	-	11	-	14
Incertidumbre	9	-	-	-
Imposibilidad	-	1	-	9
Relativas	18	-	-	-
Temporales	9	-	2	-
Finales	-	8	-	10
Condicionales	15	-	12	-
Concesivas	-	-	-	-
Causales negadas	-	-	-	-
Locativas	2	-	1	-
Modales	-	-	-	-
Causativas	-	-	-	-

Cuadro 4. Las tres generaciones.

| | Ausencia | | Presencia | |
	Contextos variables	Contextos categóricos	Contextos variables	Contextos categóricos
1a generación	16	-	60	70
2a generación	44	7	66	72
3a generación	53	20	15	33

Figura 1. Uso total del subjuntivo.

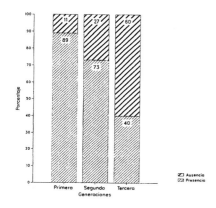

Figura 2. Contextos categóricos.

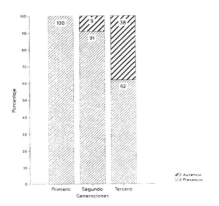

Figura 3. Contextos variables.

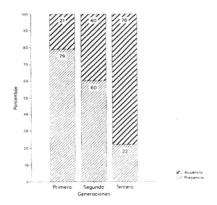

Referencias

Akatsuka, N. 1985. Conditionals and the epistemic scale. *Language* 61:3.625-39.

Bell, A. 1980. Mood in Spanish: A discussion of some recent proposals. *Hispania* 63:2.377-90.

Dorian, N. 1980. Maintenance and loss of same meaning structures in language death. *Word* 31.39-45.

Gal, S. 1984. Phonological style in bilingualism: The interaction of structure and use. En: *Georgetown University Round Table on Languages and Linguistics 1984*. D. Schiffrin, ed. Washington, D.C.: Georgetown University Press.

Silva-Corvalán, C. 1986. Tense-mood-aspect across the bilingual continuum. Trabajo presentado en NWAV XV, Stanford University.

Solé, Y., y C. Solé. 1977. *Modern Spanish syntax: A study in contrast*. Lexington, Mass.: Heath.

Actitudes hacia los cambios de códigos en Nuevo México: Reacciones de un sujeto a ejemplos de su habla

Rosa M. Fernández
The University of New Mexico

1 Introducción. La sociolingüística o el estudio de la lengua en su contexto social se concentra en el *qué, cuándo* y *dónde* de los fenómenos lingüísticos de una comunidad. Para poder comprender el *por qué* es necesario explorar también los fenómenos sociopsicológicos, es decir, la dinámica de las interacciones, identidades, motivos y actitudes de los individuos. La psicología social trata de comprender y explicar la forma en que la presencia real, imaginada o implícita de otros seres humanos, influye en los sentimientos, pensamientos y la conducta de un individuo. Sin analizar la interacción del individuo y la sociedad a través de la psicología social, nos falta saber por qué las personas escogen hablar de cierto modo en determinados contextos o por qué las variables lingüísticas influyen nuestras actitudes hacia quienes hablan.

Ya que gran parte del comportamiento social de los individuos se basa en la codificación y descodificación de mensajes no es sorpredente que una de las formas más importantes de influir a los demás es mediante el habla. Varios estudios han mostrado que el estilo de hablar (las características lingüísticas que determinan *cómo* se transmite un mensaje y no *qué* es lo que se dice) influye en la formación de impresiones y actitudes (Giles y Powesland 1975:1 y Lambert et al. 1960:48, entre otros).

1.1 La psicología social y la actitud. El concepto de actitud ha sido identificado como uno de los conceptos claves de la psicología social y constituye una de sus variables más fundamentales. No es un concepto, sin embargo, sobre el cual exista un acuerdo universal. Hay confusión entre actitud y otros conceptos íntimamente ligados con ella, tales como motivos, creencias, opiniones, valores, etc. Munn (1980:30) define las actitudes como el conjunto de creencias, sentimientos y tendencias de un individuo. Aborda la actitud desde dos perspectivas: (1) relacionándola con los motivos, y (2) como predisposición de las conductas, añadiendo que la actitud de una persona frente a algo es su predisposición a ejecutar, percibir, pensar, y sentir, en relación a ello.

Actitud y conducta suelen concordar entre sí, ya que la actitud es una preconducta que expresa una predisposición a una forma determinada de actuar. Aunque parece que sería posible anticipar el comportamiento de una persona conociendo sus predisposiciones, con frecuencia dicha persona realiza lo imprevisible y acta en contra de sus actitudes. La discrepancia entre actitud y conducta revela que no estamos entre causa y efecto, sino que ocurren una serie de factores con los cuales hay que contar. Wicker (1969:51) sugiere que estos factores son de índole personal y circunstancial, como otras actitudes relacionadas con el mismo acto de conducta, los intereses del sujeto en la situación concreta, y el miedo a la desaprobación del endogrupo.

1.2 Componentes de la actitud. Las actitudes de un individuo están integradas con su personalidad global y son condicionadas por ella. Por lo mismo, en toda actitud se hallan presentes las tres dimensiones fundamentales de la personalidad: percepción, emoción y motivación.

Los componentes de la actitud son el cognoscitivo, el afectivo y el tendencial. El componente cognoscitivo consiste en las creencias, valores y estereotipos acerca de un objeto. El componente afectivo se refiere a los sentimientos y emociones que acompañan en mayor o menor grado a toda actitud, y el componente tendencial abarca la tendencia a actuar o a reaccionar de un cierto modo con respecto al objeto. Es ése el componente más relacionado con la conducta.

1.3 Formación de las actitudes. Hay tres factores esenciales que intervienen en la formación de las actitudes: la información que recibimos, el grupo con el cual nos identificamos y nuestras propias necesidades personales. La información que recibimos nos llega mediante la enseñanza, los medios de comunicación, nuestras experiencias directas y a través del grupo en el cual nos movemos. Los grupos primarios a los que pertenecemos, como la familia, los amigos y compañeros, ejercen una gran influencia sobre los miembros. El deseo de ser aceptado y la gratificación obtenida al adoptar el punto de vista del grupo refuerzan el deseo de pertenecer, y aumentan el temor de no ser 'normal'; esto induce al individuo a incorporar las actitudes del grupo. Las actitudes se forman en el proceso de satisfacción de necesidades personales, y su signo, sea positivo o negativo, depende de si efectivamente se satisfacen o no.

2 Actitudes lingüísticas. A pesar de que el estudio descriptivo de la lengua ha indicado que no hay ninguna forma lingüística que sea por naturaleza superior, este concepto se mantiene vivo. Para comprender cómo se forman las actitudes hacia una lengua o variante lingüística es necesario explorar las fuerzas políticas y sociales que operan dentro de la historia de una nación. La forma idealizada de hablar es aquélla que se ha legitimado por el gobierno y cuyo uso se encuentra en las escuelas, los medios informativos, la literatura, los diccionarios, etc. Los maestros, los editores y otros guardianes del lenguaje se encargan de corregir y prescribir la forma legítima. O'Neil (1972:441) y Sledd (1972:450) afirman que la estandarización de una lengua es uno de los instrumentos que utiliza una nación para controlar a sus ciudadanos y así desarrollar en ellos ciertas actitudes en común.

El proceso de legitimación está íntimamente ligado al concepto del poder. Douglas (1982:78) observa que el hecho de que a un grupo se le señale por no seguir la norma crea y perpetúa la existencia de los grupos ajenos. Así a las minorías que por razones étnicas, religiosas o económicas se distinguen en su habla, se les puede impedir que tengan acceso a la cultura mayoritaria. Los causantes de esta forma de exclusión son generalmente grupos de presión u organizaciones profesionales que gozan de aceptación dentro del grupo en poder. El poder se utiliza para legitimar la lengua y la cultura del endogrupo y separarlo de aquéllos que han sido clasificados como el exogrupo.

Existen entonces aquellos individuos cuyo deseo de identificarse con grupos élites a los cuales perciben como superiores en términos sociales, económicos o políticos los lleva a tratar de imitar o adoptar la forma lingüística de más prestigio, menospreciando la propia. Sin embargo, como los miembros de una subcultura comparten entre ellos el mismo sistema de valores y creencias, tienen también una lengua o variante lingüística en común, la cual los identifica como parte del grupo. Surgen como consecuencia funciones separadas para las lenguas y las variantes empleadas en una colectividad lingüística. La forma de prestigio puede representar un alto status social, mientras que las formas de bajo prestigio reflejan solidaridad y cohesión grupal (Edwards 1985:150).

Estudios realizados por Labov (1966:293), Giles (1970:218) y otros han comprobado que los hablantes de las formas de bajo prestigio con frecuencia expresan opiniones desfavorables hacia las mismas y manifiestan actitudes negativas para quienes las usan. A pesar del desprestigio que las caracteriza y de las presiones sociales que tratan de empujar a los hablantes a substituirlas por la forma aceptada, estas variantes se mantienen en uso. Como señala Labov (1972b:297), aunque el individuo adopte las normas lingüísticas del grupo dominante, la presencia de valores opuestos apoya el uso del vernáculo. Usar el vernáculo en determinadas situaciones es un acto consciente de lealtad al grupo étnico con el cual el individuo se identifica. Este uso, según propone Giles (1973:92), puede ser convergente al tratar de acercarse a los miembros del grupo, o divergente para distanciarse del exogrupo y así establecer que el vernáculo o dialecto es el símbolo de comunicación exclusivo de sus miembros.

2.1 Actitudes hacia cambios de código. El cambio de códigos o el uso alternativo de dos lenguas dentro de un mismo mensaje es un fenómeno lingüístico característico de las colectividades bilingües. A pesar de la frecuencia con que ocurre este fenómeno en los Estados Unidos, existen actitudes negativas hacia esta variante por asociarla principalmente con la forma de hablar de grupos minoritarios impopulares. El cambio de códigos o *code-switching*, sobre todo entre inglés y español, se interpreta como una deficiencia lingüística que revela la falta de proficiencia del hablante en ambas lenguas, la cual le obliga a recurrir a la segunda lengua cuando agota su repertorio en la primera. Jacobson (1982:182) ha señalado que el cambio de códigos entre español e inglés se ve en una forma tan desfavorable que con frecuencia aquellos individuos que usan esta variante lo niegan o lo admiten con renuencia. Investigaciones hechas en los últimos veinte años han comprobado que el cambio de códigos es una estrategia lingüística con usos de índole social empleada por personas bilingües poseedoras de formas equivalentes en ambas lenguas (Valdés-Fallis:1976:84 y Fernández 1980, por ejemplo). Aún en el habla de niños bilingües Padilla (1977:98) descubrió que al igual que para los adultos, el cambiar de códigos representa no una falta de conocimiento, sino la habilidad de manejar con facilidad ambas lenguas, y un amplio conocimiento de las estrategias empleadas en la colectividad bilingüe a la que pertenecen.

2.2 Actitudes y uso del cambio de códigos en Nuevo México. El estudio aquí descrito se llevó a cabo con el fin de investigar ciertas actitudes lingüísticas y las correspondientes conductas de personas bilingües en el norte de Nuevo México. Se trató de establecer si había una discrepancia entre la actitud que los sujetos manifestaban hacia el cambio de códigos y su comportamiento lingüístico en cuanto al mismo.

Ya que la actitud negativa hacia el cambio de códigos entre español e inglés es general y no limitada a determinada región geográfica, era de esperarse que entre los participantes se encontraran sentimientos negativos similares. Por otra parte, siendo que todos eran hispanos y nativos de una región caracterizada por un alto sentido de cohesión grupal (Ornstein 1975:10) se esperaba que a pesar de su desprestigio, el cambio de códigos formara parte de su repertorio lingüístico y que lo emplearan durante conversaciones sostenidas entre ellos. La selección de los sujetos se llevó a cabo entre originarios del norte de Nuevo México siguiendo el concepto de *'introspectional perspective'* propuesto por Reyes (1976:184), es decir, que el nivel de bilingüismo así como la habilidad de alternar entre el español y el inglés de la investigadora, le permitieron juzgar la proficiencia lingüística de los participantes. Todos tenían un nivel académico de doctorado o licenciatura y todos trabajaban en algún aspecto de la enseñanza; seis eran mujeres y seis hombres, todos entre las edades de 35 y 50 años. Al conducir el experimento se agruparon los participantes en parejas y se asignaron dos tópicos para discutir, uno formal--'La importancia de la instrucción bilingüe'--y otro informal--'Recuerdos de mi infancia en Nuevo México'; y se dieron instrucciones de conducir las conversaciones en inglés, en español, o en una mezcla de las dos lenguas según desearan. Las conversaciones fueron grabadas para facilitar su análisis. Días después todos los participantes fueron entrevistados por separado y respondieron a un cuestionario que solicitaba su opinión acerca del cambio de códigos. Se les pidió también que trataran de explicar ejemplos específicos de cambios de código que ellos habían hecho durante sus conversaciones.

Los problemas de seleccionar una técnica de investigación para elicitar el habla en una forma que no afecte la validez del análisis han sido explorados por Gumperz (1972:25), quien concluyó que la necesidad de obtener muestras de conversaciones en un ámbito real se puede satisfacer mediante entrevistas con dos o más personas juntas en vez de con un solo individuo. Esta técnica constituye una forma intensiva de abordaje a los individuos que favorece la obtención de información con un grado de libertad mayor que el que ofrecen formas más estructuradas:

> The role of the interviewer in such groups is simply to act as an observer who may introduce a topic, but who then allows group processes to determine further treatment for the topic. Although it would seem difficult to induce people to speak normally while a tape recorder is operating, it has been found that when speakers are interviewed in groups, the social obligations among members frequently lead them to disregard the recording instrument and to behave as if they were unobserved. (pág. 25)

Kerlinger (1964:398) añade que el obtener entrevistas separadas con cada participante después de las conversaciones en grupo constituye una técnica de investigación que puede ser de mucha utilidad. La posibilidad de conversación que brinda una entrevista facilita en gran medida la espontánea exploración de determinadas actitudes de los sujetos.

2.3 Análisis de los datos. Para el análisis del contenido de las conversaciones la definición operativa de 'code-switching' se apoyó en la definición de Redlinger (1976:43), la cual comprende toda inclusión de una palabra, frase, oración o párrafo no asimilado de una lengua en otra. No se estudiaron en este trabajo casos de integración fonológica, ni ejemplos de palabras integradas en la otra lengua en términos morfológicos y fonológicos como sucede con formas verbales tales como *taipear, taipeas, taipiado* del inglés *to type*. Para contar la frecuencia de cambios de códigos en determinado tiempo se obtuvieron segmentos del principio, la mitad y el fin de las conversaciones para cada tópico. Ya que la duración de las discusiones varió entre 16 y 27 minutos, se determinó el punto medio de cada conversación de acuerdo a su duración y se aislaron tres minutos de la mitad, del principio y del final de la discusión de cada tópico para analizarse.

Se presenta a continuación el caso del sujeto identificado como D2 por ser el único participante que describió el cambio de códigos como algo 'malo', aunque por otra parte no fue quien efectuó el menor número de cambios entre los participantes (véase Tabla 1).

Tabla 1.

Identificación de los sujetos:	Opinión acerca de CS: good/bad/neither	Número de CS en 18 mts. de conversación:
A1	neither	18
A2	good	48
B1	neither	12
B2	neither	23
C1	neither	61
C2	good	10
D1	neither	20
D2	bad	15
E1	good	61
E2	neither	5
F1	good	6
F2	good	62

La participante D2 reconoce al español como su lengua materna ya que no aprendió el inglés hasta la edad de seis años, pero describe su habilidad en ambas como la de un hablante nativo. Pasó su infancia y juventud en el norte de Nuevo México pero salió del estado para obtener su bachillerato en Administración de Empresas, y Sociología. Después se especializó en la enseñanza al nivel primario y en la instrucción bilingüe. Recibió dieciocho horas de créditos universitarios en literatura española a un nivel postgraduado. Ha trabajado por varios años en diferentes programas bilingües en Nuevo México y Florida y ha viajado en calidad de consultora a varios países en Centro y Sur América. Opina que el cambio de códigos entre inglés y español es malo a pesar de que reconoce que investigaciones recientes han tratado de mostrar sus aspectos positivos; pero dice: *'I'm not sold on it.'* Piensa que su uso está totalmente fuera de lugar en la sala de clase donde la meta debe ser desarrollar la proficiencia del estudiante en una lengua o en la otra. Dice que tampoco cabe en situaciones formales donde tal vez el uso de una palabra aislada se permita, pero no el dividir frases u oraciones por mitades. También afirma que el cambio de códigos debe limitarse a situaciones informales, entre miembros de la familia y amistades. De no ser así, cree que la única otra justificación sería si el oyente no tuviera facilidad en ninguna de las dos lenguas y el hablarle en español exclusivamente pudiera acomplejarlo, aunque en dicho caso el uso total de inglés resolvería ese problema. Para ella, el hecho de que en una conversación el otro interlocutor tome la iniciativa y empiece a cambiar de códigos no es razón para imitarlo.

En respuesta a la pregunta si ella tiene costumbre de cambiar de códigos, la entrevistada declaró que sí, casi con todo el mundo, amistades, personas que conoce bien, pero nunca en situaciones formales. Dice que aprendió esta variante lingüística incidentalmente porque 'así hablábamos todos,' pero no sabría explicarle a alguien dónde o cómo hacer los cambios de una lengua a la otra. Ella empezó a hacerlo en la primaria donde éste era el único medio de comunicación entre el grupo. Cree que tal vez era un paso en el proceso de aprender el inglés. Al pedirle que explicara los ejemplos de cambios de código que aparecieron durante la conversación que sostuvo con la participante D1, quien es amiga suya, la entrevistada propuso las siguientes razones:

(1) Para el tipo de cambio en que el hablante repite el mismo término en las dos lenguas (como en 'No me recuerdo las palabras, pero que según, una minoría. Y yo me pregunto en qué términos quiere decir eso de *minority*. *Does she mean minority* que somos...?') la entrevistada explicó que el uso del inglés representaba una cita, mientras que el equivalente en español era su propia expresión.

(2) Para el uso de frases superfluas (*fillers*) que aparecen repetidas veces, sea al principio, a la mitad, o al final de una oración que se dijo en la otra lengua (por ejemplo, 'y bueno, tú sabes, mucho énfasis en la religión y catecismo, *you know*') ella es de la opinión que su uso del inglés aquí revela una postura más distante, menos personal y menos directa que el uso de su equivalente en español.

(3) Los cambios de código al inglés de palabras o frases cortas aisladas (por ejemplo, 'Era una ceremonia, y se compraba uno un traje nuevo y hasta iba uno al *beauty shop* y todo') los relaciona la entrevistada con el contexto en que ocurrió dicha experiencia; es decir, el salón de belleza en ese tiempo y lugar era conocido como el *beauty shop*.

(4) Un ejemplo similar de inserción de una palabra del inglés al español pero aparentemente no asociada con el contexto (como en 'Con la sociedad ahora que es tan *mobile,* pues no, no sabe uno') lo explicó la interrogada como un lapso de la memoria que le impidió recordar el equivalente en español.

(5) El tipo de cambio en que una oración está dividida en partes casi iguales entre las dos lenguas (por ejemplo, 'Yo, a mí se me hace que yo fui muy afortunada *because I went to school in a very small town*') la participante cree que es un fenómeno inconsciente pero que parece expresar el concepto aún mejor que si se hubiera dicho en una sola lengua, no importa cuál de las dos.

Ya que la base lingüística de la conversación de la participante D2 fue el español dentro de la cual insertó ocho cambios al inglés durante la discusión del tópico formal y siete en el informal, sólo se le pudo preguntar el por qué recurrió al inglés en dichas inserciones. Hay que notar las siguientes discrepancias entre la actitud expresada por la participante y su conducta lingüística, haciendo hincapié en el hecho de que las entrevistas durante las cuales manifestó su opinión y analizó sus ejemplos de cambios de código se llevaron a cabo *después* de la grabación de las conversaciones.

En términos generales la postura negativa hacia los cambios de código declarada en la entrevista contradijo el comportamiento de la participante previo al estudio; es decir, que se le había escogido por ser una persona cuyo repertorio lingüístico incluía el uso frecuente de *code-switching*, y su conducta durante la grabación de las conversaciones mostró muy poco uso de este fenómeno lingüístico. Su afirmación de que usa el cambio de códigos con familiares y amigos fue una contradicción a lo que en efecto ocurrió. Evidentemente la participante interpretó la grabación de las conversaciones como una situación formal ya que a pesar de la amistad de varios años que ha sostenido con la participante D1 y con la investigadora no le pareció éste el momento oportuno para usar la variante que normalmente usa con ellas. Fue notable cómo una vez que terminó la grabación y dejó de usarse la máquina grabadora, el cambio de códigos fue casi el único medio de comunicación que la entrevistada utilizó. Merece mencionarse también que aunque ella asocia el cambio de códigos con la informalidad, fue durante la discusión del tópico formal que ella efectuó más cambios.

En cuanto a los ejemplos específicos de alternación de inglés y español, se encuentran también algunas discrepancias. La explicación de la entrevistada acerca del uso del inglés 'minority' en el ejemplo 1 como una cita no parece válida si se observa que en la frase, 'no me recuerdo las palabras, pero que según, una minoría,' la cual se mantuvo toda en español, la hablante también está citando indirectamente lo dicho por alguien en inglés en el original. La interpretación de lo que aconteció en el ejemplo 2 con el uso de 'you know' como una estrategia que disminuye la personalización expresada por su equivalente en español es también dudosa ya que dentro de la misma oración la entrevistada había usado antes la expresión 'tú sabes'. Dada la amistad entre las dos interlocutoras y que discutan el tópico informal, no se comprende la necesidad de impersonalizar la situación.

La baja frecuencia total de cambios al inglés en su conversación sí fue efectivamente un reflejo de la opinión que expresó la entrevistada acerca de lo inapropiado de su uso en ocasiones formales, pero aún así, sí efectuó algunos cambios, y como ya hemos notado, no fue ella quien hizo el menor número de cambios de código entre todos los sujetos.

3 Conclusiones. Las conclusiones a las que se puede llegar con este estudio están algo limitadas dado el pequeño número de sujetos que se observó y porque las conversaciones fueron elicitadas y no espontáneas. Sin embargo, estos datos pueden servir de base para comparar a otras poblaciones bilingües dentro y fuera de Nuevo México, y para medir su comportamiento y actitudes lingüísticas.

Como se dijo inicialmente, el individuo con frecuencia realiza lo imprevisible y actúa en contra de sus actitudes. En el caso de la participante D2 su comportamiento y las actitudes que expresó no coincidieron. Hubo otros elementos a cuya presencia reaccionó y los cuales afectaron su conducta. No cabía dentro de los límites de este estudio inquirir en cuanto a la índole de los factores que influyeron dicha conducta. Fue evidente, sin embargo, que a pesar de su interpretación de la situación como formal, y a pesar de los sentimientos negativos que expresó, la participante mantuvo el uso de esta variante aunque en forma limitada.

El resto de los participantes también empleó el cambio de códigos en sus conversaciones con otros individuos a quienes identificaron como usuarios de la misma forma lingüística, aunque no todos expresaron una opinión favorable hacia la misma.[1]

Este estudio constituye un ejemplo más del hecho que formas de hablar impopulares persisten y se mantienen en uso por servir de símbolo de identificación y solidaridad a los miembros del endogrupo. No cabe duda que se seguirán usando mientras mantengan un significado sociopsicológico para sus hablantes, como lo confirma este estudio.

Nota

1. Es necesario aclarar que en la Tabla 1, tanto en los casos F1 y F2 como en los C1 y C2, la diferencia tan notable entre el número de cambios efectuados por los interlocutores se debe a que en ambas situaciones el sujeto con el número más alto dominó la conversación casi por completo. Los números bajos no deben interpretarse como una discrepancia entre la actitud favorable expresada hacia *code-switching* por los participantes y su comportamiento.

Referencias

Douglas, W. 1982. Reseña de E. Finegan, 'Attitudes towards English usages.' *College English* 44.72-83.
Edwards, J. 1985. *Language, society and identity.* Oxford: Basil Blackwell.
Fernández, R.M. 1980. Some social constraints in the code-switching patterns in the speech of Mexican-Americans in New Mexico. Tesis doctoral, University of New Mexico.
Giles, H. 1970. Evaluative reactions to accents. *Educational Review* 22.211-27.
_____. 1973. Accent mobility: A model and some data. *Anthropological Linguistics* 15.87-105.
_____, y P.F. Powesland. 1975. *Speech style and social evaluation.* Londres: Academic Press.
Jacobson, R. 1982. The social implications of intrasentential code-switching. En: *Spanish in the United States.* J. Amastae y L. Elías Olivares, eds. Nueva York: Cambridge University Press.
Kerlinger, F.N. 1964. *Foundations of behavioural research.* Nueva York: Holt, Rinehart and Winston.
Labov, W. 1972a. The study of language in its social context. En: *Language and social context.* P. Giglioli, ed. Middlesex, Inglaterra: Penguin Books.
_____. 1972b. The social setting of linguistic change. En: *Sociolinguistic patterns.* W. Labov, ed. Filadelfia: University of Pennsylvania Press.
Lambert, W.E., R.C. Hodgson, R.C. Gardner, y S. Filenbaum. 1960. Evaluational reactions to spoken languages. *Journal of Abnormal and Social Psychology* 60.44-51.
Munn, F. 1980. *Psicología social.* Barcelona: Ediciones CEAC.

O'Neil, W. 1972. The politics of bidialectalism. *College English* 33.439-56.

Ornstein, J. 1975. The archaic and the modern in the Spanish of New Mexico. En: *El lenguaje de los chicanos.* E. Hernández-Chávez, A.D. Cohen, y A.F. Beltramo, eds. Arlington, Va.: Center for Applied Linguistics.

Padilla, A.M. 1977. Child bilingualism: Insights to issues. En: *Chicano psychology.* J.L. Martínez, ed. Nueva York: Academic Press.

Redlinger, W.E. 1976. A description of transference and code-switching in Mexican-American English and Spanish. En: *Bilingualism in the bicentennial and beyond.* G. Keller, R.V. Teschner y S. Viera, eds. Nueva York: Bilingual Press.

Reyes, R. 1976. Language mixing in Chicano bilingual speech. En: *Studies in Southwest Spanish.* J.D. Bowen y J. Ornstein, eds. Rowley, Mass: Newbury House.

Sledd, J. 1972. Doublespeak: Dialectology in service of big brother. *College English* 33.439-56.

Valdés-Fallis, G. 1976. Social interaction and code-switching patterns. En: *Bilingualism in the bicentennial and beyond.* G. Keller, R.V. Teschner y S. Viera, eds. Nueva York: Bilingual Press.

Wicker, A.W. 1969. Attitudes versus actions; The relationship of verbal and overt behavioural responses to attitude objects. *Journal of Social Issues* 4.41-78.

Intrasentential code-switching and the socioeconomic perspective

Rodolfo Jacobson
*The University of Texas at San Antonio
and Universiti Malaya, Kuala Lumpur, Malaysia*

Two previous studies have attempted to pinpoint the relationship between the encoding practices in the speech of bilinguals to produce mixed discourse and a set of variables relative to the individual who engages in such intrasentential code-switching. The earlier South Central American Dialect Society 1983 (SCADS) study showed a significant relationship between utterances in two languages and the speaker's membership in a given socioeconomic group. When a later replication study (11th World Congress of Sociology, New Delhi, India, 1986) initially failed to confirm the same correlation, other variables, such as age and gender, were added and the interplay of socioeconomic status (SES), age, and gender were all found to be relevent factors. This interplay between and among factors, however, still left several questions unanswered. A new attempt is here being made to consider also such variables as education and place of residence in order to come closer to a more viable statement concerning the relationship between an intersententially code-switched utterance and its producer. The two earlier studies are here reported on and an expanded analysis is then conducted. Finally, some comments address the need to envision code-switching studies in a much broader perspective.

1 The SCADS study. A number of recordings of code-switching discourse were made in 1976 in order to explore the Spanish-English switching patterns common to the speech of bilingual Mexican-Americans in San Antonio. The findings of this project have been reported in the study entitled 'The social implications of Spanish-English intrasentential code-switching' (Jacobson 1977). These interviews were reexamined in 1983 in order to determine whether any additional conclusions could be reached. It then appeared appropriate to select four of these interviews because each interview represented a different socioeconomic level, thus allowing the researcher to look into a potential relationship between SES class membership and language performance. Ten sentences from each interview were finally earmarked for further analysis. The data seemed to suggest that the utterances in question fell into three different categories. The sentences were basically Spanish but had some English embeddings or they were basically English but had some Spanish embedding or they were balanced English-Spanish sentences to the extent that it was impossible to determine which language played the major and which the minor role in a given utterance. Three dual language frames were therefore proposed whereby Frame A was considered a Spanish sentence with English elements incorporated in it, Frame B the reverse, and Frame AB a balanced occurrence of the two languages in the same sentence.

The tentative findings arrived at in the SCADS study with regard to the correlation between the frame and the SES class membership were the following:

(1) There was a preference for Frame A over Frame B by low and low middle class speakers.
(2) There was a preference for Frame AB by low SES members as compared to the low middle class.
(3) There was a reduction of Frame A as far as middle SES speakers were concerned; at the same time there was an increase of Frame AB beyond what it had been for low SES speakers.
(4) The utterances of the middle SES speakers had become grammatically more complex, in the sense that one could recognize a shift from intrasentential to intersentential code-switching.
(5) Finally, there was an increase in the use of Frame B over both Frames A and AB, with respect to middle SES speakers.

The tentative conclusions reached in the study were four:

(1) A 'frame' as a unit of analysis is a viable notion.
(2) Certain variables seem to control the encoding strategies of code-switching bilinguals and these are identifiable through discourse analysis, even though some preferences must be attributed to different language proficiency levels.
(3) Preferences in the choice of frames appear to be correlatable to the membership in a given SES class.
(4) And finally, the preference for Frame B might be seen as an index of educational and/or socioeconomic achievement.

2 The New Delhi study. A broader study of the frame-SES class correlation was conducted in 1986, leading to a paper delivered at the 11th World Congress of Sociology in New Delhi, India. The questions to be asked in such a broader study included, but were not necessarily limited to, the following:

(1) Was the socioeconomic class structure used for the previous project satisfactory or should the breakdown into individual social classes be reexamined in light of recent sociological research?

(2) Was it sufficient to analyze the code-switched data on the basis of the three frames A, B, and AB, or should additional frames be considered?

(3) Should a new corpus be obtained in order to examine the validity of earlier (tentative) findings and, if so, what were the implications of a new corpus for the causes triggering the switching identified in the 1976 study?

(4) Did the interpretation of these new data warrant the addition of new variables?

(5) To what extent did the interpretation of the new data alter, invalidate, or upgrade the past findings?

2.1 The design of the follow-up study. The credit for conducting the recorded sessions for the follow-up study goes to Ms. Trinidad M. Martinez, a graduate student in the division of Bicultural-Bilingual Studies at the University of Texas at San Antonio. She selected a group of nine Mexican-Americans of different socioeconomic statuses, males as well as females, ranging from 30 to 62 years of age. Nine taped interviews served as the corpus for this analysis, representing the speech patterns of members from four different SES levels. The interviews yielded nine sets of utterances of varying length ranging from four words for the shortest utterances to 38 words for the longest. The number of utterances selected from the interviews varied depending on whether or not they were instances of mixed discourse. The total number of words included in the analysis was 1,345. Each utterance was classified in terms of frames and the overall objective was to confirm, reject, or modify the earlier conclusions.

2.2 American socioeconomic class structure. The report by Coleman and Rainwater (1980) contained a useful outline of the metropolitan class structure and the proposed class structure served as a basis for assessing each informant in terms of his/her membership in a given social class. Of Coleman and Rainwater's seven subcategories, only four could be assigned to the informants. None belonged--for obvious reasons--to the upper-upper and lower-upper of the upper Americans nor to the bottom of the lower Americans. Hence, the informants fell, on the basis of the approximate annual salary earned, into the following four groups:

(1) The upper-middle of upper-Americans,
(2) The middle class of middle-Americans,
(3) The working class of middle-Americans,
(4) The semipoor of lower-Americans.

2.3 Frames. The notion of dual language frames was again found to be a viable one as each utterance was analyzable on the basis of the function that either language had in the sentence. However, a closer look at the data suggested that two different types of A and B frames should be recognized, one in which the embedding was lexical and another in which it was syntatic. The recognition of four frames, i.e., A-lexical, A-syntactic, B-lexical, and B-syntactic, represents an intermediate position between scholars who tend to label every language alternation as code-switching and those others who tend to label many language alternation data as borrowing, alternations that should be considered code-switching (Poplack 1986). It is obvious that the Frame AB did not have to be reinterpreted along these lines, as the balance of the two languages in the sentence requires that either component follow the structural rules of the language in question. Therefore, the total inventory of frames proposed in the New Delhi Study consisted of five such frames, i.e., A-lex, A-syn, B-lex, B-syn, and AB.

2.4 Causes that may trigger switches. It is generally agreed that there is no predictive value associated with the interpretation of code-switching events. In other words, even if we understand the nature of code-switching well, we are unable to predict when the speaker will switch from one to the other language. On the other hand, just recognizing the causes that triggered the switch is a complex matter and requires an in-depth cultural understanding of the group whose members engage in this language behavior. Since linguists often work with languages with whose structure they are acquainted but without fully understanding the sociocultural setting in which they operate, it is not surprising that many of them tend to ignore this aspect of the study of code-switching. However, I believe that the causes that trigger switches can be identified when--in Pikean terminology--emic rather that etic perception is available to the researcher. In an earlier study Jacobson (1977) identified a series of such causes and proposed the classification and subclassification of switches on the basis of psychologically and sociologically conditioned variables. Within the context of the New Delhi study it appeared worth examining which variables identified in the earlier projects were also applicable to the present one and which new variables would have to be added. Such additional variables are easily encountered when more data become available. However, there were not many categories or subcategories to be added, so that it was safe to say that by and large there has been a great deal of agreement between the two corpora. Both old and new variables were then correlated with each one of the five dual language frames, producing an interesting expanded inventory of variables causing code-switching.

2.5 Design and interpretations of the new data. The utterances could now be categorized according to the larger number of frames and the results be computed accordingly. When the frame inventory was matched with the four levels of SES class, a somewhat disappointing picture emerged. The lower SES categories (semipoor and working) no longer preferred Frame A consistently; the middle categories showed no clear preference for any frame and definitely not for Frame AB; and, by the same token, the upper-middle class revealed an equally confusing picture, with one informant showing no preference at all and the other, a preference for AB but not B.

The dilemma pointed to three potential answers: (1) the new corpus was still too limited; (2) the author's initial assumption was misleading and frames cannot be correlated with SES classes; (3) other variables like gender and age had to be taken into consideration also. The last alternative seemed to be a reasonable one and four different age categories and the two gender categories were added to the evaluational design. A pattern now seemed to emerge in the sense that male speakers selected B or AB frames, depending on their socioeconomic status, and female speakers selected A or B frames, depending on their age level. The results of this analysis were, however, not clear enough to be fully convincing, so that a future project along these same lines seemed to be warranted.

3 Follow-up study 2. What are some of the lessons that we have learned from the previous studies? A correlation between a dual language frame and a set of selected variables is possible but the correlation based on SES class alone appears to be an oversimplification. Second, the variables of age and gender seem to provide valuable additional clues without which the correlation has no clear pattern and is confusing. The pattern that does emerge still appears to be in need of a greater focus by looking at some additional variables. This second follow-up study intends to examine whether the new variables might be education and place of residence within the city. These new variables, on the other hand, pose a new set of questions that is worth examining at this stage of the study: (1) Do some variables contribute to the selection of certain frames? (2) Which variables outweigh others when choosing a frame option? (3) Which shared variables, if any, favor the same frame selection? (4) What pattern emerges when focusing on a single variable? The author attempts to provide some answers to these questions in the following dicussion.

3.1 Frame preference. It appeared to be appropriate to identify each informant on the basis of the mentioned variables and to investigate to what extent the variable inventory provided some clues with respect to the language frame selected by him/her. By plotting the age category and the educational level against SES membership and interrelating each informant with each other, 23 such relationships or oppositions emerged that revealed which variables were shared and which were not in the expectation that the difference in variables would give us a clue with respect to frame preference. The choice of one specific frame on the basis of the variable inventory was inconclusive but when an either/or choice was investigated, some patterning did seem to emerge. Table 1 reveals that when certain variables differ, one out of two frames is chosen by one informant and the other by the second informant, such that one would choose A and the other B, one B and the other AB, or one A and the other AB.

Table 1. Variables not shared by informants (1:1 oppositions).

Oppositions	A vs. B A E G R S	Oppositions	B vs AB A E G R S	Oppositions	A vs. AB A E G R S
1.	X	4.	X X X	10.	X X
2.	X X X X	5.	X X X	19.	X X X X X
3.	X X	6.	X X X X	23.	X X X X
11.	X X				
14.	X X X	20.	X X X X		
16.	X X X X				

A = Age, E = Education, G = Gender, R = Residence, S = SES

The patterning is not flawless but a priority relationship emerges to tell us that, when certain variables are not shared by the two informants, the latter will opt for the selection of different frames. Accordingly, we have found the following priority range to pertain:

  (1) The choice between frames A and B seems to be contingent upon the difference in variables in the following order of priority: (1) age or education, (2) gender or SES, (3) residence.
  (2) The choice between frames B and AB seems to be contingent upon the difference in variables in the following order of priority: (1) education, (2) age or gender or SES, (3) residence.
  (3) The choice between frames A and AB seems to be contingent upon the difference in variables in the following order of priority: (1) gender or SES, (2) age or education, (3) residence.

3.2 Variables that outweigh others. The proposed priority order reveals that the place of residence in a given city is lowest for each group. As the study was done in San Antonio, it first appeared that it might be significant whether an informant grew up in the predominantly Anglo north, in the predominantly Mexican-American south or west, or in the predominantly Black east. This has not been proven, however. The other four variables appeared more significant although they were differentially distributed. Age or education, education only, and gender or SES class differences seemed to determine whether A was chosen over B, B over AB, or A over AB. As a case in point, one would expect an older person with limited education to choose A over B. Second, a female of lower socioeconomic status would be expected to make that same choice. As for the choice between B and AB, one would expect an individual to choose B first if he/she had a higher education and only second if this person was a middle-aged female of working-class or higher status and so forth.

3.3 Shared variables. This part of the study was inconclusive. In other words, there seemed to be no clear correlation between variables shared by two speakers and their selection of language frames. It might be that the number of informants was not large enough for this to be a significant aspect.

3.4 Focus on a single variable. As one focuses on any one variable, he can make a few generalizations that are, however, of limited value. Age seems to be a significant factor in the sense that lower middle age (LMA) speakers tend to choose between B and AB, whereas upper middle age (UMA) speakers select either A or B. Education as a variable shows--strangely enough--a similarity in the behavior of individuals with elementary as well as college education, since members of both groups choose between A and B, even though probably for different reasons. High school educated individuals make a choice between A and AB. The gender variable shows that males choose between B and A, and females between A and B. Residence, as already suggested, was inconclusive and SES class membership was partially inconclusive, as only the semipoor tend to agree on a choice between A and B.

The previous analysis now allows us to construct a profile of preferences. In other words, what kind of bilingual speaker would preferably use an A-frame and who would prefer a B or AB pattern? Based on the above data analysis, we are proposing the following three profiles:

A-preference: A female, preferably of low advanced age (LAA) and semipoor (SP) status;
B-preference: A female with college or university education;
AB-preference: A male with high school education and of middle or upper-middle class status.

We have now come full circle to reconfirm the author's first hypothesis in the sense that the member of the lower socioeconomic class tends to incorporate English elements in his/her Spanish discourse. The individual who is moving up socially and academically, even though still with a limited education, will utilize the resources from both languages in a fairly balanced way. Finally, it is the speaker who participates in higher education who will use English most of the time but prefers to leave room for some vernacular elements in order to show that acculturation to the mainstream society can go hand-in-hand with loyalty toward more traditional values.

4 Conclusion. It has been the purpose of this presentation to report on some ongoing research that is attempting to correlate dual language encoding strategies with a set of variables of the speaker's socioeconomic and personal background. From the consideration of SES class alone to that of SES, age, and sex, the studies have been shown to have become sensitive to greater complexity. The recent inclusion of education and place of residence has suggested the importance of the former but not of the latter. These studies, together with many others recently and currently conducted by scholars in the United States, are mostly concerned with bilingual Spanish/English speakers. But the time has now arrived to compare notes with other researchers (foreign as well as national) who are examining settings other than our own in order to categorize these phenomena more effectively in global perspective and thereby isolate the features that are truly universal.

References

Coleman, R., and L. Rainwater. 1978. *Social standing in America.* New York: Basic Books.
Jacobson, R. 1977. The social implications of Spanish-English intrasentential code-switching. *The New Scholar* (special issue) 6.227-56. Reprint 1978. In: *New directions in Chicano scholarship.* R. Romo and R. Paredes, eds. La Jolla: University of California, San Diego.
_____. 1983. Switches to English or Spanish: Does it matter? Paper delivered at the 40th Annual Meeting, South Central Modern Language Association (SCADS), Fort Worth, Tex., October 27-29.
Poplack, S., and D. Sankoff. 1986. Verification of the equivalence constraint on intrasentential codeswitching in Tamil-English constructions and some terminological issues. Paper delivered at the 11th World Congress of Sociology, New Delhi, India.

Spanish language use in West Liberty, Iowa

Nora González and Irene Wherritt
University of Iowa

1 Introduction. In 1980 over 26,000 persons of Mexican, Puerto Rican, Cuban, and 'other Spanish' descent made their homes in Iowa. The figure represents 1% of the total population of Iowa. Persons of Mexican descent accounted for 72% of the Spanish-origin population in Iowa.

Map 1 shows the three major streams of migratory patterns in the United States. The west coast and mid-continent streams both start in southern Texas and along the borders of Mexico. Both streams are composed predominantly of Mexican-Americans with some Indians, Blacks, and a few Anglos (Governor's Spanish Speaking Task Force 1980:39-40). As in the nation, persons of Spanish origin constitute the second largest racial or ethnic minority group in Iowa.

Map 1. Iowa in relation to the national migratory patterns.

Although Blacks have greater numbers (42,228, or 1.4% of Iowa's population), persons of Spanish origin outnumber Blacks in 78 of Iowa's 99 counties (Saenz and Goudy 1983:1-2). Map 2 shows the distribution of persons of Spanish origin in Iowa counties by percentage of population. The map demonstrates that residents of Spanish origin are concentrated in three areas: near the Mississippi River, in a north to south band in the center of the state, and near the western border. Many individuals arrived in the 1970s from Mexico to work as migrant workers or as laborers in food processing plants.   Few studies, if any, have documented language use in such communities. This report examines language use and language attitudes in West Liberty, Iowa, a small community in Muscatine County.

Map 2. Iowa counties by Spanish origin percentage of population.

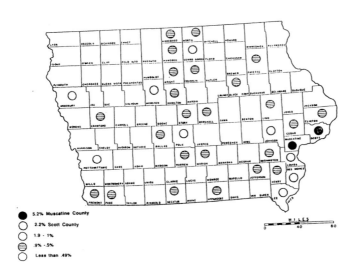

- ● 5.2% Muscatine County
- ○ 2.2% Scott County
- ○ 1.9 - 1%
- ◒ .9% - .5%
- ○ Less than .49%

Spanish speakers have inhabited the Mississippi valley in Iowa since as early as 100 years ago, principally in Muscatine County. Among the earliest settlers are individuals such as Francisco and José Villafana, who came to work with the railroad in West Liberty in 1910. The big influx of Spanish-speaking people began in 1963, when Louis Rich Foods came to West Liberty. One of the employees of the company was from Del Rio, Texas. Word traveled in the Texas town that jobs were available at Louis Rich Foods and gradually more and more families moved north. By 1976 some 300 people, or 15% of the community, were Spanish speakers from Del Rio and surrounding areas of Texas and Mexico (Miehe 1976:64). Today, Mexicans number about 500 and comprise 25% of the population of the community.

These individuals come principally from northern Mexico and Texas, and most of them work in a turkey processing plant.

The community of West Liberty is shown in Map 3. Mexicans tend to live south of the railroad tracks on First Street, A and B Streets, Prairie Street, and Short Street. Those who have resided longer tend to have either bought a home or rented a larger dwelling north of the railroad line on Fourth through Seventh Streets. More affluent homes are located northeast of the tracks.

Map 3. City of West Liberty, Muscatine County, Iowa.

1. CITY HALL
2. PUBLIC LIBRARY
3. TELEPHONE BUILDING
4. HIGH SCHOOL
5. FAIR GROUNDS
6. ELEMENTARY SCHOOL
7. POST OFFICE
8. KIMBERLY PARK & POOL
9. UNITED METHODIST CHURCH
10. CATHOLIC CHURCH
11. LUTHERAN CHURCH
12. FIRST CHURCH UNITED
13. FAITH BAPTIST CHURCH
14. MIDDLE SCHOOL
15. SIMPSON MEMORIAL HOME
16. WAPSIE PARK

In order to undertake the present study, a series of thirty brief interviews were conducted. Questions were asked relating to the backgrounds of the informants, their language choices in various situations, their participation in the community, and their language attitudes.

2 Informants and their backgrounds. Thirty subjects agreed to take part in the interviews. Equal numbers of men and women participated, ranging in age from 16 to 66. All interviews were given in Spanish by two native speakers. The majority of informants were born in Mexico, especially in the Texas border region. Map 4 shows the geographical origins of the informants. All the informants born in Mexico consider Spanish as their mother tongue; half of the informants born in the United States consider English as their native language. The majority of the group claims to notice some differences between the Spanish spoken in West Liberty and the Spanish spoken in

Mexico. The differences observed are interference of English in vocabulary, differences in phonetic features, and a mixture of Spanish and English.

The informants were asked in what language they pray, swear, think, and count. The percent of language use estimated for each function varies as indicated in Figure 1. In mental activities that are more abstract and philosophical, informants claim greater use of Spanish. In more concrete thinking related more to school activities, they claim greater use of English, although Spanish still prevails.

Map 4. Birthplace of informants.

One-half of the subjects arrived in 1969 and 1970. Another smaller group arrived in 1979. Subsequently, others have continuously arrived in small numbers. Newly arrived individuals tend to be relatives of the people who immigrated previously. The informants have lived in West Liberty between one and twenty years, and 70% perceive themselves as Mexicans rather than Chicanos.

Most of the informants have extended family who live in Mexico or Texas. The majority visit their relatives once a year or every two years, making contact with the Spanish language and Mexican culture frequent.

The subjects' education ranges from three years of elementary school to completion of high school. All informants who have children state that all of their children are attending school. Most are attending elementary or junior high school at the present time. One informant has children who attend the University of Iowa. All informants assert that school is important for their children. The majority of parents interviewed claim that their children have either American friends or a mixture of American and Mexican friends. Only 10% claim that their children have only Mexican friends; most likely they are children in new immigrant families.

Figure 1. Language use.

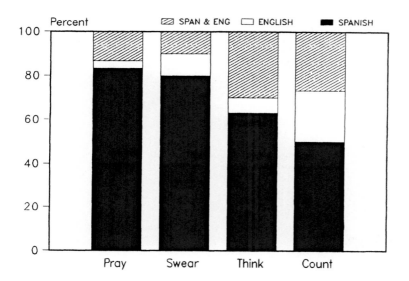

A bilingual bicultural program existed from 1982 to 1984 in kindergarten and first grade, but currently children enter school with no such assistance. ESL classes were offered at all levels from 1970 to 1985, but at present only primary school ESL classes are still given. Occasionally, night classes in English have been offered to local residents, and informants express the desire to have more such classes. Those who do not yet speak English claim they have not had the opportunity to learn it.

The Catholic church has had a Spanish-speaking priest since 1974 and mass in Spanish is offered once every Sunday. A local Mexican community cultural center, the *Centro Unido*, has been in existence since the early 1970s and sponsors cultural and service activities for Spanish-speaking residents. Cable television in Spanish is available and local residents travel frequently to nearby Muscatine to rent Spanish videotaped movies.

The principal source of employment in West Liberty is the Louis Rich turkey processing plant. English is not necessary for the work-place since most of the work is mechanical. Fifty-seven percent of the informants who work are employed at Louis Rich.

3.1 Maintenance of Spanish and domains of language use. The informants were asked what languages they use in a variety of places and situations. Figure 2 summarizes the findings. Across the bottom of the figure is a list of domains. Spanish tends to be used more in those domains toward the left side of the figure and English in those toward the right side of the figure. For more informal and familiar situations--in church, at home, at parties, and when conversing with their neighbors--informants report a much greater use of Spanish. Mass is said in Spanish, and often picnics and get-togethers follow the church service. In situations outside the Mexican culture, the informants naturally report a greater use of English and of Spanish and English. Cable television in Spanish is available, yet only five informants watch TV exclusively in Spanish. Movies in Spanish are rented from nearby Muscatine. Several informants report use of an interpreter in the bank and with their doctor.

Figure 2. Language use: General.

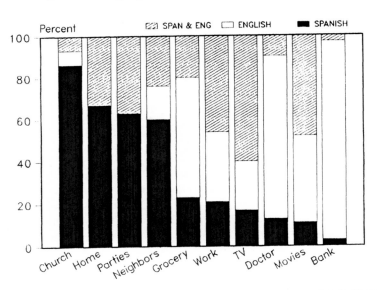

Our survey supports the findings of Fishman (1968:35-36) that in a diglossic community the low language is the one that will be selected in domains such as the family, friendship, and the neighborhood, whereas the high language will most often be used in more formal domains such as education, government, and employment.

The informants were also asked what language they used with members of their families. Figure 3 represents the informants' responses. Informants claim more use of Spanish with elderly relatives listed on the left and somewhat less Spanish use with the younger ones indicated on the right. Very few informants report exclusive use of English with all their relatives and family members, but rather only with siblings, nieces, and nephews. In some communities different language choice by younger and older speakers may simply reflect the changes in language use from one period of a person's life to another (Fasold 1984:241). Most likely, the changes noted in this report reflect a language shift as opposed to changes across time in the individual's language use. More data are needed to confirm this initial hypothesis.

Figure 3. Language use: Family.

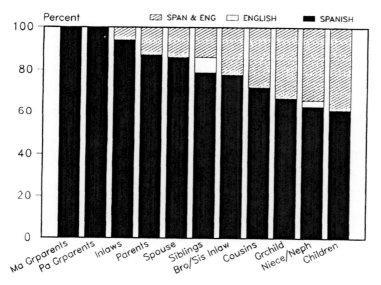

Informants who speak Spanish at home tend to rate themselves poorly in their ability to speak English, whereas those who claim to use both Spanish and English mostly rate themselves 'well' and 'pretty well' in English. Similarly, those who claim to speak both Spanish and English at home are generally those who went to school in the United States. Exclusive Spanish language use in the home is claimed more by males than females. Informants under the age of 25 are divided equally among those who use only Spanish in their homes and those who converse in both Spanish and English in this environment; on the other hand, 80% of those over 50 report exclusive use of Spanish in the home.

We asked the informants if they mix Spanish and English. Eighty percent of those who report exclusive use of Spanish at work also claim not to mix the two languages. In contrast, 82% of those who report use of Spanish and English and 50% of those who indicate exclusive use of English at work claim to practice such a mixture. We conclude that exclusive use of Spanish in the work-place helps to maintain a purer Spanish.

Questions appeared in the interviews regarding participation in the *Centro Unido* and in the Catholic church. Men and women differ somewhat in their reporting about the *Centro*. Sixty percent of the women interviewed state that they participate often or usually in the *Centro Unido*, whereas only 7% of the men report similar participation. Informal discussions after the interviews revealed that conflicts have arisen in past years as to leadership in the *Centro Unido*. Decreased interest on the part of male informants in the *Centro* may relate to such conflict among male community members. The *Centro* appears to attract those whose English is weak rather than those who have already progressed to a higher stage of proficiency in English. Fifty-seven percent of those who report high ability in English say they never or rarely attend activities at the *Centro*. In contrast, only 13% of those who speak little or no English claim similar attendance. Of those who attend usually or often, 60% state they speak little or no English. On the other hand, attendance in church is quite regular and is reported about equal by both men and women. Likewise, both report almost exclusive use of Spanish in church.

In summary, home life and participation in the Catholic church and in the *Centro Unido* are encouraging Spanish language maintenance in the community.

3.2 The effect of school on the acquisition of English. The subjects were asked to evaluate their ability to speak English on a scale using four values: 'none,' 'a little,' 'pretty well,' and 'well.' In Table 1 the answers given to this question are cross-tabulated with the variable of the age at which the informants started school in the United States. The table shows three distinct groups. The first consists of those who started school in the United States at less than twelve years of age and they estimate their ability to speak English as 'pretty well' or 'well.' The members of the second group began school in the United States between ages twelve and fourteen and their estimate is 'pretty well.' The third group consists of adults who did not attend school in the United States. The majority of this group estimates their ability in English as 'none' or 'little.'

One of the informants was born in the United States and started school in the United States at age six. She estimates her ability in English as 'pretty well'; yet, at intervals during the interview she addressed her child in native English. Other subjects appear to have underestimated their ability in English. Underestimation of ability merits further investigation in subsequent studies.

The present paper corroborates the recent research on the effect of age on the quality of second language acquisition. Evidence suggests that a distinction exists between children and adults in second language acquisition. Several hypotheses have been proposed to explain this difference. (1) The Critical Period Hypothesis (Lennenberg 1967:153) claims that the optimal period for learning languages is from age two to puberty. (2) The Cognitive Style Hypothesis (Taylor 1978:459-60) asserts that adults have a more mature cognitive system with capacity for abstraction and generalizations to which they can resort when learning a second language. (3) The Affective Factor Hypothesis (Elkind 1970:223) maintains that adolescents and adults are more self-conscious than children and thus have more difficulty in learning a second language. (4) The findings of our research are in accord with Dulay, Burt, and Krashen (1982:93-94), who state that 'some aspect of all or several of the explanations taken together are required to completely understand the effect of age on second language acquisition.'

Table 1. Ability in English in relation to age at arrival.

Age at arrival in the U.S.	Ability in English: None/A little	Pretty well	Well	Total
5			2 100%	2 6.7%
6		2 50%	2 50%	4 13.3%
7			1 100%	1 3.3%
9			1 100%	1 3.3%
12		1 100%		1 3.3%
14		2 100%		2 6.7%
over 21	16 84.3%	2 10.4%	1 5.3%	19 33.3%
Total	16 53.3%	7 23.3%	7 23.3%	30 100%

Length of residence in West Liberty does not appear to have an effect on the informants' estimated ability in English. Fifty-four percent of those who have lived in West Liberty for fourteen to seventeen years, and 40% of those who have lived in West Liberty for eighteen to twenty years claim to speak little or no English. Figure 4 shows a trend line from the data which also suggests that the number of years in West Liberty does not affect one's ability to speak English.

The sixteen adults listed in Table 1 did not attend school in the United States, and evaluate their ability in English as 'none' or 'little.' These individuals may lack the instrumental and integrative motivation (Gardner and Lambert 1972:132) necessary for successful second language acquisition. The majority of the informants in this study do not need English at work. They are not forced to learn more English to attain a better job or to survive in the English-speaking community. A little use of English at the grocery store or at the doctor's office suffices. The one informant who claims to speak no English works at home and uses her children as interpreters when necessary.

Newmark (1971:14) claims that an individual needs to pay attention to sufficient meaningful language instances in order to acquire a second language. Immersion alone in a diglossic community will not ensure success in the acquisition of a second language; motivation to learn is also necessary.

Forty percent of the subjects went to school in the United States. These individuals tend to have arrived at a younger age and to have attained a higher level of education than other informants. Also, more women than men attained a higher level of schooling in the United States. Undoubtedly men leave school to join the work force sooner than women.

Figure 4. Language proficiency: English.

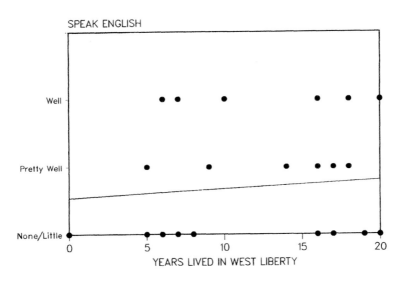

Similarly, the most successful learners of English are those informants who attended school in the United States. Eighty-five percent of those who estimated their English ability as 'pretty well' or 'well' went to school in the United States. Figure 5 shows the distribution of language use at school by informants. The figure suggests that informants who have attained a lower level of education use Spanish more, whereas those who have attained higher levels of instruction use Spanish less.

In summary, informants who have attended school in the United States appear to have found an effective communication situation for learning English. English classes for adults are much less effective for the acquisition of English: three out of four informants who had special English classes claim little or no ability in English. Length of residence in the United States does not appear to aid significantly in the acquisition of English.

4 Conclusions and future directions. This study shows the general patterns of language use in West Liberty according to domains and particular social settings. It suggests that early age of arrival in the United States and higher schooling attained in the United States encourage acquisition of English. Employment at the turkey processing plant and participation in

Mexican cultural activities appear to encourage maintenance of Spanish. The number of years which one has spent in the community is not a significant variable.

Figure 5. Language use: School.

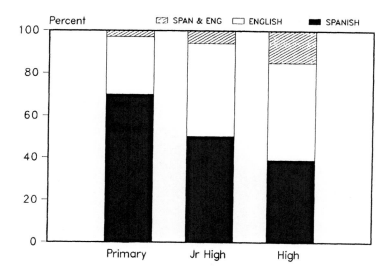

Our research suggests various topics for more detailed investigation in future studies; among these are attitudes toward language and cultural organizations, differences in language use according to gender and age, and integrative vs. instrumental motivation for learning English.

The study on West Liberty opens a new area of documentation of Spanish language use in the United States, since typically such studies deal with the Southwest or with large metropolitan areas. The findings also encourage greater cultural understanding and facilitate community decision making in education, law, medicine, and social services.

Note

This article was completed at University House, University of Iowa. The authors are grateful to Javier Rojas Cardona, who helped in conducting interviews and gathering data, and to Kathleen Taylor, who assisted in data reduction and analysis.

References

Dulay, H., M. Burt, and S. Krashen. 1982. *Language two*. New York: Oxford University Press.

Elkind, D. 1970. *Children and adolescents: Interpretive essays on Jean Piaget.* New York: Oxford University Press.

Fasold, R.A. 1984. *The sociolinguistics of society.* New York: Basil Blackwell.

Fishman, J. 1968. Language maintenance and language shift as fields of inquiry. *Linguistics* 39.21-49.

Gardner, R., and W. Lambert. 1972. *Attitudes and motivation in second language learning.* Rowley, Mass.: Newbury House.

Governor's Spanish Speaking Task Force. 1980. *Conóceme en Iowa.* Des Moines, Iowa.

Lennenberg, E. 1967. *Biological foundations of language.* New York: Wiley.

Miehe, V. 1976. The Spanish-speaking people. In: *Moving ahead with West Liberty.* West Liberty, Iowa.: Heritage Committee.

Newmark, L. 1971. A minimal language-teaching program. In: *The psychology of second language learning.* P. Pimsleur and T. Quinn, eds. New York: Cambridge University Press. 11-18.

Saenz, R., and W. Goudy. 1983. *Persons of Spanish origin in Iowa.* Ames, Iowa: Cooperative Extension Service, Iowa State University.

Taylor, I. 1978. Acquiring versus learning a second language. *Canadian Modern Language Review* 34.455-72.

The complimenting speech act among Chicano women

Rosa H. Yáñez
University of California at Berkeley

1 Introduction. Sociolinguists and ethnolinguists have recently devoted much attention to the study of conversational discourse. They are concerned about the different strategies which speakers use in order to convey a message, both directly and indirectly, within conversation. An important aspect of the analysis of conversational discourse is that of complimenting speech acts.

Recently, several such studies on complimenting speech acts that have been carried out on different groups of speakers have led to interesting findings. For example, it has been demonstrated that this speech act has several functions in our society. According to Manes (1983:97), 'a major function of compliments is the establishment or reinforcement of solidarity between the speaker and the addressee.' A related point concerns what the compliment must communicate. It characteristically expresses a positive evaluation on something which the speakers of a society agree on as being of positive value. In American society, for example, a pleasing personal appearance is considered desirable; thus, we find large numbers of compliments made about personal appearance. Possessions and newness are also features which are frequently praised.

In this paper I present my findings from a survey of the complimenting behavior in social and family settings of Chicano women from the Mesilla Valley area of southern New Mexico. I am using as my main frames of reference the work of Wolfson (1983) and the study by Valdés and Pino (1981). The former focuses on the complimenting itself, the latter on the response. Section 2 presents the findings of these and other scholars.

2 Review of previous research. Wolfson's article analyzes the syntactic structure and the semantic content of this speech act. She presents (p. 85) some of the aspects which she and Manes (1983) have come across in their studies on American-English speakers. From their findings she concludes that certain fixed syntactic patterns consistently occur in the complimenting act:

NP	is/looks	(really)	ADJ
I	(really)	like/love	NP
PRO	is	(really)	a ADJ NOUN

She further states that speakers make use mainly of adjectives to express approval; for this, the selection among adjectives is also very narrow: *nice* and *good* are the predominant ones. Regarding verbs, *to look* and *to be* are the most frequent ones. The use of so few variations in syntactic structures and lexical items leads Wolfson to conclude that compliments are mere formulas, in the same way that other speech acts like greetings, apologies, etc. are. Wolfson divides the themes of compliments into two major categories-- compliments referring to appearance and compliments referring to ability. Finally, she notes that women are the recipients and the givers of compliments more frequently than men are; she even asserts (p. 93) that 'when... appearance is the topic of the compliment, the addressee in the data so far collected seems hardly ever to be a male.'

A different approach to this speech act was taken by Valdés and Pino in their study on Mexican-American bilinguals' responses to compliments. Taking the compliment response patterns that Pomerantz (1978:89-110) presents as found among English-speaking monolinguals, they carry out a study that includes Spanish-speaking monolinguals and Mexican-American bilinguals. A very important observation in both studies is the claim that the receiver of a compliment believes that he/she has to respond to it and also has to avoid giving the impression of self-praise. Again, Pomerantz notes that there are recurring compliment response patterns:

(1) Acceptance:	(a) Acceptance with appreciation token.
	(b) Agreements.
(2) Rejections:	(a) Disagreements.
(3) Self-praise avoidance mechanisms:	(a) Praise upgrade.
	(b) Scaling down of praise.
	(c) Disagreements.
	(d) Reassignments of praise.
	(e) Returns.

Valdés and Pino (pp. 62-65) observe that the patterns described by Pomerantz are also found in the compliments used by the two groups which they studied, although with slight variations.

An important finding in their study of the Mexican-American bilingual group is the use of both Spanish and English in compliments; that is, they came across compliments which use a great amount of code-switching within a single compliment-response pair, and from this they analyzed the language choices encountered.

Valdés and Pino summarize their findings as follows:

(1) the use of all patterns described by Pomerantz;
(2) the use of mere fragments in one of the patterns used by Mexican monolinguals (i.e., the politeness formula, as explained below);
(3) the use of a second additional pattern among Mexican monolinguals-- the request for expansion and repetition of the compliment;
(4) the use of a greater variety of acceptance patterns than those which Pomerantz encountered; and
(5) the use of the two languages in both compliments and compliment responses.

Although Valdés and Pino do not state who the recipients of the compliments were, from a look at the examples recorded, one concludes that most of the recipients were women, and the predominant topic was personal appearance.

After reading the articles which I have mentioned, I undertook my own study with the following questions in mind:

(1) Will complimenting among Chicano women present strict syntactic structures?
(2) What will be the values complimented upon?
(3) What will the language choice(s) be?

3 Data collection and interpretation. In order to gather data for my study I started frequenting places where I knew Chicano women of all ages typically gather: weddings, potluck dinners, family reunions, coffee shops, department stores, church meetings, etc. In nonpublic places, acquaintances introduced me at these gatherings.

An important aspect to be noted is that the family is the nucleus of most such get-togethers among Hispanics; in this regard, it is always obvious that children have a very important place in the gathering. As a result, much attention is given to what such Chicano children say and do; they are always encouraged to participate in the activities taking place.

Very little of the data was recorded; it was mainly gathered by taking notes. During the time I carried out the research I gathered a corpus of forty-one compliments. I now interpret them according to the following schema:

(1) the language(s) used;
(2) the structure of the compliment initiation;
(3) the response patterns; and
(4) the content of the compliments.

3.1 Language(s) used. Of the 41 utterance pairs investigated, 26 were initiated in Spanish and 15 in English. Of the 26 initiated in Spanish, 17 were also responded to in Spanish, 3 in English, and (as I will explain shortly) 6 were not answered at all. All the compliments initiated in English received a response, 13 in the same language and 2 in Spanish.

Unlike Valdés and Pino, I did not find a large amount of code-switching; there are only a few examples where a word of the other language is inserted:

> (1) A: *Valerie, ¡qué bonito está tu baby! Ni sabía que tenías baby boy.*
> B: *Thank you... yes.*

The general lack of code-switching is surprising because it is well known that there is a large amount of code-switching among Chicano speakers. A possible reason for its absence in my corpus may be that it typically occurs among intimates, inasmuch as Valdés and Pino encountered it frequently in their research. However, I did come across numerous instances of compliments initiated in one language and the responses to them given in the other language.

3.2 Structure of compliment initiation. As I have mentioned, Wolfson found that fixed syntactic patterns occur among American-English speakers when complimenting. Such recurrent patterns also occur among Chicano women in both Spanish and English. In Spanish there are three basic patterns:

(a)	*Qué*	+	**ADJ**	+	**NP**		
	(2) *¡Qué*		*bonito*		*cojín!*		
(b)	*Qué*	+	**ADJ**	+	**VERB**	+	**NP**
	(3) *¡Qué*		*bonito*		*se te ve*		*el pelo!*
(c)	**NP**	+	**VERB**	+	**ADJ**		
	(4) *Oye, esta salsa*		*te salió*		*rica.*		

Again, the selection of adjectives is shown to be rather restricted. Of twenty-four adjective occurrences in the compliments, the adjective *bonito/a* occurred eleven times. Each of the other adjectives occurred either once or twice. On the other hand, the selection of verbs was too narrow to discern a numerical predominance of any of them.

The syntactic patterns which I encountered in the English compliments were the same as the first two reported by Wolfson:

(a)	**NP**	+	*is/looks*	+	**ADJ**
	(5) *You*		*look*		*great.*
(b)	**I**	+	*like*	+	**NP**
	(6) *I*		*like*		*this dress.*

However, in my corpus I did not come across the third pattern which Wolfson mentions. Although the number of examples in English is too small (only fifteen compliments) for establishing generalizations, it is apparent from these examples that the predominant verbs are *to be, to look,* and *to like.* Regarding adjectives, *pretty* was encountered eight times, *great* twice, and the others only once each.

3.3 The response patterns. The findings from my examination of the responses to the compliments coincide in some aspects with those encountered by Valdés and Pino in their study of Mexican-American bilinguals. I found most of Pomerantz's patterns, for example:

Reassignment of praise:

(7) A: *I like your combination* (referring to one's dress, necklace, and belt).
 B: *Thank you. Hermana Mary made everything.*

Acceptance with appreciation token:

(8) A: *I really like your dress.*
 B: *Thank you.*

Scaling down on compliment assertion:

(9) A: *Se ve bien con esos zapatos.*
 B: *Oh, they're comfortable.*

Qualification to compliment assertion:

(10) A: *I like this dress.*
 B: *Oh, ¿te acuerdas cuándo lo compré? Ya está viejo.*
 A: *It's still pretty.*

I also came across two patterns identified by Valdés and Pino but not mentioned by Pomerantz. One of these is a comment used alone as an acceptance response:

(11) A: *¡Qué bonito prendedor trae!*
 B: *Mira, significa todas las lenguas, y los colores todas las razas.*

The other is a fragmented politeness formula (e.g., *cuando quieras*) used among monolingual Mexicans:

(12) A: *Oye, esta salsa te salió rica.*
 B: *Ay, cuando quieras, nomás le ponemos chile colorado.*

The last example is shown to be an important one when it is contrasted with sentences (13) through (16):

(13) A: *El arroz está muy bueno.*
      B: . . .
(14) A: *¡Qué bonitos se ven los pasteles!*
      B: . . .
(15) A: *Este pay está rico.*
      B: . . .
(16) A: *Oye, ¡qué delicioso salió este pastel!*
      B: . . .

In (13) through (16) there was no response at all because these compliments were not directed at any one in particular. Therefore, even if the person who cooked whichever dish was being praised was present, (s)he did not feel obliged to respond to the compliment. The crucial word that distinguishes (12) from these other compliments is the pronoun *te*; therefore, since this compliment was directed to a particular person, that individual did feel obligated to respond. The case of (17) and (18), in which there was no response either, is again different:

(17) A: *Mira, ¡qué pestañas tiene la niña. . . enormes!*
      B: . . .
(18) A: *Ay, ¡qué bonita niña!*
      B: . . .

Both of these compliments were addressed to the same baby girl as she was being held in her mother's arms. The mother, although surrounded by people who spoke Spanish, did not seem to understand Spanish; this obviously explains her lack of a response.

On the other hand, I did not come across the response pattern that requests expansion and repetition of the compliment assertion.

3.4 Content of the compliments. The topics complimented upon were the following:

Topics:	Number of compliments:
Children	12
Clothing	7
Food	6
Personal appearance	6
Jewelry	6
Hairdos	5
Creativity	2

As mentioned earlier, children are a very important part of the Chicano family setting (as indeed they are in any culture). This explains why they are the most frequent subjects of the compliments which comprise my corpus.

4 Conclusions. On the basis of the research described here, I draw the following conclusions:

(1) Complimenting among Chicano women follows strict syntactic patterns that are very similar to those found for monolingual English speakers.
(2) Such complimenting reflects the high value which Chicano culture gives to the family institution.
(3) Code-switching in such complimentation is not as frequent as one would expect it to be.

References

Manes, J. 1983. Compliments: A mirror of cultural values. In: *Sociolinguistics and language acquisition*. N. Wolfson and E. Judd, eds. Rowley, Mass.: Newbury House. 96-102.
Searle, J.R. 1971. What is a speech act? In: *The philosophy of language*. J.R. Searle, ed. London: Oxford University Press. 39-53.
Strawson, P.J. 1971. Intention and convention in speech acts. In: *The philosophy of language*. J.R. Searle, ed. London: Oxford University Press. 23-38.
Valdés, G., and C. Pino. 1981. *Muy a tus órdenes:* Compliment responses among Mexican-American bilinguals. *Language in Society* 10.53-72.
Van Dijk, T.A. 1980. *Estructuras y funciones del discurso.* Mexico City: Siglo XXI Editores.
Wolfson, N. 1983. An empirically based analysis of complimenting in American-English. In: *Sociolinguistics and language acquisition*. N. Wolfson and E. Judd, eds. Rowley, Mass.: Newbury House. 82-95.

Becoming literate: Historias de San Antonio

René Cisneros
Metropolitan State University, St. Paul, Minnesota
Elizabeth Leone
Montclair State College, Upper Montclair, New Jersey

1 Introduction. A 1983 study on illiteracy in San Antonio, Texas, reported the alarming statistic that about 25% of that city's population was functionally illiterate (IDRA 1983). Furthermore, the areas of the city that were cited as having the highest illiteracy rates were those areas which had the greatest number of limited English proficient persons (LEPs), and in the case of San Antonio, these persons are of Mexican ancestry.

In the recent published research on literacy one often reads claims about the causes of illiteracy for the population in question. However, the IDRA investigation did not attempt to find causes; it is similarly not the purpose of the present study to establish the causes of illiteracy, nor to determine if the San Antonio Literacy Council's efforts in lowering the illiteracy rate are effective. This is especially not feasible, given the fact that although 'the majority of providers (of literacy services) are found in the areas of greatest need, . . . the numbers served are small in relation to the target population' (IDRA 1983:64). Nevertheless, our study raises questions about literacy issues in general, presents perspectives of persons in the process of developing literacy, and finally makes recommendations for research and applications of research in the area of literacy, particularly in bilingual communities.

When studies of literacy are cited, one of the chief problems is that different scholars use different definitions, so the true literacy level of different segments of a community is often never known, even in the most superficial terms (see Gray 1969). In fact, the literacy of a group is sometimes defined in reference to one of two criteria which may not be related to what the group members can do or choose to do with regard to reading and writing in their daily lives. These two criteria are (1) eight years of schooling and (2) the ability of community members to function according to certain established levels of performance for a hypothetical citizen of a country. (See APL 1977 and IDRA 1983 for discussions of literacy criteria.) However, the criterion of eight years of schooling can tell us little about the abilities which a person may or may not possess. On the other hand, performance levels are valuable tools for determining functions of literacy needed by persons in a society, even though these levels may not reflect choices about the uses of literacy of a given literacy learner.

It is the ways of using language and the choices implied by these ways that ethnolinguist Shirley Brice Heath reports on in her *Ways with words* (1983). In her long-range study of the day-to-day reading and writing activities of a working class community, Trackton, in the southeastern United States, Heath found that there were many functions of literacy for the community members. They used reading and writing for a variety of personal and social needs which took the form of lists, bills, church bulletins, and brochures, to name but a few (see Tables 1 and 2).

Table 1. Types of uses of reading in Trackton (Heath 1983:198).

---

1. Instrumental: reading to accomplish the goals of daily life (price tags, checks, bills, clocks, street signs, house numbers).

2. Social-interactional/recreational: reading to maintain social relationships, make plans, and introduce topics for discussion & storytelling (greeting cards, cartoons, letters, newspaper features, flyers, announcements of community meetings).

3. News-related: reading to learn about third parties or events (local news items, circulars from the community center or school).

4. Confirmational: reading to gain support for attitudes or beliefs already held (Bible, brochures on cars, loan notes, bills).

Table 2. Types of uses of writing in Trackton (Heath 1983:199).

---

1. Memory aids (primarily used by women): writing to serve as a reminder for the writer and, only occasionally, others (telephone numbers, notes on calendars).

2. Substitutes for oral messages (primarily used by women): writing used when direct oral communication was not possible or would prove embarrassing (notes for tardiness or absences from school, greeting cards, letters).

3. Financial: writing to record numerals and to write out amounts and accompanying notes (signatures on checks and public forms, figures and notes for income tax preparation).

4. Public records (church only): writing to announce the order of the church services and forthcoming events and to record financial and policy decisions (church bulletins, reports of the church building fund committee).

These uses of reading in Trackton were noted by Heath as important and functional for the members of the community. Equally important were the uses of writing in this community.

All of these types of reading and writing noted by Heath are integral parts of the way of life and the ways of using written language in the community she studied. These types of reading and writing reflect the situations, purposes, and forms of language in the daily lives of the Trackton community members and, therefore, would be significant information for persons who may be interested in providing services to them. Unfortunately, many teachers and researchers of reading do not know anything about the functions of reading and writing of the literacy learners for whom they attempt to prescribe assistance. By not knowing about a community's use of written language, it is logical that the educator would be less successful in providing assistance to the members of the community. This is often because the community members would not be taking an active role in deciding how to use the reading and writing skills that they are acquiring nor in informing the educator how they hope to use these skills.

Emphasizing the active and interactive role of literacy learners is the work of researchers who focus on the schema that a reader brings to a text and which then determines the meaning the reader derives from the text (see Carrell 1983). The foundation of a schema theory of reading is the well-known notion that we can learn ideas only insofar as they are somehow related to what we already know. If this is true, then in order to be able to understand how literacy learners conceptualize the world the educator needs to know what the literacy learners already know and what they value. And it is by means of an ethnographic approach to the language use and culture of these learners that an educator can (1) grasp this perspective of the literacy learners and (2) assist these learners in connecting literacy to their daily lives and needs, by means of a critical-thinking, problem-posing process such as the one proposed by Weinstein (1984). And so, a reading process that is not related to the learner's sociolinguistic and cultural situation will be only a mechanical decoding process, one without objectives in the real world of the learner (Freire 1970). And, it would not be likely for such a mechanical process to be effective in producing functional literacy or critical thinking as its outcome.

On the other hand, when educators and learners together take the opportunity to examine critically the reading materials which they use, to be sure the texts are meaningful to the learner and that the purposes, functions, and forms of language studied are those chosen by the learners, then the outcome will certainly be more functional and rewarding for both learners and educators. (See Auerbach and Burgess 1985 and Wallerstein 1983 for examples of Freirian learner-centered and problem-posing approaches to language teaching issues.) Such educators can find out precisely why their students want to learn to read or to improve their reading, and how the students already use and plan to use their developing literacy skills outside the classroom in order to assist them in their day-to-day lives. It is this orientation that the present study has taken in investigating the literacy stories of a group of adult literacy learners in San Antonio, Texas.

2 Methodology

2.1 The interview. The twenty-five participants in the study were contacted by telephone or in person to find out if they were interested in participating in the study. Those who agreed (most who were contacted did agree) arranged a time to meet the interviewer, usually before or after class in the same community center where they were enrolled in literacy classes, ESL or pre-GED primarily.

The interview itself usually lasted from 45 to 75 minutes and took place in a secluded corner of the library of the community center. The setting provided a degree of privacy and made the tape-recording more audible for later transcribing. Nevertheless, the low voices or whispers used by both interviewer and interviewees seemed to make the interview more intimate, perhaps encouraging greater self-disclosure.

2.2 The participants in the study. The twenty-five persons who participated in this research project represent a unique and important sample of literacy learners. However, the sample of literacy learners is not necessarily representative of all literacy learners in major metropolitan bilingual/ bicultural populations of the U.S. Southwest. The twenty-five adult participants were predominantly in their thirties and forties, had offspring who were in their teens and early twenties, had worked in the service-related work-force as hotel housekeepers, restaurant employees, and store clerks between five and ten years prior to this interview, attended literacy classes after work hours or on Saturdays, and had about six years of education in Mexico before immigrating to the United States. In addition, this group of learners volunteered to participate in the study with the understanding that they would be asked to give an account of their literacy learning experiences, that their anonymity would be protected, and that their accounts would provide educators as well as other literacy learners with an in-depth understanding of literacy not found in other more generalized studies.

The sample of literacy learners in this study is important because it is clear that the literacy learners interviewed are striving to develop their literacy while faced with limiting economic constraints, physically taxing work conditions, and demanding family obligations, all of which present seemingly insurmountable odds against success. In other words, they constitute a sample of highly motivated literacy learners who are striving for success in literacy, their work, and family life, with the hope of improving their own and their family's literacy and (consequently) economic lot. It is important to see how this population sample has dealt with the literacy experience, so that we may better understand the interaction of the literacy experience with the dynamics of day-to-day life, the work place, and the home and school settings.

2.3 The interview questionnaire. An interview was used to elicit the narrative accounts of the literacy experiences as perceived, conceptualized, and articulated by the twenty-five participants of the sample. The twenty-two interview questions were of the type generally associated with the ethnographic method. Examples of six types of ethnographic questions used in the interview are given here in the original Spanish interview form followed by their English translations:

(1) *Why*--explanation questions. *Cuénteme, ¿por qué decidió usted asistir a las clases de alfabetización en inglés?* 'Tell me, why did you decide to take the English literacy classes?'

(2) *How*--instrumental questions. *Cuénteme cómo prepara sus tareas de alfabetización.* 'Tell me how you prepare your literacy homework assignments.'

(3) Functional questions. *¿Para qué propósito utiliza la escritura y lectura en su trabajo?* 'For what purpose do you read and write at work?'

(4) Semantic link (X is a type of Y) questions. *¿Alguna vez ha tenido usted la experiencia de no entender alguna cosa escrita en inglés y haber deseado saber leer en inglés? Déme un ejemplo.* 'Have you ever had the experience of not understanding something written in English and wishing that you knew how to read in English? Give me an example.'

(5) Distribution check questions. *¿Y los otros empleados en la empresa, saben ellos leer y escribir?* 'The other employees at work, do they know how to read and write?'

(6) Contrast questions. *¿Cómo ha cambiado su vida ahora que aprende a leer en inglés?* 'How has your life changed now that you study English literacy?'

During the interview, the literacy learners were encouraged to exemplify their answers with personal anecdotes from their lives and to elaborate as much as possible. In addition, the use of the ethnographic-type of information questions plus the open-ended features of *Cuénteme . . .* 'Tell me . . .' or *Explíqueme . . .* 'Please explain . . .' contributed to the dynamic and natural quality of the interviews. Once each interview was in motion, requests for clarification and/or elaboration were made when necessary. (For further discussion of ethnographic interview questions, see Agar 1980.)

The interview questionnaire covered four aspects of the literacy experience. The first set of questions requested accounts of the learner's rationales for developing literacy skills. The second set of interview questions requested accounts of the learner's strategies for literacy development. The third set of questions requested accounts of the learner's literacy experiences and use of literacy in the workplace, and the fourth set of interview questions requested accounts of the literacy learner's and her or his family's educational biographies. These four areas constitute the four parts of the findings section of the paper: rationales, strategies, literacy and work biographies, and literacy and educational biographies.

3 Findings

3.1 Rationales for developing literacy skills.

In the first area, the rationales for developing literacy skills, the analysis of the interview data produced the following seven clusters of concepts and explanations.

3.1.1 Self-determination.

One set of rationales clusters around the notion of self-determination. The literacy learners who participated in the study expressed their decision to determine their own lives and break away from dependent roles, situations, and settings in which they were completely dependent on others for their livelihood and for communication in public life. The informant quoted here expresses this rationale quite clearly.

Y ahora que me veo sola, yo quiero y deseo y necesito abrirme paso para poder valerme por sí misma para no tener que estar dependiendo de alguien.

In expressing their desire for self-determination, the literacy learners conceive of literacy skills not only as tools for encoding and decoding messages, but also, and more importantly, as tools for transcending their oppressive conditions. The data include accounts of persons depending on others for all important communications in the work-place and in the sphere of legal decisions and legal documents. The powerlessness that grows from having to depend on others for one's livelihood and all important decisions was clearly expressed in the literacy learners' accounts. They clearly visualize the empowering effect and consequences that literacy will bring to them when they are finally able to read all important documents in the work-place and in their personal business.

3.1.2 Economic needs.

A second cluster of motives revolves around specifically economic issues. This rationale expresses the adult literacy learner's decision to develop literacy for the purpose of meeting the prerequisites for a more dignified and economically sound employment opportunity, the type of employment that the person has always wanted. The narratives provided by the participants reveal that the persons are aware that higher levels of literacy skills are a prerequisite to the type of employment they want. This is exemplified well in the following text, in response to the field-worker's (FW) query. Of course, this motive is related to the first motive of the literacy learners' decision to self-direct their lives.

FW: *¿Qué trabajo tiene?*
I: *Andaba buscando trabajo y en ese day care center me dijeron que sí tenían trabajo, . . . pero que no me daban porque no tenía GED. Yo pienso también que el motivo, que no sé suficiente inglés . . . y ya ve . . . que se requiere.*

3.1.3 Work needs. Related to the world of work, the third set of motives focuses on the literacy learner's decision to develop literacy skills in order to accept more responsibility at work. Often, in this case, the learner has developed work-related skills and gained experience in a Spanish-language working environment. Subsequently, he or she has chosen to develop English literacy skills in order to utilize completely his or her previously developed work skills and apply these to new jobs in the English-speaking environment.

At the time of the interview, these literacy learners had already developed what could be called labor-related Basic Interpersonal Communicative Skills (BICS) in English, and now, wanted to develop their labor-related Cognitive and Academic Linguistic Proficiency (CALP) in English. To expand on Cummins' (1979) concept of BICS and CALP, the authors propose the concept 'labor-related BICS.' These basic interpersonal communicative skills are language skills utilized to carry out daily work tasks in many of the less skilled service-oriented employment settings. The labor-related CALP refers to the more complex context-free linguistic proficiency (including literacy), a requisite for most skilled-employment opportunities. It is evident that the interviewee speaking in the following text is concerned about these work advancement opportunities that his language learning will afford him.

FW: *¿Cuáles son sus metas?*
I: *Bueno, pues, yo . . . mi meta es que aprendiendo inglés yo quiero trabajar en un trabajo en el que yo pueda hacer lo que yo sé. Y seguir superándose [sic]. Porque ya ves, después de allí sale otra cosa.*

3.1.4 Family needs. Strongly related to the family domain, a fourth set of motives clusters around the adult literacy learner and parent who has enrolled in literacy classes in order to serve as a model for his or her young adult offspring and consequently to motivate the latter to complete their high school education. This includes motivating the offspring to continue their education and not to drop out, or motivating them to return to secondary school or to enroll in a GED program. These parents openly expressed their concern for the education of their offspring and a concern for the future of their daughters' and sons' self-determination and future employment opportunities. The following text illustrates this concern very clearly.

Y también, esto yo lo hice . . . agarrar clases en inglés para que también mi hijo se sintiera motivado. Ir adelante. Porque el que está tan joven. Este, yo no quiero que él se quede así. Y porque son muy inteligentes. Yo sé que él sí se puede desenvolver.

3.1.5 Family lifestyles. Also tied to family concerns, a fifth set of motives for making the decision to take literacy classes focuses on the fact that the adult literacy learner's children have grown up and the adult now has more time to spend in literacy classes. This set of motives usually cooccurred with other motives, such that persons made a decision on the basis, for example, of the age of their offspring and one or more of the other motives listed in this section of the study. The fact that the interviewee in the following text was a widow, for example, may also be related to her decision to take classes.

Vine (a las clases) porque cuando me quedé viuda no me quise salir de mi casa por mis hijos. Ya que se casaron todos . . . ya están casados todos, dije: 'voy a hacer algo para mí.'

3.1.6 Family relationships. Tying motives more directly to relationships between family members, a sixth area of rationales reveals that sometimes the literacy learner decided to develop her literacy skills without the support of her spouse. That is, one spouse (the husband in all cases) explicitly discouraged the other spouse from attending literacy classes. However, as a result of a change in marital status or as a result of pressing economic needs, the woman decided to pursue literacy classes in order to compete better in the labor-market. In fact, the interviewee in the following text explicitly refers to her husband as being the reason she did not develop her English language skills for so many years.

Pero yo pienso que no aprendí . . . porque yo ya debía saber el inglés. Pero como le digo . . . según como uno vive . . . su vida en su hogar . . . Yo siento que a mí me troncó todo eso, ¿verdad? Fue el mal vivir . . . la cosa es que yo pienso que mi esposo siempre fue el motivo de que yo no me desenvolviera.

3.1.7 Older learners' needs. Revealing the special needs of a certain age group, the seventh and last set of motives deals with the older literacy learners in the study. These learners explained that they were not developing their literacy skills in order to seek employment, because they saw themselves as too old to find employment in the service sector as housekeepers, cooks, and the like. They explained that they were developing their language and literacy skills to communicate effectively in health, social service, and transportation settings. The older literacy learners said that they need to communicate effectively about vital daily concerns with nurses, doctors, technicians, social workers, housing officials, Medicare officials, and transportation providers.

The statement given by the interviewee in the following text exemplifies this point.

Porque muchas veces se enferma uno . . . va uno a un hospital. No sabe qué decir . . . No sabe qué le dijeron. Y es muy necesario para uno mismo. No estoy diciendo para trabajar. A mí ya no me dan trabajo.

In conclusion, the analysis of rationales for developing literacy reveals that the literacy learners want to develop their reading and writing skills in English primarily for two reasons: (1) to have more choices in the domains of work, social, and family life; and (2) to motivate their offspring to continue their education so that they will also have more choices and self-determination.

3.2 Strategies for language skill development. The second area of the findings reports on the analysis of the strategies utilized for literacy skills development. Participants in the study were asked to explain how they resolved situations in which they did not understand what was written nor what was said in English. The literacy learners were also asked to elaborate on their learning and study strategies at home and in public life. The analysis of the interviews reveals several clusters of learning strategies.

3.2.1 Using family assistance. The first cluster focuses on the literacy learning assistance given by literate family members to family members who are literacy learners. Family literacy learning assistance took four forms. One was the literacy learning assistance that young literate high-school-aged and junior-high-aged sons and daughters offered their parents who were literacy learners. The text given here exemplifies this strategy.

FW: *¿Solicita la ayuda de sus hijos, para estudiar?*
I: *Les hablo para que me digan si estoy bien . . . o lo que no entiendo. Yo les pregunto, '¿Qué quiere decir aquí, hijo,' . . . lo que no entiendo . . . '¿Y cómo se pronuncia para decirlo correcto?' A veces lo digo mal, ¿verdad? Y ellos están listos. Como ellos saben, muy bien, retequebién. 'No mami,' me dicen, 'no mami, no se dice así, corrígelo pa'que lo hables bien.' Cuando no es uno, es el otro, el que viene y me dice . . . me ayuda.*

A second form of family literacy learning assistance is that which a literate spouse gives to the spouse who is an adult literacy learner. Reports include both female and male literate spouses helping the illiterate spouse develop his/her literacy.

Another form of family learning assistance is that given by parents literate in Spanish to their sons or daughters who already are literate in English, but who are also developing their literacy in secondary school Spanish classes.

And a fourth form of family literacy learning assistance is the two-way reciprocal assistance that occurred between secondary school-aged offspring who were developing their literacy and their parents who were also developing their literacy, either attending the same class together or the parent enrolled in a night class and the offspring in a day class. These family literacy strategies are sometimes mentioned in the literature in terms of the learning assistance given by parents to their offspring. However, the variety of family literacy learning assistance found in our data for the most part has not been previously investigated by literacy researchers.

3.2.2 Maintaining early reading habits. A second set of strategies for developing literacy skills revolves around the literacy learner's affinity for reading since childhood. Some interviewees stated that during their few early years of schooling, reading always had been their favorite subject. Others mentioned that when they dropped out of elementary school they continued to read the school texts that belonged to their brothers and sisters who were in school. Others gave accounts of frequently reading on their own. Throughout their lives they read in a variety of forms: newspapers, magazines, romance novels, detective stories, and religious materials, as noted in the following text.

> *Leo periódicos y revistas y libros de detectives. Y todo lo leo en inglés. Las listas de mandado las hago en inglés porque a veces mando a los muchachos.*

Some of the interviewees read the materials in Spanish; others read them in English.

Another literacy learner mentioned that much of what she knew had been learned through independent reading she had done since she dropped out of the fourth grade in Mexico. The early reading habits first cultivated in Spanish and then carried over to English reflect the contemporary theoretical notion of transference of cognitive and academic skills from one language to another among bilinguals (see Cummins 1979). Even though not all the successful literacy learners reported having cultivated early reading habits, the cultivation of a reading habit might be an important goal for all literacy learners.

3.2.3 Using the media. Referring to the role of television and radio, a third and related cluster of literacy learning strategies includes reports on literacy learners' use of the mass media as input for literacy development. Participants who are at the intermediate and advanced levels in their English language proficiency mentioned that they consciously made an effort to watch television and listen to the radio in English to help them develop their language and literacy skills.

It is important to remember that these students of literacy were also students of English as a second language. They were working on their language proficiency in both oral and written English. And, as higher level linguistic skills develop in oral English, these skills can immediately transfer to their literacy development and vice versa. That is, literacy learners who are limited in their cognitive and academic English language proficiency will build up their English language proficiency to complement their efforts in literacy development (Cummins 1979). Interestingly, consistent with theoretical works in bilingualism by Cummins and others, the members of this community see their literacy development in global terms. They perceive themselves as developing all four English language skills: listening, speaking, reading, and writing. They usually did not talk of developing literacy alone. Rather, seeing the four skills as one whole set of interdependent language skills, they gave accounts of learning to speak, listen, read, and write. Such is the case in the following text, where the literacy learner speaks about both watching English language television/movies and reading books in English:

> Lo único que yo he tomado mucho como experiencia es que en vez de agarrar un libro en español, lo agarren en inglés. Si van al cine, que no sea el cine mexicano, que sea el cine en inglés. Si ven un programa en la televisión, no lo miren en español, sino en inglés.

3.2.4 Practicing at work. Focusing on the area of work, a fourth set of literacy-learning strategies involves practicing literacy skills in the work setting, even though literacy learners specifically reported that the opportunities to practice language skills in the work-place are severely limited. These limitations reflect the minimal literacy skills required in the service oriented work-place. These work-places include but were not limited to meat-packing plants, construction, housekeeping, food retail places, and some light-industry assembly plants.

A specific strategy in this cluster involves practicing the literacy skills with English-speaking co-workers or supervisors. In the following text one participant narrated the experience of reading packing orders and keeping track of items in a food warehouse. The packing orders were in English and the delivery men and some of the clients were English speakers.

> Y en el trabajo, todos los trabajadores hablan español. Uso el inglés con los que van, como el milkman, o, este, ¿cómo se dice?, 'delivery man,' ¿verdad? Todos los que entregan la mercancía . . . todos . . . la mayoría . . . trato de hablarlo, y de hacerme entender en inglés. Porque tengo que hacerlo . . . Y con los clientes, todo el tiempo en inglés.

In the following text, another participant narrated the experience of having an English-speaking supervisor who was very much interested in developing his Spanish language skills. This supervisor and worker in a bilingual restaurant setting had agreed to help each other with their language and literacy skills. The supervisor would practice his Spanish by addressing the worker in Spanish, and the worker, in turn, would practice her English by addressing him in English.

Les digo que si ellos me corrigen el inglés, yo les corrijo su español. Así siempre estamos hablando . . . mi patrón . . . yo le hablo a él en inglés y él me hablaba en español. Si yo estoy mal, él me corrige, y si él está mal, yo lo corrijo.

However, most of the literacy learners cited the experience of having the opportunity to practice only the basic interpersonal communication skills (BICS) needed to carry out work tasks in the work setting. The literacy learners learned and practiced only the BICS--the limited set of context-bound communications spoken or written in English and which are necessary to carry out the work assignments in the work setting. The participants in the study stated that there were few or no opportunities to practice or develop the higher level language skills (CALP) in their work setting. Other participants reported working in settings where written or spoken English was rarely or never utilized to carry out the work tasks, and where Spanish served as the exclusive medium of oral communication in the work-place.

3.2.5 Finding things out. A fifth cluster of strategies reveals a desire to be well informed and not to be always dependent on others for information related to the work-place, work assignments, work responsibilities, and other important facets of everyday life. This strategy involves always taking the initiative to find out on one's own, and secondhand from other bilinguals, the information needed to make important decisions at work and in the realm of personal and family life. (See the parallel discussion of motives and rationale, section 3.1 ff.) For example, in the following text the speaker states that she wanted to make her own decisions and not to be influenced by others who might urge a more dependent role for her.

Yo recomendaría que la gente sea como yo soy. Una gente me dice 'mira no vayas allí, porque allí te van a preguntar esto . . .' No, no, me gusta sursurarme por mí misma. Nunca dejo que la gente me influya negativamente.

To be able to be independent and not always in doubt about things, she needed to develop her literacy CALP and critical thinking skills.

3.2.6 Encouraging friends. A sixth strategy deals with the literacy learner's concern not only with her/his own literacy development but also with that of colleagues and neighbors. In the interviews, the literacy learners mentioned that they had either been invited or informed of the classes by friends or that they had invited friends and colleagues to come to the literacy classes:

> *Una señora que está allí . . . que se llama Elena . . . que está viniendo a esta clase . . . Nunca quería venir. Yo la convencí de que viniera. Vino ella, y su hija, y su hijo. Ahora, hay palabras, hay cosas que aunque ellas solas se rían, de cómo las hablan . . . y todo eso . . . pero las habla en inglés. Y hay cosas que dicen y ella entiende lo que están diciendo. ¿Por que? Porque está viniendo.*

Thus it can be seen that by encouraging friends to take classes the literacy learner can build a support group for motivation and assistance in the literacy learning process.

3.2.7 Requesting assistance. A seventh literacy-learning strategy reveals that in addition to literacy assistance from one's family, outside the home the literacy learner turns to trusted friends, neighbors, or work supervisors for assistance. Nonfamily members helped the literacy learner to decode legal documents related to marital status, housing, real estate, and citizenship. The following text explains how a work supervisor helped an employee understand documents pertaining to important transactions involving the buying of a house and filing for a divorce.

> *Bueno, por ejemplo, cuando estaba comprando mi casa, cuando me estaba divorciando . . . en varias oportunidades de experimentar eso . . . ¿verdad? . . . de no entender. Nunca firmaba algo sin saber lo que estaba haciendo. Y si yo no sabía entender el idioma, porque estaba escrito en español . . . en inglés . . . siempre buscaba una persona que me lo tradujera. En este aspecto, mi patrón me ha ayudado mucho, ¿verdad? Yo le digo: '¿Qué quiere decir esto.?' Y él me dice: 'Mira, esto quiere decir esto . . . esto otro, esto otro, esto otro. Y si a ti te conviene; está bien . . . si no, bueno, tú lo dices.'*

While on one hand literacy assistance from family members was primarily in the domain of class assignments, the assistance requested from trusted friends was limited to documents related to legal transactions.

3.2.8 Doing homework. Preparing literacy homework assignments is an eighth literacy-learning strategy. The literacy learners pointed out the difficulties encountered in reconciling conflicting work schedules, family obligations, and homework assignments. Literacy learners report that they have limited time to prepare their lessons. Some of the learners arrive at the community center one-half hour to one hour before class to prepare their lessons. Others make time to study after dinner and others come with little or no preparation because of their long working hours and family commitments. The literacy students who have been laid off or who are retired, of course, explain that they have ample time for their lesson preparation. The literacy learners whose offspring are teenagers mentioned that they had more time to attend classes now as compared to when their children were younger. An additional positive factor that accompanied having teenage offspring was that their teenagers' literacy skills enabled them to assist in their parents' literacy learning. The text given here illustrates a student's account of how she arrives at school prior to class time to prepare the literacy assignments and to check out books from the library:

FW: *¿En casa, qué lee o escribe?*

I: *Pos, lo único es cuando vengo a la escuela. Siempre llego, y siempre me gusta escribir. Cuando vengo aquí siempre checo libros . . . que son los libros que estoy estudiando. Como yo sé que no son míos, siempre estoy escribiendo todo lo que quiero aprender . . . espeleando las palabras. Si no sé cómo se espelean, las busco en el diccionario, y sé cómo escribirlas. Y tengo también la ayuda de los muchachos . . . de mis hijos . . . que . . . cuando, no sé algo les pregunto a ellos, y todo eso.*

3.2.9 Developing metalinguistic awareness.   The development of a metalinguistic and metacommunicative awareness--a consciousness about the forms of language and communication--is the ninth literacy-learning strategy. The participants reported becoming more aware of forms and uses of speaking and writing. They noted that as a result of literacy classes they had become more interested in how, why, and when people said or wrote what they did, as illustrated here.

FW: *¿Ha notado diferencias desde que está tomando sus clases?*

I: *Pues . . . que antes . . . yo no me interesaba por saber qué se decía, o qué no se decía . . . o cómo se hablaba. Y . . . ahora sí. Tengo interés en fijarme, ¿cómo están hablando? . . . ¿Qué es lo que están hablando?, para poderlo entender y leer . . . y escribir también.*

In contrast, before the literacy classes, the literacy learners had been concerned with the content of the communication only. According to the literacy learner just quoted, the occurrence of this literacy-learning strategy demonstrates that a metalinguistic and metacommunicative awareness contributes to successful literacy development.

    In conclusion, the analysis of strategies for language skill development reveals a profile of a self-initiating literacy learner who seeks support for learning from family and trusted friends, utilizes the media and the work-place for practicing language skills, maintains reading habits, and pays attention to metalinguistic and metacommunicative competencies. These traits of a successful literacy learner have learning and teaching implications for other adult literacy learners and adult literacy educators.

3.3 Literacy and labor biographies. The third part of our findings is a report on the analysis of the literacy learners' work and literacy histories.

3.3.1 Physical work. The first cluster of experiences narrated in the interviews refers to the physically tiring nature of work tasks in the service-labor sector. The literacy learners repeatedly mention that service jobs involve low pay, hard physical work, no choice in terms of work schedules, no permanence, and no benefits. This is pointed out in the following text:

> I: *You don't have any education. It's too hard for people. They work too hard. And it's hard . . . hard work. Because all the places . . . they work you too hard if you don't have education. So that's why I want to continue my education. Because it's the service type work! Too hard.*

The literacy learners gave accounts of leaving one job and going on to another because of the difficult working conditions and poor pay. Other accounts tell of finding a job which is somewhat better but then being laid off, or of having to quit the job to take care of an ill and elderly person in the family and subsequently having to look for another job.

These narratives also include mention by learners of feeling caught in a circular predicament where they are too tired physically to attend literacy classes after work hours but know that they need to sharpen their literacy skills to compete in the labor market. They express the desire to develop literacy skills in the work-place but also the frustration of discovering that often literacy skills are a prerequisite to employment. At the same time, several participants report that employers take no interest in developing the language and literacy skills of their employees, as exemplified by this text:

> I: *Y ése es el problema mío . . . donde he ido a hacer aplicación para buscar trabajo aquí. Entonces, yo necesito más conversación. Aunque yo entiendo y sé del trabajo; lo puedo hacer.*

3.3.2 Definitions of literacy. Another cluster of experiences revolves around the literacy learner's definition of literacy. The literacy learners in this sample do not see themselves as *analfabetos*/illiterates. For the literacy learners, an *analfabeto* is a person who has no formal education and no notions about the writing and reading system. Most of the participants have had from five to seven years of schooling in Mexico; so they perceive themselves as literate in Spanish, even though the typical definition of a functional illiterate in the United States is a person with less than eight years of education. This raises the question: but what about persons who have had six years of education in another language and in a different educational system? These findings poignantly demonstrate that it would be wise to use the terms illiterate/*analfabeto* carefully with community persons. For them, an illiterate person is one who cannot read, not a person who cannot read English. The following text bears out this point.

> *Porque aunque uno sepa hacer muchas cosas. . . si no sabe el idioma . . . creen que uno tiene mucha ignorancia . . . O es analfabeto. O que no puede desempeñar nada, porque no sabe el idioma.*

3.3.3 Others' perceptions. Another type of experience reported by the participants, many with five to seven years of schooling in Mexico or the United States, is that because of their limited English language and literacy skills, employers and the population in general perceive them as completely incompetent for various types of work. Many also cited the years of work experience in another country and their skills in Spanish literacy and mathematics, only to discover that U.S. employers regarded them as inexperienced and illiterate, and therefore often not employable. This demonstrates a need to educate U.S. employers in ways of assessing their employees' work experience in another country and their literacy in other languages, and a need for employers to formulate plans to utilize and develop the literacy of their employees in the work-place.

3.3.4 Work BICS. The interviewees' experiences learning English language labor-related BICS in the work-place comprise the fourth cluster of labor biographies. The literacy learners tell of learning the spoken and written English BICS in the work-place for a variety of purposes, and, for example, give accounts of using these BICS to carry out inventory tasks in clothing stores or food-handling businesses. In the following text, a restaurant waiter narrates his experiences learning the labor-related BICS:

FW: *¿En el trabajo entiende todo?*
I: *Lo entiendo todo por completo. Si, por ejemplo, si llega una gente le digo 'What would you like,' o 'What you order,' y me dicen la orden en inglés, lo entiendo perfectamente, de todo. Cuando me dicen 'no tomato,' o 'no onions,' o que no quieren esto, 'no tamale, no enchilada, extra enchilada,' o si trata de trabajo, lo entiendo perfectamente.*

Another literacy learner describes the labor-related BICS developed as a restaurant cook:

> *Sí, leemos las órdenes en inglés. Las escribimos también, pero son cosas básicas: arroz, beans, fries, beans, beef tacos, chicken tacos . . . Sí, las escribimos, half a pint of rice, half a pint of beans . . . Es todo, nada más.*

In a more skilled area such as bricklaying, one literacy learner gave an account of learning all the written and spoken vocabulary needed to do bricklaying tasks.

These same persons were aware of the limitations of their spoken and written English BICS and often discussed their desire to develop the higher level CALP skills as in the texts cited below. In the first text, the literacy learner explains that her job requires such limited basic interpersonal communication skills (BICS) in English that she sees no reason to continue ESL classes:

> *También fue motivo por que ya no fui a estudiar inglés. Porque con lo poquito que me aprendí allí, ¿verdad?, oyendo, para mí era lo suficiente como para trabajar. En la oficina . . . era cuando oía palabras. Oía uno. Simplemente cuando iban americanas o americanos a pedir mercancía. La pedían. Y ya por una palabra, ¿verdad?, entonces ya uno, ya contaba, ya sabíamos, cómo habían pedido aquello que querían. Y así. Pero no era, verdad, lo suficiente.*

The literacy learner cited in the next example points out that his communication is limited to the BICS and that he lacks more developed skills to handle conversations beyond these BICS skills.

> FW: *¿Sería más difícil si va a una oficina?*
> I: *Sí, aha, sí. Por ejemplo, cuando voy a comprar algo, por ejemplo, le digo, 'I'm looking for something,' sí, me hago entender. Pero ya si se trata de más conversación . . . ya de mucho, esto o el otro . . . entiendo muchas palabras. Pero con una sola que no entienda, allí se me echo a perder todo.*

Some literacy learners also mention that they have to explain their level of language proficiency as carefully as possible to employers, so as not to be accused of misrepresenting themselves. The literacy learners explain to their employers that they know sufficient English to handle the basic communications related to their immediate service-oriented jobs, but not enough to handle discussions beyond their immediate work context.

In conclusion, analysis of the literacy and labor biographies of literacy learners reveals a picture of a linguistically limited work-place where English language communications are limited to labor-related BICSs without opportunities to further develop language skills. It is a work-place with long hours of physically taxing work with little or no motivation for educational improvement, a work-place where employers perceive English literacy learners as totally incompetent in spite of the learners' literacy in Spanish and their previous work experience.

3.4 Literacy and educational biographies. This last section of the findings presents analysis and discussion of the narratives given by the literacy learners about their own and their families' educational and literacy backgrounds.

3.4.1 Schooling in Mexico. The first cluster of accounts reveals that, of the twenty-five literacy learners in the sample, twenty-three had had from five to seven years of schooling in Mexico. One learner had had no schooling and two had had from five to eight years of schooling in the United States. The learners who had been educated in Mexico had resided in the United States for over twelve years and most had teenage offspring. Of course, the study had already been limited to participants who had had less than nine years of schooling. The following texts give clear narrative evidence of the types of experiences shared by the participants. The interviewees in the following two texts had attended school in Mexico in their youth. The learner in the first narrative had completed the fifth grade and the learner in the second narrative had completed the seventh grade. Both learners had dropped out of school. The first one had dropped out because her 'old-fashioned' father had ordered her to stay at home and help her mother with the housework; the second one had dropped out to get married.

FW: *¿Fue a la escuela?*
I: *A los seis años empecé la primaria. Al llegar a los diez años estaba en quinto año. Eramos una mujer y ocho hombres en la familia. Entonces, mi papá era un hombre inculto y hombre chapado a la antigua. No quiso que yo siguiera estudiando. Y dijo: 'Tienes que ayudar a tu mamá en el quehacer de la casa.'*
FW: *¿Fue a la escuela?*
I: *Fui por siete años a la escuela.*

FW: *¿Le gustó la escuela?*
I: *Sí, sí, me gustaba. Porque aprendía cosas que yo no sabía. Y porque yo quería ser alguien. Quería prepararme. Me gustaba escribir a máquina. Me gustaba bastante.*

FW: *¿Por qué no continuó en la escuela?*
I: *Dejé la escuela porque me casé.*

3.4.2 Offsprings' education. Focusing on offsprings' educational experiences, the second cluster of educational biographies shows that the sons and daughters of these adults form two groups: those that drop out of school in the eighth or ninth grade and those that are doing well in school. There are about the same number of accounts of both. The first group includes families in which the parents, sons, and daughters had dropped out of schools in the United States. This group of families with school dropouts is one about which we must be concerned. Some of these same adult literacy learners have siblings who had dropped out of school also. In fact, it is very probable that there are groups of families, beyond this sample, in which members of two or three generations are caught in a cyclical pattern of functional illiteracy.

In contrast, other literacy learners narrate accounts of having children who did well in school. Five of the participants had offspring who were attending college or who had attended college. In fact, it is possible that the persons in these classes were precisely those who had decided to challenge the problem of functional illiteracy in the community and were studying and working on developing their literacy skills to insure that their families were functionally literate.

The following texts illustrate the educational experiences of offspring. The first text is an account of those who stayed in school. The second illustrates the experience of those who did not, and those who came back to school.

FW: *¿Y su familia, sabe leer y escribir?*
I: *Toda mi familia sabe leer y escribir. Nadie es analfabeto. Pues, mi hijo tiene diecisiete años. Va a entrar al twelfth grade, y mi hija va a entrar al décimo grado.*

Another participant narrates a different experience:

Y cuando vino aquí no le gustó a la muchacha, y dejó de ir. Mistió el año (de Dallas). Nomás fue como dos meses a Lanier, y se me amachó que ya no quería. Y también se me fue para allá, con mi mamá y mi papá en México. Y después yo estuve hablando con ella y dándole consejos que volviera comoquiera a la escuela, ¿verdad?, porque le iba a hacer mucha falta más allá. Ella aceptó otra vez venir. Y entró de vuelta, y ya acabó el año ahora. Ya lo acabó . . . el nueve. Y va al diez.

3.4.3 Generational differences. A third cluster of educational biography experiences demonstrates that some of the older literacy learners (in their sixties) talk about their childhood in poverty in Mexico and rural Texas, where they had had little schooling. Some narrate accounts of learning to read and write in Spanish from a relative at home. Others give accounts of teaching Spanish literacy to their sons and daughters who became literate in English in U.S. schools.

The younger foreign-born participants (the ones in their thirties and forties) tend to have more education than those in their sixties. This coincides with research conducted by Bustamente (1986) on Mexican immigration to the United States showing that the contemporary Mexican immigrant to the U.S. has more education than the immigrants of earlier years. In one ESL/literacy class, the field-workers met young immigrants in their twenties who had had twelve years of schooling in Mexico. (From the U.S. perspective, it is desirable that we have immigrants with a better educational background than before, but from the Mexican perspective, we need to be concerned that the young educated emigrants are draining Mexico of a precious resource.)

3.4.4 Schooling in two countries. Accounts of families in which the older siblings were educated in Mexico and the younger ones were educated in the United States make up a fourth cluster of experiences. The literacy learners note that the younger siblings have developed their language skills and literacy in English. However, they also note that the older siblings who were in their midteens when they immigrated to the U.S. did not develop their literacy as well as the younger ones. The literacy learners claim that the older teenage siblings were placed in elementary school classrooms which did not meet their needs and where they felt humiliated and embarrassed and subsequently dropped out of school. The report in the following text illustrates this point.

Yo tengo ocho hermanos; uno es radiotécnico; otro es licenciado; otro es capitán piloto aviador; otro es agricultor. Nada más él y yo no estudiamos. El que sigue de mí, estudió bastante, unos quince años.

The significant factor in this account is one of experiencing humiliation and embarrassment, rather than an age factor. Research by both Skuttnabb-Kangas (1979) and Troike (1978) shows that immigrant teenagers with developed academic skills in their mother tongue have a higher success rate in school in the host country than younger immigrant students who come to the host country before developing their early cognitive and academic skills.

3.4.5 Education interrupted. A final cluster of educational experiences focuses on the experiences of participants (mostly immigrant women from Mexico) who narrate that their brothers who had stayed in Mexico had continued their education in Mexico and now had good employment there. For these women, coming to the United States had meant an interruption in their education and development, even though now they have resumed classes in Texas to develop their literacy and English language skills. We might wonder what their opportunities would have been like in Mexico if they had stayed. Would they have had an interruption in their education there like they had here? And would they have returned to school in Mexico, if it had been interrupted?

In conclusion, the analysis of the literacy and educational biographies of adult learners presents a profile of an adult immigrant population with five to seven years of schooling in Mexico, about fifteen years of residence in the United States, and with teenage children in U.S. schools. In some cases, the teenagers are successful in school; in others, they are not. Many of these adult learners have been enrolled in literacy classes for about one year, after not having gone to school for at least a dozen years. Some of the adult learners' younger siblings had attended U.S. schools, but the older siblings had not because of family and work obligations or because of encountering school settings that did not meet their needs or which were openly discriminatory and hostile to them (cf. Cisneros and Leone 1985).

4 Conclusion. This ethnographic literacy study concerns the shared ways of thinking about literacy in a particular community of literacy learners on the west side of San Antonio, Texas. The first stage of this study has yielded important findings in four areas: (1) their motivation for literacy learning, (2) their strategies for literacy learning, (3) the learners' literacy vis-à-vis work experience, and (4) their literacy vis-à-vis school experience--all from the perspective of the literacy learners themselves. Now that these findings have been presented, noncommunity persons need to become cognizant of and to understand the perspective of the literacy learner as a prerequisite to participating in the literacy development of adults in the Spanish/English speaking communities in the United States.

Just as significant as the shared ways of thinking of the literacy learners of this community will be the ways in which the literacy learners explain and narrate their experiences. These explanations and ways of using language--the focus of the second stage of this study--will shed light on both the ways of thinking and the discourse of the literacy learners; this will then be useful for persons working with and assisting them in their Spanish/English literacy development.

4.1 Future directions. As findings from this study point out, from an ethnographic perspective there are several areas of research on literacy that need to be pursued. These include (1) the macrosociocultural context of literacy, (2) the perspectives on literacy use, especially with regard to schooling and work, (3) the reasons for persons to pursue greater literacy abilities, (4) the strategies of literacy development, and (5) the perspectives on the changes encountered in private and public life and attitudes of persons who have developed greater literacy skills. But, in order to constitute an ethnography of communication, a study of the areas and questions analyzed in this study would need to be consistent theoretically and methodologically with research directions explained and exemplified by Hymes (1972), Freire (1970), Agar (1980), and Heath (1983).

As mentioned earlier, the sociocultural context of the adult literacy learners is of primary importance in getting to know the role of literacy and the role of language in general in the lives of literacy learners. In the case of San Antonio, the macrocontext of the present study, the relation between language and culture has been much in the consciousness of both Mejicanos and Anglos residing there, as in other areas of the United States (Sánchez 1983:16; Attinasi 1985:29; and Elías-Olivares and Valdés 1982:29). This consciousness is due to a number of factors, including the politicization of bilingual education programs, the recent English-only movement, the local emphasis on U.S.-Mexico business collaboration, the second strong term of the city's first Spanish/English bilingual mayor, and the recent redistricting of city political boundaries, which has already had far-reaching effects in every aspect of city life--all of this within the nation's tenth largest city, about two-thirds of whose inhabitants are of Mexican-American ancestry.

With respect to the other areas covered in this study (perspectives on literacy use, reasons and strategies for developing literacy, and expected changes as a result of literacy development), information on literacy use by other literacy learners, their families, and friends is vital not only for educators but also for all others interested in communicating with the literacy learner and furthering his or her critical thinking and learner autonomy. That is, more and different types of literacy learners need to be consulted and asked many of the same questions asked in this study. Some of these groups include:

(1) first-generation persons, especially between the ages of eighteen and thirty, but also in other age groups;
(2) second- and third-generation persons of different age groups;
(3) persons residing in other parts of the country, such as border areas, northeastern and midwestern regions, and migrant groups; and
(4) persons who did not immigrate to the United States on a permanent basis but who have had some extended residence in the U.S.

Future work also needs to take into account the blossoming research in the area of learning strategies and, to the extent possible, address specific concerns in this area, as exemplified in the following questions:

(1) What strategies do these learners find most useful and how have they discovered the usefulness of the strategies?
(2) How did the literacy learners learn these strategies--from someone else or through discovery on their own?
(3) What specific strategies do learners use for pronunciation, grammar, vocabulary, organizing learning material, remembering material, understanding directions, communicating in social situations, and engaging in work-related communication? (cf. Rubin 1975, O'Malley et al. 1985, and Wenden 1987.)

Applications of this literacy research can also take several directions, including especially ethnographic teaching methods such as problem posing (not problem solving) and self-assessment, to name a few (Wallerstein 1983; LeBlanc and Painchaud 1985). In the area of literacy materials, Auerbach and Burgess (1985:490ff.) suggest a careful examination of 'the hidden curriculum' in our texts, and a revision of curriculum as needed to reflect the learners' needs to think critically and to make choices in daily communicative activities. In these ways, we can become better acquainted with and develop our understanding of literacy learners and those with whom they come into contact, and therefore, encourage their autonomy and self-determination (Wenden 1987 and Rubin 1975).

Finally, for language planners in both educational and employment environments, the implications of the study are significant. An example of a successful literacy program would be one which plans with family literacy in mind, not just individual literacy. Another example would be the collaboration of commercial businesses in the literacy classes, in more than just a financial capacity. That is, the employer could not only give work incentives for employees to develop their literacy skills, but also encourage educators and literacy learners to incorporate specific work-related communication into the language and literacy curriculum. Finally, literacy learners could then participate in the posing of problems and the creating of solutions for these problems, both in the work area and in other domains of their daily lives.

Other language planning implications of this study point toward several areas of application. A few of these are:

(1) Employers need to provide more opportunities for employees to use and therefore to develop CALP and higher level language skills on the job.
(2) Businesses need to utilize fully these persons' literacy skills and other prior experiences which use both Spanish and English.
(3) Educators need to integrate into literacy classes (a) the dynamics of literacy assistance given to adult learners by family and friends, (b) the cultivation and maintenance of reading habits, and (c) metalinguistic and metacommunicative strategies.
(4) Researchers need to use the term 'functional illiteracy' carefully in a bicultural setting where the community members' literacy expands across two languages, often with a higher level in one language and a lower one in a second language.

Note

The authors would like to thank the staff and students at the Bazan Library for their assistance with the interview collection for this study.

References

Adult Performance Level Project. 1977. *The final report: An adult performance level study.* Washington, D.C.: Department of Health, Education, and Welfare.
Agar, M.H. 1980. *The professional stranger: An informal introduction to ethnography.* New York: Academic Press.
Attinasi, J.J. 1985. Hispanic attitudes in northwest Indiana and New York. In: *Spanish language use and public life in the USA.* L. Elías-Olivares et al., eds. New York: Mouton. 27-58.
Auerbach, E.R., and D. Burgess. 1985. The hidden curriculum of survival ESL. *TESOL Quarterly* 19:3.475-95.

Bustamente, J. 1986. U.S. Mexico relations. In: *Encuentro: El chicano y el mejicano*. Symposium conducted at La Universidad Nacional Autónoma de México at San Antonio, San Antonio, Texas.

Carrell, P.L., and J.C. Eisterhold. 1983. Schema theory and ESL reading pedagogy. *TESOL Quarterly* 17:4.553-73.

Cisneros, R., and E.A. Leone. 1983. Contact and recontact: Mexican-American language communities in the Twin Cities. In: *Spanish in the U.S. setting: Beyond the Southwest*. L. Elías-Olivares, ed. Arlington, Va.: National Clearinghouse for Bilingual Education. 181-209.

Cummins, J. 1979. Linguistic interdependence and the educational development of bilingual children. *Review of Educational Research* 49.222-51.

Elías-Olivares, L., and G. Valdés. 1982. Language diversity in Chicano speech communities: Implications for language teaching. In: *Bilingual education for Hispanic students in the United States*. New York: Teachers College Press. 151-66.

Freire, P. 1970. *Cultural action for freedom*. Cambridge, Mass.: *Harvard Educational Review* and Center for Study of Development and Social Changes.

Gray, W.S. 1969. *The teaching of reading and writing*. Glenview, Ill.: UNESCO and Scott Foresman.

Heath, S.B. 1983. *Ways with words*. New York: Cambridge University Press.

Intercultural Development Research Association. 1983. *The status of illiteracy in San Antonio*. San Antonio, Texas: IDRA.

Hymes, D. 1972. Models of the interaction of language and social life. In: *Directions in sociolinguistics*. J. Gumperz and D. Hymes, eds. New York: Holt, Rinehart, and Winston. 35-71.

Le Blanc, R., and G. Painchaud. 1985. Self-assessment as a second language placement instrument. *TESOL Quarterly* 19:4.673-86.

O'Malley, J.M., et al. 1985. Learning strategy applications with students of English as a second language. *TESOL Quarterly* 19:3.557-84.

Rubin, J. 1975. What the 'Good Language Learner' can teach us. *TESOL Quarterly* 19:3.41-51.

Sanches, R. 1983. *Chicano discourse*. Rowley, Mass.: Newbury House.

Skutnabb-Kangas, T. 1979. *Language in the process of cultural assimilation and structural incorporation of linguistic minorities*. Arlington, Va.: National Clearinghouse for Bilingual Education.

Troike, R. 1978. Research evidence for the effectiveness of bilingual education. *NABE Journal* III:1.13-24.

Wallerstein, N. 1983. The teaching approach of Paulo Freire. In: *Methods that work*. J.W. Oller, Jr. and P.A. Richard-Amato, eds. Rowley, Mass.: Newbury House. 190-204.

Weinstein, G. 1984. Literacy and second language acquisition: Issues and perspectives. *TESOL Quarterly* 18:3.471-84.

Wenden, A. 1987. Promoting learner autonomy: A curricular framework. Paper presented at the 21st Annual Convention of TESOL, Miami.

On the question of 'standard' versus 'dialect': Implications for teaching Hispanic college students

Margarita Hidalgo
San Diego State University

1 Introduction. In spite of the serious attempts to explain language variation within the framework of both traditional dialectology and contemporary sociolinguistics, this phenomenon continues to create a problem for the teacher of standard language. The problem may stem from various sources: (1) the thorough impact that the standard theory of language has had on students of language and linguistics,[1] and (2) the general intolerance toward forms of speech which do not conform to the model accepted as a national or local standard. The study of language as a fixed system of interrelated structures seems to be well established in our teaching of language and linguistics. However, the problem of variation versus nonvariation in language is magnified when we teach an accepted standard to speakers of varieties which are lacking in prestige. Spanish-speaking students enrolled in American colleges and universities in Spanish for Native Speakers (SNS) courses provide an excellent opportunity to explore some of the most relevant issues related to this sociolinguistic phenomenon. In this regard, this paper discusses three major points: (1) the theoretical distinction of standard versus dialect and the pedagogical and societal implications of bidialectal education in several educational systems; (2) the most striking structural differences between Chicano and Puerto Rican Spanish, on one hand, and a proposed supraregional and suprasocial standard model that can be accepted among all U.S. Hispanics, on the other; and (3) the implications of such differences for teaching Spanish to Hispanic college students in the United States.

1.1 Standard versus dialect: Theoretical considerations. The standard/ dialect dichotomy has been addressed by scholars from different viewpoints. From a historical/sociolinguistic perspective, the standard language is considered to be merely the regional or social dialect that acquired prestige because of political and economic reasons and therefore became the instrument of communication of central administrations, educational systems, and national literatures (Fishman 1972; Giles and Powesland 1975). Trudgill (1979) offers one of the clearest discussions of the origins of the standard. He points out that standard British English descended from dialects originally spoken in the southeast of England; for this reason 'differences between standard English and non-standard dialects of the south of England, while socially very significant, are linguistically rather trivial, and few in number' (p. 11). However, since standard English or Received Pronunciation may be learned in the large public schools or through conscious effort and training, this variety is, within England, genuinely regionless.

The distinction between language and dialect can also be drawn on national criteria. For example, Norwegian, Swedish, and Danish are usually referred to as distinct official languages even though they are mutually intelligible. In spite of the political autonomy of each of the three Scandinavian countries, the linguistic situation in Scandinavia can be described as a continuum of dialects from Norway in the north to Denmark in the south. On the other hand, the various dialects of the Arab world are characterized by far greater differences than those held in Scandinavia but the ideals of religious and cultural unity motivate Arabs to minimize these differences (Edwards 1983:46-47). Likewise, some of the 'dialects' spoken in China exhibit more differences among themselves than do the Scandinavian languages mentioned above. Nonetheless, the eventual dominance of the Peking variety over all the others seems to characterize mainland China (Ray 1962:95). In summary, the criteria for establishing the distinction between a language and a dialect are not well defined.

Once a prestigious dialect is elevated to a standard variety, it is likely to disseminate over the region or nation that is dominated by the political system supporting it. In many modern nations a prestigious dialect has become a superposed variety with ample functions and sociohistorical attributes which demonstrate a consistent tendency to affect social attitudes toward them (Stewart 1962:17-18).[2] Furthermore, in some Latin American countries the speech variety spoken in the national capital represents the ideal linguistic norm and a model worthy of imitation. Although the norm has not been defined from the purely linguistic point of view, the concept of the norm is widespread throughout Spanish-speaking countries and supported by linguistic research (e.g., as in the international project entitled *Estudio coordinado de la norma lingüística en las principales ciudades de América*). In contrast, in the United States the linguistic norm seems to refer to those forms of inflectional morphology and syntax which are universally undenigrated. Differences in pronunciation, on the other hand, are associated with region, generally tolerated, and often expected. Moreover, idiosyncrasies of pronunciation and intonation seem to encompass the components of one's native dialect that inevitably emerge when one speaks the standard language (Smith and Lance 1979:131; Fromkin and Rodman 1983:458).

Nevertheless, some researchers consider that the standard variety should be understood as an idealization rather than as a fact. In this vein, Escobar

(1976:55, 1978:143, 162) claims that the linguistic norm is defined as an abstraction or as an average representation of language whose variability is not questioned. Along the same lines, Fromkin and Rodman (1983:251) doubt that the standard is spoken by a readily identifiable group of people. They state: 'Standard American English (SAE) is a dialect of English that many Americans almost speak; divergences from this "norm" are labeled "Philadelphia dialect," "Chicago dialect," "Black English" and so on. SAE is an idealization. Nobody speaks this dialect, and if somebody did, we wouldn't know it because SAE is not defined precisely.'

In various countries, however, a notion of the standard as the most acceptable form of language is propagated through the school, language academies, and dictionaries. Although the correct forms of language are not always clear, even to users of the standard language, there is a general consensus that the variety (or style) used in public or official events, the language of the media, and the language of educational institutions should be considered more correct or more appropriate than the variety (or style) used in everyday affairs.

1.2 Educational implications. The traditional response of the school, as well as of the larger society, to linguistic diversity has been an attempt to eradicate varieties other than the perceived standard. The rationalization given is that the standard language used in teaching is commonly the vehicle for general communication and has already been implemented to serve public functions and to write works of art, literature, science, and technology. In contrast, a dialect is considered to have informal daily functions that hinder its use in the former fields. The position of educators with respect to the dialect/standard dilemma is similar to that held for the mother tongue/foreign language issue.

Bilingual education (BE), as an instructional strategy, has traditionally been examined from two apparently mutually exclusive perspectives: (1) those who promote BE believe that individuals and communities should be given the opportunity to be educated in and use their other-than-English language and (2) those who support monolingual education maintain that BE inflicts a personal and societal damage, since individuals must learn the language of the dominant society in order to succeed. Those who argue in favor of the second position often overlook the advantages of BE, whose major goal is to enrich the linguistic and cultural repertoire of the individual. The proponents of the first position, on the other hand, fear that monolingual education will ultimately foster assimilation. These rather generalized positions actually represent a wide range of opinions which are normally influenced or constricted by the context in which the decisions about educational policy are made. For many teachers, the inflammatory nature of the controversy in BE causes confusion and contradictory attitudes which inevitably affect what they do, want to do, or refuse to do in the classroom. Likewise, trends in bilingual education reflect multivaried attitudes toward standard and dialect. The main issues discussed by researchers and educators have to do with the societal values of standard and dialect and the implications derived from teaching both, or from choosing one of the two for classroom use. The standard/dialect dichotomy also brings about problems of structural dissimilarities between the two varieties. Moreover, the existence of such a dichotomy obliges researchers to address the long-term consequences of favoring the standard over the dialect or vice versa, since depending on this choice, one's job opportunities and general success in society may be either enhanced or jeopardized.

In recent years, numerous researchers and educators have claimed that a pedagogically sensitive shift from dialect to standard and the retention of the former may positively effect the educational well-being and cultural repertoire of many dialect speakers (Baratz and Shuy 1969; Dillard 1978; Fasold and Shuy 1970; Fishman and Lueders-Salmon 1972; Keller 1982; Moses et al. 1976; Trudgill 1979; Valdés-Fallis 1976, 1978; and Valdés et al. 1981). One of the most coherent positions with respect to the question of standard versus dialect is that put forth by Ammon (1977), in his response to Fishman and Lueders-Salmon (1972). Comparing Swabian speakers of southeastern Germany with speakers of Black English, the latter authors describe the use of dialect in education and the consequences of such a practice, but they do not strongly advocate the teaching of the superposed variety. In his response, Ammon gives convincing evidence that an imposition of the standard and a total disregard for dialect is more academically, economically, and psychologically detrimental than beneficial to Swabian speakers. Ammon's elaborate response to Fishman and Lueders-Salmon culminated in a series of studies dealing with specific social aspects of dialect in highly industrialized nations, educational problems, and quests for their solutions (see Ammon 1979).

Although with respect to the standard/dialect issue there seem to be as many opinions as researchers, the response to language variation in BE in the United States has been the implementation of programs or courses commonly referred to as bidialectal. According to Moses et al. (1976), 'Typical school practices continue to emphasize either eradication, or some version of bidialectalism.' For the past fifteen years scholars such as Shuy, Wolfram, Labov, and others have addressed the study of the structure of Black English, but the controversy on bidialectal education has been standing at an impasse. Textbooks for speakers of Black English have been prepared with great care by experts on the subject, but their implementation has often been blocked by political rather than academic interests (Dillard 1978). More recently, however, a lawsuit on behalf of eleven Black children who charged the Ann Arbor School District with violation of federal law has brought hopes for all Black-English-speaking students, for the decision in that case will force school administrators and teachers to become acquainted with this variety and to prepare correspondingly suitable materials for classroom use (Farr Whiteman 1980).

2 Spanish for native speakers: Theory and practice. The endeavors of educators committed to bilingualism and biliteracy for U.S. Hispanics are reported in Valdés et al. (1981) and revealed in the many textbooks written for such college students. The SNS tracks that now exist in some American colleges and universities aim at improving the students' language skills in the areas of speaking, listening, spelling, reading, writing, and formal grammar. The SNS curricula have been designed along the lines of those who promote bidialectalism and appreciation of dialect differences (Valdés-Fallis 1976, 1978). According to Valdés-Fallis 1978:106):

> A comprehensive language development program is based upon the fact that 'teaching' the standard language is not adequately handled by presenting long lists of features labeled 'non-standard.' It begins by insisting that materials be used which show an awareness of the varying sources of non-standard features which are accepted universally. The students are made aware of regional differences and encouraged not to change those aspects of the speech which are accepted in educated speakers of the same region. At the same time they are also made aware of how special phonological features may themselves create special spelling problems; for example, the use of [l] for [r], or the use of [∅] for [y] will create problems in the spelling of *muerte, silla, gallina,* etc. for speakers of varieties which have those characteristics.

In addition, students are made aware of style and register appropriateness and when they begin to write they are taught which forms are peculiar to casual rapid speech and which are accepted in writing.

Whereas most educators involved in SNS courses seem to have concentrated their efforts on writing skills and formal grammar, very few of them have revealed their legitimate preoccupations for the effects that formal education in Spanish may have on the spoken language. This shortcoming may have to do with the limited information we have available on actual differences between spoken standard and dialect, with the fragile definitions of standard/dialect in the Spanish-speaking world, and with the contradictory information we have with respect to the teaching of the standard. Valdés and other SNS proponents assume that the variety spoken by educated speakers is nonstigmatized and should therefore serve as a model for U.S. Hispanics. However, since the latter are a heterogeneous group they may find themselves trying to decide which standard they should study or imitate, since the Spanish-speaking world offers several and sometimes conflicting alternatives. The following sections of this paper provide an outline of the potentially stigmatized features of two U.S. varieties--Puerto Rican and Chicano Spanish--that may serve to illustrate the relationship between standard and dialect at the spoken level.

2.1 Caribbean Spanish: Principal characteristics. The following remarks taken from Lipski (1986) indicate the main characteristics of this variety of U.S. Spanish which are relevant for SNS instruction:

(1) Preconsonantal and word-final /s/ are routinely aspirated and deleted.

(2) The liquid consonants /l/ and /r/ are frequently interchanged in pre-consonantal and word-final positions. Moreover, final /-r/ may be lost in infinitives (e.g., *trabajá*) and a consonant preceded by /l/ or /r/ may result in a geminate cluster (e.g., *puerta* > *puetta, algo* > *aggo*).

(3) Intervocalic and word-final /d/ often disappear (e.g., *marido* > *marío, ciudad* > *ciudá*).

(4) Multiple /r̃/ may be pronounced like /h/ or as a uvular, similar to the French /r/.

Some of the aforementioned characteristics carry a social stigma in specific speech communities, although the degree of stigmatization has not been clearly identified. Whereas Guitart (1981) claims that the pronunciation of /r/ as a post-velar fricative trill and the confusion of /l/ and /r/ in syllable- and word-final positions are denigrated features by both in-group and out-group speakers, Lipski (1986) states that the postvelar fricative trill may be prestigious and even carry a nationalistic value of Puerto Rican identity. Both scholars agree, however, that the leveling of /l/ and /r/ is socially stigmatized to varying degrees.

As compared to other dialects of the Spanish-speaking world, Caribbean Spanish is considered a 'radical' dialect because of its obvious segmental and sequential phonological and phonetic differences from standard Spanish (Guitart 1982:168). Although no Hispanic dialect is devoid of assimilatory phenomena, Caribbean Spanish is characterized by a consonant simplification which has two manifestations: (1) phonetic reduction (e.g., the aspiration of /s/) and (2) phonetic neutralization (e.g., the realization of /r/ as [l]). Consonantal simplification is counteracted, however, by two factors: (1) a tendency toward maintaining distinctness when extreme phonetic radicalism interferes with communication (e.g., *Van a venir la muchacha*) and (2) a tendency toward monitoring casual speech when factors of style and prestige intervene in the speech event (Guitart 1983:159-63). For example, the phonetic leveling of /l/ and /r/ decreases in favor of the flap /r/ when Puerto Rican Spanish (PRS) speakers read aloud; thus, /r/ is realized more closely to an ideal standard if the speaker is careful, that is, if (s)he dedicates a sufficient amount of energy to that segment (Guitart 1981:54).[3] Since the presence of the written text exerts a considerable influence on the production of speech, it is reasonable to assume that certain phonetic processes (aspiration, deletion, neutralization) are *not* executed in formal contexts.

In the same vein, Terrell (1983:135-48) concludes that the aspiration of /s/ is most frequent among educated PRS speakers, whereas deletion predominates among the uneducated. In addition, Poplack (1980) demonstrates that several constraints affect plural /s/ deletion: the grammatical function of the token within the string, the nature of the following phonological segment and the following stress, and the number of preceding plural markers. As already indicated, there seems to be a tendency to retain semantically necessary information and, consequently, to pronounce the phoneme /s/ in order to keep a phrase or sentence free of ambiguity.

2.2 Pedagogical implications for Caribbean Spanish speakers. Since, as Guitart and Terrell show, formal contexts and the educational level of the speaker are correlated to choices in pronunciation, educators may engage in a series of exercises conducive to teaching the standard language. Specifically, reading aloud for a few minutes each day may not only draw forth the desired pronunciation, but may also help students feel confident about their native skills. In my own courses for Hispanic students, I encourage all of them to read aloud one short passage each day. In a classroom setting it is impractical to undertake a statistical analysis of standard versus nonstandard production, but after many hours of careful observation I am convinced that Guitart's variationist hypothesis is correct.[4] When reading aloud, Caribbean speakers tend to minimize consonantal simplification, inasmuch as the text indicates where the /s/ should be pronounced. In addition, in such circumstances I have observed that aspiration is rarely practiced and that deletion is virtually nonexistent.   In writing, however, the instructor finds that redundancy is avoided and the dialectal features which contrast with standard pronunciation become apparent, as in the examples discussed in section 2.3.

2.3 Morphosyntactic characteristics of Caribbean Spanish. Written samples of Caribbean speakers demonstrate that a marker of plurality is typically retained in a noun phrase (NP), thereby confirming Poplack's functional hypothesis that the expression of plurality is not completely lost:

(1) Si hablan *diferente idiomas,* tienen que decidir qué idioma van a aprender los niños.
(2) En *esto tiempos* es muy necesario que uno sepa hablá dos idiomas.
(3) Debemos conocer la cultura de *nuestro países.*
(4) *Los matrimonios interracial* son muy comunes hoy.
(5) El merengue y la salsa son *dos tipos de baile muy diferente* al bolero.

Sometimes an adjective indicating a quantity automatically causes /s/ deletion:

(6) El idioma español se puede usar de *muchisima manera.*
(7) *Mucho latino* en los Estados Unidos sí conservan su cultura propio.
(8) Hoy tengo *mucha amistade* en esta universidad.

A singular predicate adjective often describes a plural NP subject:

(9) *Los puertorriqueños son americano* por ley.

(10) *Muchos están recien llegado.*

In a coordinate NP containing two or more plural nouns, the plural marker /s/ is normally retained only in the first noun:

(11) Uso el español para leé *los libros y periódico* de mi país.
(12) Estudiar *las ideologías, cultura y sistema político* de otra nación será de gran ventaja.
(13) *Mis primos menore y sobrino pequeño* han aprendido los dos idiomas.

Of course, a plural subject whose plural suffix has been deleted is often disambiguated through subject-verb agreement:

(14) *La mujer desempeñan* un papel subordinado.

Finally, the deletion of /s/ may cause apparent lack of agreement between a subject and an object complement as well as between a conjunctive and a disjunctive pronoun:

(15) *Ellos se sienten orgulloso* de los hijos que han tenido.
(16) Apenas *lo veo a ellos* discutiendo.
(17) Tengo dos primas que se casaron con hombres de otra cultura y *se le hace incómodo a ellas* traer su esposo a las reuniones familiares, porque allá solamente se habla español, y sus esposos no entienden nada.

In all of the foregoing examples, the notion of plurality is not absent since Caribbean speakers reorganize the system of plural marking in such cases. From a pedagogical perspective, then, what are the effects of correction concerning /s/ deletion in these cases? Do speakers use the standard in writing after being corrected, or, as Valdés-Fallis (1978) puts it, after being made aware of the differences between the standard and nonstandard forms? There are several types of reactions among students in such circumstances: (1) Nonmonitor users avoid plural redundancy *ad infinitum.* (2) Careless monitor users may employ plural markers inconsistently, following the redundancy principle in a few phrases at the beginning of a paragraph or composition, or they may resort to hypercorrection (e.g., La música hispana me llena de alegría y me hace mover *las cinturas; La población hispana vas* a crecer tremendamente; En Nueva York siempre nos juntamos en la bodega o el parque para saber *los que está pasando* en la comunidad). (3) Careful monitor users are more successful in writing, and after seeing the 'errors' corrected on paper they maintain the redundancy principle of the standard written language, although they may occasionally (once or twice in a paragraph which contains ten to thirteen plural NPs) omit the plural markers, normally at the end of a paragraph or composition.[5]

Another structural difference between standard Spanish and Caribbean Spanish spoken in the United States concerns the gender of nouns and gender agreement. Most textbooks prepared for college students contain a chapter on the gender of nouns which often highlights masculine gender nouns of Greek origin ending in *-ma* and *-ta* (e.g., *el programa, el idioma, el clima, el planeta,* etc.). U.S. Hispanics sometimes tend to treat such words as feminine gender nouns. In addition, gender agreement is often violated both within an NP and in copulative sentences; in such cases the masculine form of the adjective is used with a feminine gender noun:

(18) Hay *muchas canciones que son muy bonitos* y que son sensitiva y a la vez muy romántica.
(19) Ellos van a conservar su *cultura propio.*
(19) La población de quí es de *habla inglés.*
(20) Debemos enseñar a nuestros hijos a hablar su *lengua castellano.*

In their study on Puerto Ricans in New York City, Pousada and Poplack (1982:221-34) reveal that in a community of relatively uneducated speakers the Spanish verb system remains virtually unchanged in relation to that of standard Spanish. The exceptions constitute only a miniscule proportion (about one percent) of the total verbal output. Pousada and Poplack further indicate that the present, imperfect, and preterite are the most frequently used tenses; however, they not only maintain their usual functions but also encroach upon those of other tense forms. The areas of greatest divergence between the popular and the standard varieties are: (1) the relative absence in the former of the inflected future, which has been practically replaced by the periphrastic future; (2) a lesser incidence of the subjunctive; and (3) a more widespread use of the present progressive. In contrast to Pousada and Poplack's claim concerning the infrequent occurrence of exceptions to standard usage, the written samples which I have collected from my Puerto Rican students show that considerably more than one percent of the sentences which require the subjunctive contain a form of the indicative, as in the following examples:[6]

(21) *Es necesario que conservamos* el español en los Estados Unidos.
(22) *Necesitamos gente que pueden* hablar español con los recien llegados.
(23) *No hay ninguna persona* en los Estados Unidos de segunda generación *que puede* llamarse totalmente americano.
(24) *Es muy común que* en los países latinoamericanos los gobiernos *cambian* de la noche a la mañana.
(25) Escogí esta clase *para que yo puedo* hablar español más claro.

(26) *¡Qué lástima que* algo que está al alcance de todos y que algún día podrá ser ventajoso para uno, inexplicablemente no *es* utilizado!

Although quantitative analyses similar to that of Pousada and Poplack are sorely needed to ascertain variation in verb usage, equally important are qualitative studies on language change among U.S. Hispanics. One such study is Lantolf's (1978) paper on the selection of mood among Puerto Ricans from Rochester, New York; in that article Lantolf points out that the subjunctive is giving way to the indicative in both dubitative sentences and presuppositions. Although such studies are normally based on acceptability judgments rather than on the elicitation of spontaneous speech, they give important cues to pedagogical problems resulting from contrasts between dialect and standard.

2.4 Phonological characteristics of Mexican/Chicano Spanish. Mexican-American Spanish (M-ASp), Chicano Spanish, or Southwest Spanish is the variety of U.S. Spanish spoken in Mexican-American communities throughout the American Southwest. Although there are several geographic dialects of Spanish within this vast area, all are mutually intelligible dialects which share many characteristics with Mexican Spanish as well as with other dialects of Latin America. M-ASp has been researched from both the traditional descriptive and contemporary sociolinguistic perspectives and the literature on the topic is abundant.

The phonological characteristics of M-ASp have been examined by scholars who have recorded 'the presence of numerous phonetic variants, frequent in the popular varieties of Mexico, the rest of Latin America, and Spain. These studies generally document the laxing or loss of fricatives . . ., the diphthongization of *hiatos*, the reduction of diphthongs, the simplification of consonant clusters and other phonetic changes like aphaeresis, epenthesis, apocope, syncope and lateralization' (Sánchez 1983:91). These studies indicate that common phonological processes which are characteristic of popular speech in general are also in operation in the informal speech of Mexican-Americans. When the Spanish of Mexican-Americans is analyzed at the informal level, it may seem to be what Guitart (1982) has called a 'radical' dialect. However, M-ASp can become a 'conservative' dialect when factors of style, prestige, and the like intervene in the speech act. M-ASp can therefore be standardized when some phonological rules which are idiosyncratic to popular speech are not applied. One way to foster such standardization is, as Guitart (1982:175) suggests, to engage students in conservative modes of speech, a goal that may be achieved by making them text-oriented and by increasing their literacy level to that of an educated speaker, so that they acquire the phonological idiosyncrasies of the latter.

2.5 Morphosyntactic characteristics of M-ASp. It has been observed that speakers of M-ASp, like their Caribbean counterparts, also tend to assign the feminine gender to nouns of Greek origin ending in -*ma* and -*ta* (Sánchez 1982:33), although many times the feminine alternates with the masculine gender (Hensey 1976:32, 35).

Those who study M-ASp consistently report the addition of /-s/ in the second person singular of the preterite (*dijistes, trajistes*), columnar stress in the first person plural of the present subjunctive (*váyamos, téngamos, puédamos, duérmamos*), and the substitution of /n/ for /m/ in the first person plural of the imperfect indicative (*íbanos, comprábanos, salíanos*), among other nonstandard phenomena.

In addition, the two most complete works on the morphosyntactic features of M-ASp (Sánchez 1982 and Hensey 1976) reveal that the subjunctive is sometimes replaced by the indicative and that the gerund can be used instead of the infinitive. Berk-Seligson (1980:88-89) has highlighted Sánchez's analysis of indicative/subjunctive usage in contrary-to-fact sentences, since she finds that the mood of the verbs in such sentences can be uniformly subjunctive, uniformly indicative, or subjunctive/indicative, or vice versa. More recent and more sophisticated research on the Spanish spoken in East Los Angeles indicates that the traditional use of some structural complexities of the standard language (e.g., the indicative/subjunctive opposition, the use of subordinate clauses, and indirect speech style) is notoriously decreasing across three generations of Mexican-American speakers (see Gutiérrez 1989 and Ocampo 1989, both of which appear in this volume).

3 General pedagogical considerations. Even though there is a general consensus that the mastery of standard Spanish is a goal to be achieved in SNS courses, educators still confront methodological problems which in turn derive from ill-defined concepts. One such poorly defined concept is, of course, the standard/dialect dichotomy, and within this opposition, the concept of standard itself. One of the most reasonable approaches to the standard/dialect question is Smith and Lance's (1979) discussion of American English, in which they imply that variability in suprasegmental features of language (i.e., accent and intonation), in phonetic-phonological characteristics, and in the lexicon is rather accepted and often expected in light of the diverse geographic backgrounds of the speakers of the language. But morphosyntactic characteristics (i.e., grammar) are expected to be stable, and when they vary from the perceived norm, they single out speakers of nonstandard social dialects. As a result of this difference in perceptions concerning the various components of language, we make the following suggestions in preparing teaching materials for students in SNS courses:

(1) Suprasegmental features should not be taught in SNS courses since they do not pose a major problem in communication. We have to admit, however, that some accents or types of intonations are more prestigious than

others, but it should not be part of our educational program to change such features in the idiolects of native-speaking students. The general educational level of the speaker and the use of a formal style will minimize what we know as 'accent.'

(2) The research on styles of pronunciation reveals that speakers have at their disposal a range of choices (e.g., between [s], [h], and ∅ among Caribbean speakers) which depend primarily on social constraints, and that, in fact, they produce the most appropriate choice depending on the social circumstances.

(3) The lexical differences that are peculiar to varieties of U.S. Spanish do not inhibit communication among Spanish speakers, although they may create temporary confusion between speakers of different groups, a confusion which is readily resolved after brief contact has taken place (Lipski 1985). Although we are committed to respecting and teaching lexical differences between popular and standard Spanish, such lexical contrasts are not the major goal of SNS courses inasmuch as lexical items are almost never stigmatized.

(4) The identification of morphosyntactic variation should be the primary goal of SNS courses. For example, teaching the generally accepted genders of Spanish nouns as well as teaching the standard verb system is a practice justified on a pervasive written tradition and is not psychologically harmful to speakers of U.S. Spanish.

3.1 Morphosyntax: The core of the standard. Nonstandard morphosyntactic features are likely to be stigmatized because they are associated with socioeconomic background rather than with regional origin. The variations examined by researchers of M-ASp, and especially those discussed by Sánchez (1982 and 1983), suggest that speakers have to become aware of differences in the verb systems of standard and popular Spanish. Examples of such differences are shown in Table 1.

As seen in the table, most instances of nonstandard verb morphology have to do only with the change of one or two phonemes in radical-changing verbs, with the addition of /-s/ in the second person singular of the preterite, with columnar stress, etc. It is not known, however, if users of such nonstandard forms can reorganize the system and adjust to standard models in two or three academic semesters. Spanish morphosyntactic structure does not offer stylistic alternatives to speakers; hence, it is desirable to be aware of the standard forms.

The research carried out by Wolfram (1970:106-8) among speakers of Black English suggests that a primary pedagogical consideration in the presentation of materials to dialect speakers 'must be the way in which social groups are separated from one another on the basis of linguistic features.' Wolfram distinguishes two basic types of sociolinguistic stratification: (1) 'Gradient stratification refers to a progressive increase in the frequency of occurrence of a variant between social groups without a clearly defined difference between contiguous social groups.' For example, the pronunciation of postvocalic /r/ among Black speakers in Detroit gradually decreases in the speech of members of progressively lower social classes.   Gradient stratification among Caribbean speakers is illustrated by the aspiration and loss of /s/, which also decrease according to the educational level of the speaker (Terrell 1983). (2) Sharp stratification, on the other hand, entails significant differences in the incidence of a grammatical variable, such as the omission of word-final /-s/ in the third person singular of the present indicative of verb forms among some speakers of Black English.   This omission occurs in high percentages in the lower classes but is virtually non-existent among middle and upper-middle class speakers. Wolfram asserts 'that linguistic features revealing sharp stratification are of greater social significance than those showing gradient stratification.'

Table 1. Random samples of standard and nonstandard verb forms.

Popular Mexican-American Spanish	General standard Spanish
1. *vivemos*	1a. *vivimos*
2. *durmemos*	2a. *dormimos*
3. *pidemos*	3a. *pedimos*
4. *traiba*	4a. *traía*
5. *fuites, fuistes*	5a. *fuiste*
6. *dijites, dijistes*	6a. *dijiste*
7. *cómamos*	7a. *comamos*
8. *siéntanos*	8a. *sintamos*
9. *estábanos*	9a. *estábamos*
10. *cayí*	10a. *caí*
11. *(yo) ha*	11a. *(yo) he*
12. *(nosotros) hamos*	12a. *(nosotros) hemos*

It is not known if the grammatical variations found in M-ASp, especially those related to verb morphology and syntax, are in fact stigmatized in the community or in the country where they originated, that is, Mexico. I have indicated elsewhere (Hidalgo 1987) that at least three features (the addition of /-s/ in forms like *salistes,* columnar stress in subjunctive forms like *vuélvamos,* and the substitution of /n/ for /m/, as in *estábanos*) identify the speaker's social class and educational level to Mexican urban dwellers. It is difficult to ascertain, however, if any of these features have negative social values among speakers of Mexican-American communities. In her analysis of codes and styles among Chicanos, Sánchez (1983:102-3) found that 'except in the case of language-conscious Chicano speakers, morphosyntactic shifts generally do not occur. Phonetic shifts, on the other hand, are numerous as are lexical shifts.' Moreover, 'speakers whose codes are characterized by particular morphosyntactic variants retain these . . . even though they may shift phonetically or lexically.' Sánchez assumes that language instruction may lead to rejection of -nos and adherence to -mos. It is certainly reasonable to assume that once the person has learned the morphosyntactic features of the standard, (s)he will use them in combination with suprasegmental and phonological features of the dialect. Inasmuch as speakers cannot as readily switch morphosyntactic codes as they do phonological ones and since the use of morphosyntactic features is sharply stratified, we should concentrate our efforts on identifying potentially denigrating forms and ways of dealing with them. We can resort to techniques used for speakers of Black English, as presented by Feigenbaum (1970), and we can also study the speech of those who have been in our programs, so that we may find out if switches between standard and nonstandard forms are in fact possible. I assume that at least some individuals exposed to SNS courses may become actively proficient in the standard language.[7] Some factors that have proven beneficial in the process of second language acquisition may also account for progress in second dialect acquisition, namely, aptitude, attitude, and motivation.

However, learning the standard variety of a literary language in a context in which the language does not have official functions is rather difficult, because speakers are minimally exposed to the standard and are unable to acquire it naturally and effortlessly, as it is acquired in monolingual communities (Fishman 1977). Changing the status of Spanish from a vernacular to a semi-official language will not only institutionalize it but will create the appropriate use domains that will guarantee its preservation. Until this happens, we should be committed to teaching the standard, to discovering the areas of major morphosyntactic discrepancies between standard and dialect, and to transmitting the most practical orientation for the acquisition of the former and the retention of the latter.

Notes

1. I refer, of course, to the theory of language based on the traditions of Ferdinand de Saussure and Noam Chomsky, who conceived the speakers of a language as constituting a homogeneous speech community.

2. The four attributes proposed by Stewart (1962:17) are: (1) historicity, (2) standardization, (3) vitality, and (4) homogenecity. These attributes seem to determine language type which, in turn, is 'a major factor in determining whether or not a language will be accepted by the members of a national society as suitable for some specific role, such as the use in education or as an official language.'

3. This hypothesis is based on the data provided by Ma and Herasim-chuck (1971).

4. When I was a professor at SUNY-Binghamton, many of my students were Puerto Ricans and Dominicans from New York City. The examples of their written language presented herein are indiscriminately called Caribbean

Spanish or Puerto Rican Spanish (PRS) inasmuch as both varieties tend to delete and/or aspirate final /-s/, to interchange /r/ and /l/, etc.

5. I base these assumptions on Krashen's monitor theory and the examples of individual learners offered in his numerous articles. See, for example, Krashen (1981) and specifically pp. 1-50 therein--'Individual variation in the use of the monitor,' 'Attitude and aptitude in second language acquisition and learning,' and 'Formal and informal linguistic environments in language acquisition and language learning.'

6. My sample consists of two hundred compositions of about 240 words each.

7. Some researchers have expressed skepticism about the feasibility of teaching the standard in the classroom, e.g., Valdés (1981) and the authors cited in her article, whereas others believe that only the written form of the standard can be taught (Trudgill 1979:22-23). Although doubts about teaching the standard seem to be legitimate, doubts about learning it should be dispelled, at least with respect to Spanish, since, as I have suggested in this study, the gap between standard Spanish and dialectal Spanish is not as wide as it may be in other languages, e.g., English and German. Chicano intellectuals who at some point in their lives were speakers of Chicano Spanish are the living proof that mastery of standard Spanish by U.S. bilinguals is indeed possible. Their testimonies and insights can provide valuable information for those of us who are committed to teaching the standard variety in the classroom.

References

Amastae, J., and L. Elías-Olivares, eds. 1982. *Spanish in the United States: Sociolinguistic aspects.* New York: Cambridge University Press.

Ammon, U. 1977. School problems of regional dialect speakers: Ideology and reality: Results and methods of empirical investigations in southern Germany. *Journal of Pragmatics* 1:47-68.

_____, ed. 1979. Dialect and standard in highly industrialized societies. *International Journal of the Sociology of Language* 21.

Baratz, J.C., and R.W. Shuy, eds. 1969. *Teaching Black children to read.* Washington, D.C.: Center for Applied Linguistics.

Berk-Seligson, S. 1980. A sociolinguistic view of the Mexican-American speech community: A review of the literature. *Latin American Research Review* 15:2.65-110.

Bowen, J.D., and J. Ornstein, eds. 1976. *Studies in southwest Spanish.* Rowley, Mass.: Newbury House.

Cazden, C.B., V. John, and P. Hymes, eds. 1972. *Functions of language in the classroom.* New York: Teachers College Press.

Dillard, J.L. 1978. Bidialectal education: Black English and standard English in the United States. In: Spolsky and Cooper, eds. (1978:293-311).

Edwards, V. 1983. *Language in multicultural classrooms.* London: Academic Press. Batsfor: Educational Ltd.

Elías-Olivares, L., ed. 1983. *Spanish in the U.S. setting: Beyond the Southwest.* Rosslyn, Va.: National Clearinghouse for Bilingual Education.

Escobar, A. 1976. *Language.* Lima: Instituto de Investigaciones.

_____. 1978. *Variaciones sociolingüísticas del castellano en el Perú.* Lima: Instituto de Investigaciones Peruanas.

Farr Whiteman, M., ed. 1980. *Reactions to Ann Arbor: Vernacular Black English and education.* Arlington, Va.: Center for Applied Linguistics.

Fasold, R.W., and R.W. Shuy, eds. 1970. *Teaching standard English in the inner city.* Washington, D.C.: Center for Applied Linguistics.

Feigenbaum, I. 1970. The use of non-standard English in teaching standard: Contrast and comparison. In: Fasold and Shuy, eds. (1970:87-104).

Fishman, J.A. 1972. *The sociology of language: An interdisciplinary social science approach to language in society.* Rowley, Mass.: Newbury House.

_____. 1977. Standard vs. dialect in bilingual education: An old problem in a new context. *The Modern Language Journal* 7.315-24.

_____, and R.L. Cooper, eds. 1971. *Bilingualism in the barrio.* Bloomington: Indiana University Press.

_____, and G.D. Keller, eds. 1982. *Bilingual education for Hispanic students in the United States.* New York: Teachers College Press.

_____, and E. Lueders-Salmon. 1972. What has the sociology of language to say to the teacher? On teaching the standard variety to speakers of dialectal or sociolectal varieties. In: C.B. Cazden et al., eds. (1972:67-83).

Fromkin, V., and R. Rodman. 1983. *An introduction to language.* New York: Holt, Rinehart, and Winston.

Gardner, R.C. 1979. Social psychological aspects of second language acquisition. In: Giles and St. Clair, eds. (1979:193-220).

_____, and W.E. Lambert. 1972. *Attitudes and motivation in second language learning.* Rowley, Mass.: Newbury House.

Giles, H., and P.T. Powesland. 1975. *Speech style and social evaluation.* European Monographs in Social Psychology. London: Academic Press.

_____, and R.N. St. Clair, eds. 1979. *Language and social psychology.* Oxford: Basil Blackwell.

Guitart, J.M. 1978. Conservative and radical dialects in Spanish: Implications for language instruction. *The Bilingual Review/La Revista Bilingüe* 5:1-2.57-64.

_____. 1981. The pronunciation of Puerto Rican Spanish in the mainland: Theoretical and pedagogical considerations. In: Valdés et al., eds. (1981:46-58).

_____. 1983. On the contribution of Spanish language variation studies to contemporary linguistic theory. In: Elías-Olivares, ed. (1983:149-64).

Gutiérrez, M. 1989. Sobre el mantenimiento de las cláusulas subordinadas en el español de Los Angeles. [This volume.]

Hensey, F.C. 1976. Toward a grammatical analysis of southwest Spanish. In: Bowen and Ornstein, eds. (1976:29-44).

Hidalgo, M. 1987. Español mexicano y español chicano: Problemas y propuestas fundamentales. *Language problems and language planning* 11:2.163-95.

Keller, G.D. 1982. The ultimate goal of bilingual education with respect to language skills. In: Fishman and Keller, eds. (1982:71-90).

Krashen, S. 1981. *Second language acquisition and second language learning.* Oxford: Pergamon Press.

Labov, W., ed. 1980. *Locating language in time and space.* New York: Academic Press.

Lantolf, J.P. 1978. The variable constraints on mood in Puerto Rican Spanish. In: Suñer, ed. (1978:193-217).

Lipski, J.M. 1985. Central American varieties, Mexican and Chicano Spanish. Paper read at the National Conference on Research Needs in Chicano Spanish, University of Texas at El Paso, June 13-16.

_____. 1986. Principal varieties of U.S. Spanish. Unpublished MS, University of Florida.

Ma, R., and E. Herasimchuck. 1971. The linguistic dimensions of a bilingual neighborhood. In: Fishman and Cooper, eds. (1971:225-43).

Moses, R.A., A. Hurvey, and R.A. Gundlach. 1976. Teachers' language attitudes and bidialectalism. *International Journal of the Sociology of Language* 8:77-92.

Ocampo, F. 1989. El subjuntivo en tres generaciones de hablantes bilingües. [This volume.]

Poplack, S. 1980. The notion of plural in Puerto Rican Spanish: Competing constraints on /s/ deletion. In: Labov, ed. (1980:55-67).

Pousada, A., and S. Poplack. 1982. No case for convergence: The Puerto Rican Spanish verb system in a language-contact situation. In: Fishman and Keller, eds. (1982:207-39).

Ray, P.S. 1962. Language standardization. In: Rice, ed. (1962:91-104).

Rice, F.A., ed. 1962. *Study of the role of second languages in Asia, Africa and Latin America.* Washington, D.C.: Center for Applied Linguistics.

Sánchez, R. 1982. Our linguistic and social context. In: Amastae and Elías-Olivares, eds. (1982:9-46).

_____. 1983. *Chicano discourse: Socio-historic perspectives.* Rowley, Mass.: Newbury House.

Smith, R.B., and D.M. Lance. 1979. Standard and disparate varieties of English in the United States: Educational and socio-political implications. In: Ammon, ed. (1979:127-40).

Spolsky, B., and R.L. Cooper, eds. 1978. *Case studies in bilingual education.* Rowley, Mass.: Newbury House.

Stewart, W. 1962. An outline of linguistic typology for describing multilingualism. In: Rice, ed. (1962:14-25).

Suñer, M., ed. 1978. *Contemporary studies in Romance linguistics.* Washington, D.C.: Georgetown University Press.

Terrell, T.D. 1983. Sound change: The explanatory value of the heterogeneity of variable rule application. In: Elías-Olivares, ed. (1983:133-48).

Trudgill, P. 1979. Standard and nonstandard dialects of English in the United Kingdom: Problems and policies. In: Ammon, ed. (1979:9-24).

Valdés-Fallis, G. 1976. Language development vs. the teaching of the standard language. *Letkos* (Dec.):20-32.

_____. 1978. A comprehensive approach to the teaching of Spanish to bilingual Spanish-speaking students. *The Modern Language Journal* 3.102-10.

Valdés, G. 1981. Pedagogical implications of teaching Spanish to the Spanish-speaking in the U.S. In: Valdés et al., eds. (1981:3-20).

_____, A.G. Lozano, and R. García-Moya, eds. 1981. *Teaching Spanish to the Hispanic bilingual: Issues, aims, and methods.* New York: Teachers College Press.

Wolfram, W. 1970. Sociolinguistic implications for educational sequencing. In: Fasold and Shuy, eds. (1970:105-19).

Teaching Spanish to the
Hispanic bilingual college student in Miami

Ana Roca
Florida International University

1   Introduction.   Over a decade ago, the Executive Council of the American Association of Teachers of Spanish and Portuguese published a report which included recommendations for teaching Spanish to Hispanic bilingual students in schools and universities in the United States (AATSP 1972). That report claims (p. 20) to have had its roots in the merging of two movements of that time: 'the growing acceptance by the Spanish teaching profession of responsibility for maintaining and developing the Spanish that is spoken natively in the United States, and the struggle of the nation's native Spanish speakers for a greater measure of self-determination, including a greater role for Spanish in their lives.' The force of the AATSP report, however, lies not only in its origins, but also in its political stance reflected in its major recommendations:

> Whenever in the United States there are pupils or students for whom Spanish is the native tongue, at whatever level from kindergarten to the baccalaureate, there be established in the schools and colleges special sections for developing literacy in Spanish and using it to reinforce or complement other areas of the curriculum, with correspondingly specialized materials, methods, and teachers.

Many schools and colleges have already created special courses for such bilingual students, but more than ten years later the profession has not followed up this report with investigative or comparative surveys that provide data on the type of instruction recommended in 1972. In order to evaluate Spanish-S programs in the schools or colleges, practitioners in the field first need to acquire information about current practices at the local, regional, and national levels. To date, no such surveys dealing specifically with current practices in the teaching of Spanish to U.S. Hispanic bilingual students have appeared.   The knowledge obtained from questionnaires and surveys addressed to practitioners in the field will ultimately yield many direct benefits to both instructors and students.

The AATSP report was based primarily on the teaching of Spanish-S in the schools. Its recommendations, therefore, were geared for Spanish-S instruction in the public schools, e.g., programs developed in Dade County Public Schools in the 1960s when the large Cuban refugee influx began. As a result, the AATSP report does not directly address many questions regarding the programmatical needs of Spanish for native speakers (SNS) instruction at the university level. In an attempt to raise some issues which the report did not explicitly cover, Frances Aparicio of Harvard University has written a brief but incisive article regarding SNS programs at the college level which, as she points out (Aparicio 1983:232), is 'the level with which research has been least concerned.' In her study, 'Teaching Spanish to the native speaker at the college level,' Aparicio identifies specific pedagogical problems in teaching Spanish to bilingual students at the university level. She bases her investigation on the literature of the almost analogous situation found in teaching standard English to Black Americans, the scanty research on instruction for native Spanish speakers in the United States, and her own teaching experience. She describes some of the major problems she has encountered, suggests issues for further discussion, and offers a variety of recommendations for teaching. Like other instructors who have been concerned with teaching Spanish to Hispanic bilingual students in this country (Valdés 1981, Sánchez 1981, Solé 1981, and Barkin 1981), Aparicio (p. 232) stresses the need for further research:

> There is still much work to be done in this area. The more we teach Spanish to Hispanics in the United States, the further the need to investigate the problems and idiosyncrasies of this student population, their needs, the best teaching methods, the training of teachers, and the relevance of available materials.

Instructors who work routinely in the areas of (1) college language placement testing, (2) the development of foreign language graduation requirements regarding bilingual students, (3) syllabus and curriculum design, and (4) the writing of teaching materials, will find Aparicio's urgent call for further research in this new and challenging area provocative. In spite of the increase of literature on the subject (so well represented in Valdés, Lozano, and García-Moya 1981), it is clear to those of us who teach Spanish to bilingual students that a number of issues remain to be discussed, debated, and investigated. What, for example, is a fair and practical method for the Spanish language placement testing of large numbers of bilingual students? How can Spanish instructors teach students to maximize their literacy skills in English? How can current research on the teaching of reading and writing in a first and a second language help us in the development of sound instructional materials and a practical curriculum for teaching this student population at the university level? In the 1980s interest in this area has already increased, but instructors and researchers have yet to compile basic information on current Spanish-S programs and attitudes toward such instruction in our nation's colleges. What follows is a formal and comprehensive survey on the teaching of Spanish to the Hispanic bilingual college student in the Miami area.

2 Background survey data. The survey had two chief goals. One purpose was to serve as a point of departure for obtaining information on current practices and attitudes toward teaching Spanish-S at the university level in Miami; the second objective was to provide an opportunity for colleagues with similar instructional needs to share concerns and recommendations. Ideally, the project will begin a program of collaborative efforts at the local and national levels. The results of the survey offer insights into practices and materials used in teaching Hispanic bilingual students. In addition, the data are invaluable to practitioners who are in the process of assessing pedagogical needs and preparing new and improved materials.

The survey was mailed to approximately fifty foreign language college instructors in the greater Miami area. It consisted of forty-five multiple choice questions; space was provided on the survey forms so that the respondents could expand on their answers or offer additional information. Responses to the questionnaire were marked on a General Purpose-NCS-Computer Answer Sheet which was provided along with the survey. The responses were analyzed by means of a program commonly used to obtain a variety of statistical information from questionnaire responses. In this case, the program provided an item analysis which included missing cases, adjusted frequencies, histograms, and other tabulations. Part-time and full-time instructors from the following colleges and universities received the survey: the University of Miami, Florida International University (FIU), Barry University, St. Thomas University, Florida Memorial College, and the various campuses (North, South, Bilingual Studies Division, and the [Downtown] New World Campus) of the nation's largest community college--Miami Dade Community College. An introductory letter explained the purpose of the project and promised to send respondents the results of the survey as soon as the project was completed. The respondents had the option to remain anonymous. Approximately half of the questionnaires which were mailed out were completed and returned.[1]

In recent years Dade County has seen its institutions of higher education grow at a rapid rate. FIU, 40% of whose students are of Hispanic background, has grown from a 'senior' or upper-division institution into a full four-year university which offers many undergraduate and graduate programs in a variety of disciplines. FIU's undergraduate Spanish language program has also expanded since 1981. Moreover, its SNS section of a regular grammar course has developed into a popular course which has been well established in the curriculum for several years and is currently going through further curricular growth (i.e., the establishment of a special two-course or two-level 'track' for Hispanic bilingual students). In the last few years, private universities like the University of Miami and Barry University, as well as the various independent campuses of Miami Dade Community College, have also created and expanded special SNS courses in an attempt to respond to the educational needs of Miami's bilingual college students.

3 Schedules, course levels, and placement. The first questions on the survey deal with administrative and scheduling matters. Some institutions, for example, offer SNS courses only during the first semester, but the two largest schools--the University of Miami and FIU--offer such courses during both semesters; FIU also offers the courses in both of its mini summer sessions. More than half of the respondents (54%) said that their institution offered three to four sections of SNS courses per calendar year. The University of Miami offers various such sections during the fall and spring semesters. FIU regularly offers approximately eight sections of SNS courses which fill to capacity, with 'overloads' being the rule rather than the exception. FIU is the only university which regularly offers these special courses in the evening. The reasons for regular scheduling of these courses at night are twofold: FIU has many part-time students who attend in the evenings, and its Department of Modern Languages offers not only a major in Spanish but also several new certificate programs in translation and interpretation studies. Many Hispanics interested in majoring in Spanish or in completing those other programs are advised to take SNS courses before enrolling in the more advanced language courses required for a major or for certification. According to the responses to the survey, FIU is the only university in Miami which offers SNS on a noncredit basis through a Continuing Education-Off Campus Office. In the last two years that office has been offering 'Spanish for Hispanic Professionals,' a course that meets once a week for three hours, does not carry college credit, and is geared toward Hispanic professionals who attend class at night to improve their control of Spanish.

The survey also reveals that the University of Miami offers two levels of SNS courses, that FIU offers only one such course at the junior level, and that Barry University and Miami Dade Community College offer only one course, and consequently, one level. Since the summer of 1986 FIU has provided two separate SNS courses--one at the intermediate and the other at the advanced level. Barry University, which does not have a foreign language graduation requirement, provides dual tracks in Spanish, one for SNS and the other for nonnative speakers. One of the respondents from Barry University commented that most of their SNS students are from various parts of Latin America and already have a good background in Spanish. This allows Barry to emphasize literature in its SNS courses; those students who want to focus on grammar take the advanced courses for native speakers as well as the advanced courses for nonnative speakers. Although all of Barry's literature courses are offered at the upper-division level, native speakers can enroll in these courses even if they are freshmen.

With regard to the question of *who* teaches SNS courses, 80% of the instructors are native speakers of Spanish. While the typical instructor has had at least some formal instruction in linguistics, 92.3% of the respondents who teach SNS courses in Miami are trained primarily in Spanish literature.

On the subject of placement testing of bilingual students, the responses to the survey indicate that in the majority of cases placement is left up to the chairperson, the advisors, and the instructors of the SNS courses. None of the universities or colleges administers a formal placement test designed especially for students of Spanish origin. Spanish speakers, it seems, take the same placement test that all other students take in order to be placed in the appropriate course or be exempted from the foreign language requirement (where applicable). Once the students are enrolled in a SNS class, however, 54.5% of the instructors give an impromptu composition and/or an informal interview in order to determine the students' general proficiency in Spanish; 27.3% administer their own diagnostic-placement test during the first week of classes. These techniques, it should be pointed out, are not used as a way of exempting students from the school's language requirement, but to determine whether they belong in a lower or higher level Spanish language course, be it in a SNS track or a regular track at the more advanced upper-division level.

The survey data reveal that SNS instruction is offered at different levels in the various institutions. The University of Miami, for example, offers such courses at the freshman and sophomore levels. FIU and Barry University offer courses at the junior level, and Miami Dade Community College at the sophomore level. The disparity in levels causes problems where transfer students are concerned. For example, should students who transfer from Miami Dade to FIU receive credit for taking FIU's junior level course if they have already taken the similar sophomore level SNS course at Dade? At first, an advisor might conclude that such a student should be allowed to receive credit for the higher level course at FIU. A closer look at the survey data, however, informs us that Miami Dade South, for example, currently uses the same text as that used at FIU. It is obvious that the student should not be allowed to repeat receiving credit for the same material studied in an earlier course.

Regardless of the level of SNS courses, all the colleges and universities surveyed which have a foreign language requirement count such courses toward satisfying that requirement. At FIU, for instance, bilingual students who are not exempted from the ten credit language requirement are expected to complete a minimum of three credits in the SNS track in order to meet the language requirement. When speaking to individual students it is evident that most understand and speak Spanish; however, a few do not 'place out' each year. Since 1982 the philosophy of the Department of Modern Languages at FIU, and now the current policy of the university, is to require these 'bilinguals' to improve their Spanish language skills. Even if these students are 'bilingual,' their low placement test scores are an indication of their poor vocabulary and grammar and are evidence of problems in reading in Spanish at a basic level. Those Hispanics who do not pass the placement examination must take formal instruction in Spanish in order to improve their ability in standard Spanish.

4 Materials. The next series of questions in the survey deals with the textbooks currently used in the various SNS courses. *Español escrito: Curso para hispanohablantes bilingües* (Valdés and Teschner 1984) is the text of first choice for a first-level course; 46% of the respondents use this text, 27.3% use *Mejora tu español: Lectura y redacción para bilingües* (de la Portilla and Varela 1979), and the rest use other books. It is interesting to note that a significant percentage (27.3%) use *Mejora tu español* in the first-level course even though the text has been described in reviews as suitable for advanced level bilingual students. A more detailed examination of the survey also shows that Miami Dade Community College, North, uses *Mejora tu español* in its first level course, while the other major campus--Miami Dade, South--uses *El español y su estructura* (Burunat and Starcevic 1983), a self-proclaimed intermediate level text, for the same course. This situation clearly indicates a lack of communication and curriculum planning among the various campuses of the community college. The use of texts of different levels for the same course offered at both campuses is perhaps an oversight or a case where too much academic freedom interferes with proper language education planning. Regarding the overall general quality of the texts available for teaching Hispanic students at the college level, 40% of the respondents rate as poor or unsatisfactory the quality of the photographs, drawings, graphs, and other realia. Sixty-five percent of the respondents indicate that they are not satisfied with the materials currently available. Moroever, although 25% of the respondents describe their texts as satisfactory, they clarify that they are satisfactory *only* when supplemented with other materials; 58.3% rate their texts as 'very good but tedious at times'; they also agree that 'the texts could have been more imaginative.' In fact, nearly half of the respondents have adopted a book of readings in order to supplement the main text(s) used in the course. Among the books used as supplementary readers are *Nuevos horizontes* (Fernández and García 1982), *Al tanto* (Kuperschmid 1984), and *Aventuras literarias* (Jarvis, Lebredo, and Mena 1983).

Eighty percent of the respondents say that they favor the use of self-correcting exercises in order to make more class time available for discussion of readings or topics of interest. Yet, in spite of the high percentage favoring semiprogrammed instruction to assist in individualizing learning to some extent, current texts--with the exception of *Cuaderno B* of the *Avanzando* materials, which contains an answer key--do not feature self-correcting exercises.

5 Instruction and class activities. The survey provides data on actual instruction, that is, on the kinds of learning activities, exercises, and strategies which instructors claim that they use and encourage. Eighty percent of the respondents, for example, regularly encourage their students to read magazines and the local newspapers in Spanish and to bring articles of interest to class in order to comment on them. Sixty-eight percent, however, have not experimented with having their students tape their speech so that they can hear what they sound like and also so that the speech samples can be used as topics of discussion in class; 73.3% of the respondents do not use recordings to provide samples of the different Hispanic accents so that students can become more aware of the various Spanish pronunciations which exist.

Although the majority of instructors do not bring recorded speech samples to the classroom, 73.3% do encourage or assign students to watch Spanish television in Miami (e.g., the Spanish International Network--Channel 23, HIT Cable TV, Galavision, or the new Channel 51). While some respondents (25%) assign news programs like '24 Horas' from Mexico, as well as the local news in Spanish, others (also 25%) ask students to watch the popular award-winning bilingual comedy '¿Qué pasa USA?' Many respondents do not favor one television program over another but encourage their students to watch a variety of programs, including soap operas from various countries, as these expose them to phonological and lexical varieties within standard Spanish as it is used today.

Only 14.2% of the respondents use translation exercises on a regular basis in their SNS course(s); 42.9% use such exercises during the course of a semester; 35.5% rarely use them; and 7.1% never do.

The following statistics indicate the extent to which the respondents require their students to give oral presentations in class on a selected topic: 28.6% always require it; 14.3% almost always do so; 21.4% usually or at least 60% to 75% of the time use this activity; 21.4% rarely do so; and 14.3% never do.

The survey shows that 66.6% of the respondents give their students the opportunity to see a film or a play in Spanish and hand in a *reseña* of the work.

The majority of the respondents (73.3%) are not in the habit of taking their SNS classes on field trips; the 26.7% who do include such trips in their class agendas indicate that they have taken their students to a variety of outings, such as (1) a Hispanic film, play, or *zarzuela,* (2) a Hispanic art exhibit, (3) a *charla* given in Spanish on a topic of general interest, and (4) a Hispanic restaurant.

At least 45% of respondents have guest speakers from the community in their classes to serve as models on the importance of being literate in both English and Spanish. Such speakers range from local corporate executives and health professionals to attorneys, journalists, translators, and poets.

6 Attitudes and perceptions on problem areas. The last part of the survey concentrates on attitudes and reveals that of the instructors surveyed, (1) 66.7% agree that a large number of their bilingual students have a deprecating attitude toward their language skills in Spanish; (2) 80% believe that students enroll in SNS courses because of work-related or professional reasons or because of personal motives (e.g., encouragement from their families and the desire to improve native language skills); (3) only 30% of the respondents believe that students enroll in these special courses for academic reasons.

The respondents point out that they consider the following or a combination of the following as being the most serious problems in their teaching Spanish to bilingual students: (1) the lack of pedagogically sound texts (13.3%), (2) the problems of different linguistic proficiency levels so often encountered among students in the same class (27.7%), (3) the overwhelming amount of material which they believe needs to be covered in such a short time and the consequent sense of frustration caused by expecting too high results in an unrealistic period of time (33.3%).

Concerning students' attitudes, 64.3% of the instructors believe that students perceive their basic problem to be primarily their inability to speak like an educated native speaker who can handle unknown situations and discuss topics in formal Spanish; 38% believe that a lack of reading and writing abilities due to little or no formal training in Spanish is the students' greatest concern.

The last question of the survey reads as follows: 'If one of the local colleges or universities in cooperation with Dade County Public Schools were to organize a one-day workshop on Teaching Spanish to Hispanic Bilinguals, would you attend?' An overwhelming 93.4% of the respondents said that they would attend and 27.7% of that 93.4% also indicated that they would not only attend but also help in planning the workshop; only one respondent commented that he would not participate because of a lack of interest.

7 Concluding remarks: Strengths and weaknesses. One of the strengths of the survey lies in the fact that it provides space, where appropriate, for the respondents to make additional comments. Another important feature is the fact that the respondents had the choice of remaining anonymous. They could also respond more fully by letter, telephone, or by meeting with me personally. Their interest in the subject can be informally measured by the number of instructors who took the time to follow up the survey with a telephone conversation (three instructors), a formal letter (one instructor from St. Thomas University), and informal meetings (with three instructors).

Of course, the survey has its limitations. One of its weaknesses is the fact that it is only local and, as a result, the number of conclusions which may be extrapolated from it is limited. Nonetheless, the survey still provides practitioners and researchers with valuable information pertaining to a specific geographical area and a particular student population. Inferences and pedagogical recommendations for other areas and populations may be made to some extent. Finally, in addition to the data obtained and the opinions expressed by respondents who currently teach SNS courses in the city of Miami, the survey data offer for the first time an overview of current practices in a given city.

Note

The author expresses her deepest gratitude to all of the community college and university instructors who took the time to answer the survey questions.

References

American Association of Teachers of Spanish and Portuguese. 1972. *Teaching Spanish in school and college to native speakers of Spanish./La enseñanza del español a estudiantes hispanohablantes en la escuela y en la universidad.* No. HE 5.210:10087. Washington, D.C.: U.S. Government Printing Office.

Aparicio, F. 1983. Teaching Spanish to the native speaker at the college level. *Hispania* 66:2.232-38.

Baker, P. 1981. *Español para los hispanos: A guide to Spanish for native speakers.* Skokie, Ill.: National Textbook Co.

Barkin, F. 1981. Establishing criteria for bilingual literacy: The case of bilingual university students. *The Bilingual Review/La Revista Bilingüe* 8:1.1-13.

Blair, R.W. 1982. *Innovative approaches to language teaching.* Rowley, Mass.: Newbury House.

Burunat, S., and J. Burunat. 1984. *Nuevas voces hispanas.* New York: CBS College Publishing.

____, and E. Starcevic. 1983. *El español y su estructura: Lectura y escritura para bilingües.* New York: Holt, Rinehart, and Winston.

Dade County Public School Board. 1984. *Course of study: Spanish for native speakers (Spanish-S).* Miami: The School Board of Dade County.

de la Portilla, M., and B. Varela. 1979. *Mejora tu español: Lectura y redacción para bilingües.* New York: Regents.

Fernández, J.B., and N. García. 1982. *Nuevos horizontes.* Lexington, Mass.: D.C. Heath.

Jarvis, A.C., et al. 1983. *¡Continuemos!* 2d ed. Lexington, Mass.: D.C. Heath. 3d ed., 1987.

____. 1983. *Adventuras literarias.* Lexington, Mass.: D.C. Heath.

Jiménez, F. 1981. *Mosaico de la vida.* New York: Harcourt, Brace, Jovanovich.

Kuperschmid, G.S., ed. 1984. *Al tanto.* Boston: Houghton Mifflin.

Lequerica de la Vega, S., and C. Salazar Parr. 1978. *Avanzando: Gramática española y lectura.* New York: Wiley.

Mejías, H.A., and G. Garza-Swan. 1981. *Nuestro español: Curso para estudiantes bilingües.* New York: Macmillan.

Mullen, E.J., and J.F. Garganigo. 1980. *El cuento hispánico.* New York: Random House.

Sánchez, R. 1981. Spanish for native speakers at the university: Suggestions. In: Valdés et al., eds. (1981).

Scholberg, K.R., and D.E. Scholberg. 1980. *Aquí mismo.* Rowley, Mass.: Newbury House.

Solé, C., and Y. Solé. 1977. *Spanish syntax: A study in contrast.* Lexington, Mass.: D.C. Heath.

Solé, Y. 1981. *Consideraciones pedagógicas en la enseñanza del español a estudiantes bilingües.* In: Valdés et al., eds.

Teschner, R. 1983. Spanish placement for native speakers, non-native speakers, and others. *ADFL Bulletin* 14:3.37-42.

Valdés, G. 1981. Pedagogical implications of teaching Spanish to the Spanish-speaking in the United States. In: Valdés et al., eds. (1981).

____. 1978. Code-switching and the classroom teacher. In: *Language in education: Theory and practice 4.* Arlington, Va.: Center for Applied Linguistics.

____, and R.V. Teschner. 1977. *Spanish for the Spanish-speaking: A descriptive bibliography of materials.* Austin, Texas: National Educational Laboratory Publishers.

_____. 1984. *Español escrito: Curso para hispanohablantes bilingües*: 2nd ed. New York: Scribner.

_____, A.G. Lozano, and R. García-Moya, eds. 1981. *Teaching Spanish to the Hispanic bilingual: Issues, aims, and methods.* New York: Teachers College Press.

Yates, D.A., and J.B. Dalbor, eds. 1983. *Imaginación y fantasía.* New York: CBS College Publishing.

Enseñanza de español y sensibilidad cultural a los profesionales de la salud

Teresa González-Lee
University of California at San Diego

1 Introducción. Está surgiendo en la actualidad, entre las escuelas profesionales, una nueva inquietud, que es la de desarrollar entre los futuros profesionales de la salud, una noción de sensibilidad hacia las diversas culturas que coexisten con la cultura anglosajona principal. Tal es el caso de la cultura hispana en las zonas fronterizas bilingües y biculturales. El propósito de este trabajo es mostrar la incepción de algunos programas de español en la Escuela de Medicina de la Universidad de California en San Diego, donde me ha tocado actuar como parte del personal docente.

En esta universidad, los miembros del profesorado junto con los estudiantes del Departamento de Medicina de la Comunidad están conscientes de que la cultura afecta el cuidado de la salud entre los individuos pertenecientes a un grupo social y por lo tanto los profesionales de la salud deben esmerarse en conocer esos patrones culturales. El enfoque utilizado por la Universidad de California en San Diego se basa en la siguiente premisa: 'Culture forms an important part of the identity of every patient and culture-related stresses are known to induce illness' (Kristal et al. 1983:683). La implicación es que el individuo enfermo es parte de una unidad familiar, así como de una comunidad y de una cultura, es decir, no es un ente aislado, sino que participa en la dinámica social de su grupo, cuyas normas culturales determinan ciertos modos de conducta que pueden provocar enfermedades.

La posición geográfica de San Diego con su proximidad a la frontera internacional con México, crea un tráfico constante de población mexicana y latinoamericana que busca servicios médicos en los Estados Unidos. A estos grupos se suma el número de inmigrantes mexicanos ya establecidos en la región, elevando así el porcentaje de pacientes potenciales aproximadamente a un 25% de personas que hablan español en esta zona bilingüe y bicultural.

La concepción humanista del paciente del Departamento de Medicina de la Comunidad ha llevado a la creación de dos programas de español que están actualmente en operación: uno en el segundo año de subgrado de la Escuela de Medicina y el otro a nivel de post-grado, para los médicos residentes en el hospital. Estos programas se ofrecen independientemente en el campus universitario y en el hospital universitario, y aunque tienen objetivos similares, difieren en algunos aspectos metodológicos.

2 Descripción de los programas. Los programas de español y sensibilidad cultural tienen dos componentes principales: uno propiamente académico, integrado en el curriculum de Medicina Inter-Cultural, y el otro una experiencia clínica de inmersión en la cultura. Los estudiantes de medicina al igual que los médicos residentes practican español durante una media jornada por semana y se les ubica en ambientes donde puedan escuchar y comprender los historiales de pacientes cuya lengua materna es el español.

El programa a nivel de subgrado para los estudiantes de medicina se ha dividido en dos grupos de quince estudiantes cada uno, separados en dos niveles: uno de principiantes y el otro de intermedios. El componente de inmersión cultural consiste en una sesión clínica de tres horas con médicos y pacientes de la comunidad hispana que abren sus consultorios a los estudiantes de medicina para la experiencia médico-cultural. El tiempo de contacto directo con el idioma es de seis horas semanales durante un año académico, a lo que se suman seis horas más de ejercicios de comprensión auditiva en el laboratorio y de instrucción asistida por computadoras para establecer las bases gramaticales de la lengua.

Las sesiones clínicas representan oportunidades de practicar el español dentro de un contexto médico y cultural, exponiendo a los estudiantes a las historias de los pacientes que contienen datos tanto científicos como sociales y políticos. Los preceptores son médicos de la comunidad hispana que tienen gran número de pacientes que hablan español y cuya especialidad médica se presta a una situación de aprendizaje de español médico, en particular medicina de la familia, medicina interna, pediatría, etc. Estos preceptores actúan como médicos-profesores de varios modos. Proveen el escenario donde estudiantes y pacientes pueden llevar a cabo las entrevistas, sirviéndoles de modelos; también los preceptores proveen ayuda en cuestiones biculturales que se refieren a la salud y, además comparten sus conocimientos médicos con los estudiantes. La actitud receptiva de los pacientes hispanos facilita la adquisición del lenguaje ya que ellos manifiestan su aprecio por el esfuerzo hecho por los estudiantes.

Ahora pasamos a la discusión del programa de español y sensibilidad cultural para los médicos residentes de medicina de la comunidad. Los varios componentes de este programa fueron descritos por Kristal et al. (1983:683) y consisten en (1) un curso de español, (2) una rotación en una clínica colocada en la frontera mexicano-estadounidense, (3) un entrenamiento en salud mental que se refiere específicamente a los hispanos y (4) una serie de actividades interculturales destinadas a fortalecer los conocimientos de la ciencia del comportamiento. El programa fue establecido en 1979 bajo los auspicios de la *Health Manpower Commission* y se integró al curriculum obligatorio. Se implementó hasta 1985 con un sistema tutorial de clases individualizadas e incluyó a todos los médicos residentes del segundo año y a algunos miembros del profesorado. En la actualidad este programa está siendo revisado y está experimentando cambios entre los cuales ya se ha establecido el sistema de clases en grupos de tres o cuatro médicos para permitir un mejor control de tiempo. El elemento de inmersión cultural en la clínica de San Isidro se ha conservado porque este contacto lingüístico y cultural acelera el proceso de adquisición del lenguaje en gran medida.

3 Metodología. El programa de español tiene por objetivo desarrollar la proficiencia oral de los médicos, es decir, su capacidad de comunicarse con un paciente y de comprender su lenguaje. Considerando las limitaciones de tiempo de los profesionales en cuestión y la ventaja de la inmersión cultural, se seleccionó el Método Natural de Krashen y Terrell (1983). La organización de los dos programas mencionados, con un componente académico (seminario) y la inmersión cultural (sesión clínica) se conforma con el doble proceso de 'adquisición' y 'aprendizaje' del Método Natural.

Partiendo de la hipótesis de Terrell de que adquirimos una segunda lengua por medio de la adquisición de datos lingüísticos que se nos proveen para nuestra comprensión, y que la adquisición del lenguaje es más importante que el aprendizaje mecánico de reglas, entonces podemos decir que uno de los factores determinantes en cualquier programa de lenguas para profesionales debe ser la asimilación de los datos lingüísticos, puesto que contienen un mensaje que nos interesa conocer y están colocados en un contexto significativo. En las palabras de Krashen y Terrell (1983:55):

> According to the input hypothesis, language acquisition can only take place when a message which is being transmitted is understood; i.e., when the focus is on *what* is being said rather than the *form* of the message. This could be referred to as the Great Paradox of Language Teaching. Language is best taught when it is being used to transmit messages, not when it is explicitly taught for conscious learning.

La tarea de descodificar datos lingüísticos que proveen información médica estimula la actividad intelectual y eleva el nivel de motivación del estudiante, ya que se personaliza la experiencia con un tema que es de interés profesional--la cuestión médica.

La adquisición de la lengua es fundamental en estos programas de español para profesionales donde la comunicación de información es esencial en la relación médico-paciente. En las clases de español, sólo ocasionalmente ocurren discusiones en inglés de cómo funciona la lengua y es para responder a una curiosidad intelectual propia del aprendizaje. El foco principal de la clase se concentra en actividades comunicativas complementadas con materiales audiovisuales que facilitan la 'adquisición' natural del idioma.Varios textos de español médico han sido utilizados para estos programas pero el eje principal del curso consiste en la adquisición de técnicas de entrevista para la obtención de la historia médica del paciente. Estas técnicas varían según el tipo de relación establecida entre médico y paciente. Existen aquéllas de índole abierta en que el paciente toma la iniciativa y establece un diálogo abierto con el médico; también hay otras, más estructuradas, en que el doctor elige un papel activo y guía la entrevista por medio de preguntas generales o específicas. Por último se dan aquéllas de mutua cooperación en que tanto el paciente como el médico interactúan en un diálogo de iguales (Bowden et al. 1983:100-17). Con cualquiera de estas técnicas, se trata de conseguir información sobre la queja principal, la historia médica actual del paciente, su historia médica pasada, la historia de las enfermedades de la familia y la historia social, ocupacional y cultural del paciente.

Las diferencias socio-económicas y el grado de educación del paciente pueden determinar el estilo de entrevista. La tarea de entrevistar al paciente resulta más compleja cuando la entrevista está llena de digresiones con signos históricos, folklóricos y personales, todo lo cual se convierte en dato lingüístico a procesarse para darle sentido y adquirir la información médica necesaria.

4 Conclusiones. Las experiencias con estos dos modelos de programas en la Escuela de Medicina y en su Hospital Universitario me han llevado a la conclusión de que existe una nueva concientización entre los profesionales de la salud por cultivar cualidades de sensibilidad cultural por medio de la adquisición de las lenguas. Muy importante es el caso del español en las zonas bilingües y biculturales donde son ostensibles los altos porcentajes de población flotante y arraigada.

Algunos de los factores claves en este nuevo acercamiento a las minorías culturales han sido influídos por grandes cambios en la evolución de la profesión médica. Starr (1982:421-25) sugiere la idea de que existe una crisis actual y en aumento, creada por un 'surplus' de estos profesionales cuyo *modus operandi* tendrá que cambiar para adaptarse a las transformaciones sociales futuras.

Entre estos cambios sociales cabe señalar la existencia de alternativas para el cuidado de la salud de que dispone el paciente moderno y sofisticado. Además, el mayor acceso a todo tipo de información en esta época altamente informativa le concede al paciente un poder nunca antes percibido en la historia y que se basa en el conocimiento adquirido de su propio cuerpo y de su salud, todo lo cual crea un paciente menos dependiente y con más opciones. Por otro lado el profesional trata de adaptarse a los cambios y busca nuevos horizontes ya que está colocado en una coyuntura histórica de la cual depende su porvenir. Entonces amplía su visión, se internacionaliza y se acerca a las minorías culturales ayudado por las humanidades y las ciencias sociales.

En conclusión, estamos presenciando cambios sociales que nos afectan a todos y que crean nuevos problemas y nuevas soluciones. El ejemplo de la

Escuela de Medicina de la Universidad de California en San Diego demuestra la necesidad de aumentar y multiplicar programas de esta índole dentro del país y en especial en las zonas donde la población hispanohablante requiera de servicios médicos que sean sensibles a su cultura para así conseguir el retorno de su salud y su reintegración a la vida activa en su comunidad.

Referencias

Almeyda, J., S. Mohler y R. Stinson. 1981. *Descubrir y crear*. 2a ed. Nueva York: Harper and Row.

Bowden, C., y A. Burstein. 1983. *Psychosocial basis of health care*. Baltimore: Williams and Wilkins.

González-Lee, T., y H. Simon. 1990. *Medical Spanish: Interviewing the Latino patient. A cross-cultural perspective*. Nueva York: Prentice Hall.

Jarvis, A., y R. Lebredo. 1980. *Spanish for medical personnel*. 2a ed. Lexington, Mass.: Heath.

Krashen, S., y T. Terrell. 1983. *The natural approach: Language acquisition in the classroom*. Oxford: Pergamon Press. Hayward, Calif.: Alemany Press.

Kristal, L., P. Pennock, S. Foote et al. 1983. Cross-cultural family medicine residency training. *Journal of Family Practice* 17.683-87.

Starr, P. 1982. *The social transformation of American medicine: The rising of a sovereign profession and the making of a vast industry*. Nueva York: Basic Books.

Teed, C., H. Raley y J. Barber. 1983. *Conversational Spanish for the medical and health professions*. Nueva York: Holt.

Werner, D. 1981. *Donde no hay doctor: Una guía para los campesinos que viven lejos de los centros médicos*. Palo Alto, Calif.: Hesperian Foundation.

Williams, S., y R. Burgos-Sasscer. 1981. *Exploraciones chicano-riqueñas*. Nueva York: Random House.

Spanish in the United States:
The struggle for legitimacy

Lourdes Torres
State University of New York at Stony Brook

Despite its hostile atmosphere for languages other than English, the United States continues to be a multilingual country. In an update to his 1966 study on language loyalty in the United States, Fishman (1983) found that, according to the 1970 census, 111 languages other than English were declared as mother tongue by 35 million people, and 2.4 million reported that they spoke no English. The largest non-English language background group is Hispanic, with 14.6 million claimants, according to the 1980 census. The number of Latinos in the United States has tripled in the last three decades; and by 1990, if the growth continues at its present rate, there will be an estimated 25,000,000 Hispanics in this country and they will constitute our largest minority group.

Given this context, it would seem that bilingual education would be recognized as a logical tool to deal with this obviously multilingual situation. Clearly, however, bilingual education continues to be a controversial issue in the United States. In the last few years we have seen particularly hostile attacks on bilingual education programs (for example, in *The New York Times,* January 26, 1986; *Time,* October 7, 1985; and *U.S. News and World Report,* October 7, 1985) and not unrelatedly, a renewed effort to render English the sole official language of the society. As an expression of their opposition to the use of Spanish in the United States, policymakers continue to be successful in designating English as the only legitimate language of the country. This is accomplished through a variety of strategies, the most effective of which involves the cooptation of individual Latinos to serve their cause; this occurs despite the belief among many Latinos that use of their own language is also legitimate in the U.S. context. In this essay I examine the struggles over the legitimacy of the use of Spanish in this country as exemplified in the controversies surrounding Richard Rodríguez' autobiography, *A hunger of memory* (1982).

1 *Hunger of memory*--one Hispanic's story. This is the autobiography of a Mexican-American, the son of working-class parents, who grows up in a

white middle-class neighborhood in Sacramento, California. Rodríguez went to a Catholic grammar school and a private high school. He received his B.A. degree from Stanford University, was a Rhodes scholar, and went on to receive a Ph.D. degree in English Renaissance literature from the University of California at Berkeley. He was offered academic positions at Yale and other prestigious universities but rejected all of them and dedicated himself to writing.

Language, Rodríguez states, is the subject of his book. As a school-aged child he discovered a split between public and private languages. Through his experiences at home and in the public sphere he came to identify Spanish as a private language, a family language, which implied for him softness, emotions, warmth, and security. English, in contrast, he identified as the public language, a clear, authoritative language, booming with confidence, and a language which he associated with reason and reflection. Encouraged by his teachers and Spanish-speaking parents to acquire English, he feared a loss of security at first, but soon became an enthusiastic, self-motivated student. As a thirty-two-year-old adult, looking back on his youth, he acknowledges that he suffered a loss of his culture and first language, but reasons that this was justified, given the gain of a public identity. He states that the loss of what he terms 'private individuality' is the necessary price a minority member must pay in order to become an American citizen and to enjoy all the benefits that such citizenship confers on the individual. Rodríguez declares that he feels fortunate *not* to have experienced a bilingual education since this would have postponed his acquisition of a public identity. Though himself a recipient of affirmative action dollars which financed his postsecondary education, Rodríguez aligns himself against affirmative action; he claims that it aids primarily middle-class minorities and ignores the needs of those it should seek to aid--the working class. He refuses opportunities for academic positions because he believes that they are offered to him only because of his minority status.

Rodríguez writes his book as an apology--an apology in the literary sense of autobiography, but also in the sense of its more common meaning. He wishes to apologize to working-class minorities for taking advantage of programs meant for them; however, he acknowledges that it will not be they, but rather literate Anglos, who will read his book. He is correct on this point; in fact, the book has been reviewed in a variety of academic journals, such as *The American Scholar, Harvard School of Education Journal, UCLA Chicano Law Journal,* and *Language Learning,* as well as in several respected magazines and newspapers, including *The New York Times, The New Yorker, Commentary, Commonweal,* and *The Village Voice,* and it has even been reviewed in popular weekly news and gossip magazines, such as *Newsweek, Time,* and *People Magazine.* Because of its political nature, especially its attack on bilingual education and affirmative action, it has received much more attention than is usually conferred on minority publications. The book has generated much controversy among educators, policymakers, and others who are interested in issues of language and ethnicity.

2 A theory of language and ethnic group relations--subordinate group strategies. The issues raised by Rodríguez and his critics may be understood most clearly within the context of the theory of language, ethnic identity, and intergroup relations which Giles et al. (1977) propose. The latter explore the use of dominant and subordinate group strategies to maintain or change the social structure as it relates to language and ethnic group issues. The proposed theory hypothesizes that members of ethnic groups will be motivated to change the existing intergroup situation to the extent that they perceive the situation as unstable and illegitimate, as well as according to how they rate the vitality of the group language. By applying this theory one can analyze the strategies that dominant and subordinate groups employ to maintain or alter power relations that exist in multilingual contexts. When members of minority language groups perceive that the relationship between the dominant group and themselves is legitimate and stable, they will defend the status quo; however, when they view the situation as illegitimate and unstable, they may feel that alternatives to their status in the larger context are possible and thus they may attempt to alter the imbalance. In response, the dominant group will develop new strategies aimed at maintaining their legitimacy and silencing the dissension (Giles et al. 1977:308-33). This theory is especially useful because it is dynamic, allowing one to see how minority groups may bring different factors into play to initiate change, and how dominant groups may react to strategies utilized by subordinate groups.

In what follows, I discuss some of the dynamics involved in the question of Spanish language legitimacy in the U.S. context by focusing on subordinate and dominant group strategies as articulated by Rodríguez, his admirers, and his detractors. It is important to understand how these strategies work in order to avoid being duped by those, like Richard Rodríguez and his defenders, who claim to speak in the interest of the Latino population, but who are really arguing for the elimination of Latino language and culture in the United States.

3 Subordinate group strategies. Rodríguez sees the situation of his ethnic community within the U.S. context as both stable and legitimate; he does not perceive any alternatives to the relationship and accepts the superiority of the dominant group and the inferiority of his ethnic group. Thus, his solution is to attempt to achieve distinctiveness from his ethnic community by becoming acculturated and even more Anglo than the Anglos. In complete agreement with the dominant society, he advocates acculturation (acceptance of the imposition of a second language and value set) as a prerequisite to assimilation (economic, social, and political equality). Rodríguez (p. 26) writes:

Today I hear bilingual educators say that children lose a degree of 'individuality' by becoming assimilated into public society. But the bilingualists simplistically scorn the value and the necessity of assimilation. They do not realize that there are two ways a person is individualized and consequently they do not further realize that while one suffers a diminished sense of private individuality by becoming assimilated into the public society, such assimilation makes possible the achievement of public individuality.

Rodríguez (p. 27) repeatedly emphasizes the public gain while down-playing the private pain: 'If I rehearse here the changes in my private life after my Americanization, it is finally to emphasize the public gain. The loss implies the gain.' Thus, Rodríguez argues that you can't have both: one must give up his or her ethnic language in order to reap the benefits of assimilation.

The assimilationist position renders Rodríguez's book dear to the majority of critics who praise *A hunger of memory*. It is the position that dominates in the reviews, for instance, in *Newsweek, Time, Phi Delta Kappan,* and the *New York Times Review of Books*. For example, Smith (1982:289) argues in *Phi Delta Kappan* that private languages, when used in public settings, lose their intimacy and therefore should be kept private. Furthermore, he states (p. 289): 'English-speaking children in the U.S. grow up away from their families through education, and they embrace their public identities, so should Spanish-speaking children. To try to preserve an intimate language in the public setting of the classroom denies children the necessary first proving ground for their public selves.'

In his review of *A hunger of memory* for the *New York Times Review of Books,* Zweig (1982:1) also praises Rodríguez for recognizing that the function of education is to take the child from his private world and 'give him access to the public world, which in the U.S. is negotiated in standard English, embodied by a set of attitudes, a voice, which is everywhere recognized as a passport to all the larger ambitions the public world makes possible.'

However, although many second- and third-generation ethnic minorities accept the philosophy of the dominant group and shift to English, they usually find that acculturation is not necessarily followed by incorporation into the mainstream economy and society as the myths would have working-class minorities believe (García 1982:43). Ironically, Rodríguez is a case in point. Although he has accepted and even welcomed acculturation and thus rejects the term 'minority' for himself, the dominant culture continues to see him and categorize him as a minority. In all the reviews of his book he is referred to as a minority writer or a Chicano writer; when he is asked to speak, it is as a minority speaker. In an interview with Marzán (1982:46) of *The Village Voice,* Rodríguez complains that he is only asked to contribute his works as a minority writer and in collections of works by minorities. Therefore, despite his total willingness and eagerness to assimilate he will never be accepted as a 'legitimate' member of the dominant society.

When the subordinate group perceives that there are alternatives to the unequal relations between groups, and when they believe that the system is unstable and illegitimate, they will undertake entirely different strategies. For example, they may seek to gain some control over the political, economic, cultural, and linguistic affairs of the society in an attempt to modify the unequal distribution of resources. In their review of Rodríguez's book, Torres and Morales (1984) argue for cultural pluralism; they point out that there is no such phenomenon as the melting pot, and that society in general gains by the inclusion of different cultures, with their specific characteristics. Others argue that Spanish has a three-hundred-year history in the United States and the Latino population continues to increase, and thus the educational system must acknowledge this situation and incorporate Latinos into the mainstream, while at the same time allowing them their cultural expression in order to ensure, at the very least, their social and psychological well-being. Those who support cultural pluralism advocate maintenance bilingual programs that treat both languages equally so that content subjects are taught in both languages. One of the aims of bilingual education should be to demonstrate that Spanish is as valid an instrument of communication as English. Bilingual education supporters have never advocated doing away with English, but rather doing away with the superiority notions associated with English so that children will think more positively about their cultural heritage, their parents, and the first language that they usually grow up speaking (Hortas 1982:356).   The preceding strategy entails an attempt to change the educational system to be more inclusive of diverse ethnic populations and their languages.

Another subordinate group strategy discussed by Giles et al. (1977:338) involves the redefinition of negative characteristics. The subordinate group reinterprets characteristics that have been negatively defined by the dominant group. A positive reaffirmation of attributes ensues which challenges the dominant cultural stereotypes. Unable to understand this strategy, Rodríguez criticizes the behavior of Chicanos on college campuses during the seventies. He claims (p. 159) that when Chicanos dress in ethnic garb or speak Spanish loudly and proudly in public places, they are living in the past and/or trying to establish a false link between themselves and their ancestors, a link which, according to Rodríguez, is lost when a Chicano becomes educated. However, Torres and Morales (1984:126) argue that such Chicanos are not attempting to escape their present reality but rather are trying to identify and legitimize in a positive way a particular approach to their participation in society. The authors go on to say that such Chicanos are in the process of legitimizing their cultural experience within the context of a society which has previously denied the importance of their specific identity.

Subordinate ethnic group members thus take a variety of approaches in response to an unequal social situation. Like Rodríguez, they may accept the unequal system as just and therefore attempt an individual solution which entails losing one's culture through acculturation, or, if they perceive alternatives to the illegitimate and unstable situation, they may try to modify the system. Strategies for the latter approach include struggling for cultural pluralism, and reclaiming and redefining negative stereotypes imposed by the dominant-group culture.

4 Dominant group strategies. One of the major problems facing dominant groups in multilingual, multicultural societies is establishing and maintaining legitimacy. In order to maintain its superiority, the dominant group must convince people that the institutions and processes that distribute social and economic goods are legitimate and just (Rocco 1977:194-95). Giles et al. (1977:341) argue that when the legitimacy of their control is threatened, elites will not accept a new situation; rather, they will attempt to reestablish legitimacy and ensure that stability is reinforced.

In his review of Rodríguez's book for *The Harvard Educational Review,* Hortas (1983:356) identifies one of the strategies which the dominant group uses to maintain its legitimacy. That is, he points out that the dominant culture is very successful at convincing ethnics that their culture is inferior and not worth maintaining. Ethnicity is identified with poverty and acculturation with advancement. Hortas quotes Smolicz (1983:357-58):

> Probably the most potent weapon that the majority can use to subjugate minority groups is to attempt to persuade them of their cultural and social inferiority. Schools, for example, may lead ethnic parents to believe that ethnic cultural diversity is harmful and that they have an inexorable choice to make between their children's economic and educational advancement, on the one hand, and the retention of their culture on the other. In the past, such advice has been forthcoming in the face of research that pointed in the opposite direction.

Rodríguez's parents, for example, accept this theory; when the nuns came into their home and told them that they must speak only English to their son so that he would be able to progress, they complied. Indirectly, they were being told that their language, and by extension their culture, would potentially harm their son's well-being. Out of love for their son and because of their firm belief in the institution of education (and the Catholic Church) they acquiesced despite the awkward situation that resulted, since they themselves could barely speak English. This process has the effect of inhibiting and limiting family interaction, and causes great emotional and psychological stress. Unfortunately, many Latino parents are similarly convinced. Others, however, do not wish to choose between cultural identity and increased social and economic opportunities--they want both. While they acknowledge that learning English is required in order to compete for good jobs and economic security, they believe that this does not imply the involuntary loss of Spanish or of an indigenous culture.

Another strategy of the dominant culture is to create and support an educational system which does not challenge students to think, but rather trains them to accept the interests of the dominant culture (its government, education, media, and religion) as their own. Rodríguez does not question the assimilationist ideology nor the rationale against bilingual education. He accepts the status quo, despite the very painful process of his own education. A critical thinker would challenge this process and explore other alternatives which would not have resulted in such profound alienation; but Rodríguez is incapable of such a leap, which would force him to question the values of the society of which he so urgently desires to be a part. As Kerr (1983:26) states, '[Rodríguez] feels that retaining Spanish, even as a second language, would have retarded his mental growth and makes no conjecture about how such retention might have expanded it.' Another example of how the educational process stymies critical thought is evident by the fact that, as Marzán (1982:36) points out, Rodríguez believes that his desire to assimilate is solely motivated by his educational experience. He denies the effects of social and media pressures which subtly and blatantly reinforce dominant group values, while unceasingly degrading minority group values and culture. Marzán writes:

> Whether or not Rodríguez was right to assimilate or feels, as he says he does, 'well adjusted,' is less relevant than that his book fails because he writes as if he never truly felt socially pressured to assimilate--as if he didn't have an obligation to himself to consider whether he acted or merely submitted to a grander scheme. In other words, his squeamish book lacks verisimilitude. In real life, the Hispanic child's vision of Hispanics is more repellent and the Anglo's more attractive. Between these two extremes runs the magnetic impulse to assimilate.

Thus, Richard Rodríguez is a good example of the results of a U.S. North American education. Within the latter, students are trained to view the world from a very narrow Anglo perspective which assumes that all that is European and white is superior, and all else is insignificant and inferior. The dominant culture (the media, the government, and religion) plants the seeds of racism, and the educational system reinforces and nurtures this ideology. Even brown and black people emerge with this point of view; they emerge as Rodríguez does, filled with self-hatred, and with little knowledge of, curiosity about, or respect for their own cultures.

A related dominant group strategy entails the cooptation of a minority group member to serve as spokesperson for dominant group interests. Romero (1983:3) suggests that Rodríguez is an example of how the school system works to separate a few minority students from their ethnic group, and to socialize them into believing themselves different and better than others in their ethnic group. The fragmentation of experience, which in Rodríguez's case surfaces as a split between the public and private languages, is thus 'internalized as an inevitable process based on individual experiences' (Romero 1983:3). In that same context Romero writes:

> Every time minority students attribute 'I' as the sole agent for their educational success, the history of minority students is violated. Increased minority

enrollments, minority student programs, student aid and EOP opportunities were obtained and maintained through the constant struggles of many. By redefining the failure of the individual, minority students are taught the yo-yo theory and the bootstrap myth of social mobility is passed on to another generation.

Rodríguez defends the interests of the ruling class when he speaks out against affirmative action even though 'minority dollars' financed his way through college and graduate school. Rodríguez represents one of the select few minorities who is allowed to make it through a system that, for the most part, excludes minority voices and perspectives as well as critical thinking. He is expected to return to the community to espouse the ideology of the majority. Thus, he is an example of the individual whom the dominant group trains, coopts, and then encourages and sponsors. It is this type of minority whose books are published by major presses, who are paraded before society by the media, and invited to speak on the lecture circuit by the academicians. The message from Rodríguez to all Latinos and other ethnic minorities is clear: you too can succeed if you pull yourself up by your own bootstraps. According to this perspective, if a minority person fails it is not because of the failure of the system but because of the failure of the individual and if he/she succeeds it is likewise due to individual effort. The 'exceptionalist' explanation that Rodríguez uses to explain his success denies the long and continuing history of struggle by people of color for equal access and opportunity.

In his review of *A hunger of memory* in *The American Scholar,* Porter (1983:280-81) also chastises Rodríguez for his ahistorical point of view. He points out that Rodríguez mouths the dominant society's claims when he argues that middle-class ethnics and those who are students should not be considered minorities because they have had access to education, which Rodríguez sees as the great equalizer. According to Rodríguez, these groups should not benefit from affirmative action programs. Porter shows that this is a myth; for instance, Blacks who are of the middle class and are educated still suffer from racial discrimination. In the source just cited Porter writes: 'Furthermore, racism is a curious and illogical thing. Although some of the Black students who were admitted during affirmative action's heyday might not have been socially oppressed or economically deprived, some were nevertheless victims of racism's poisonous effects.' In conclusion, he notes that especially prior to affirmative action the few Blacks who graduated from first-rate universities could only find appointments at Black colleges.

One final example of a dominant group strategy is the skillful repression of dissent which would undermine the dominant group's legitimacy. The ruling class recognizes that the most effective and efficient means of preventing or diffusing challenges to the power structure is to absorb such challenges into the system. The dominant group is aware that the importance of language choice is most powerfully felt when an individual is denied use of his/her mother tongue; such an individual correctly interprets that denial as an indication of the lack of importance which the dominant society gives to that person's language and to his/her cultural heritage. Thus, so-called bilingual education programs are created in order to facilitate rapid acculturation and work to the benefit of the ruling class. Although some who struggle for bilingual education argue for bilingual programs which acknowledge the importance of languages other than English and which encourage cultural pluralism, the dominant group has, for the most part, successfully undermined this challenge. Kjolseth (1972:109), in a review of bilingual education programs in the United States in the seventies, found that well over eighty percent of bilingual education administrators subscribed to an acculturation model rather than to a pluralistic model:

> This is to say that in most cases the ethnic language is being exploited rather than cultivated--weaning the public away from his mother tongue in what amounts to a kind of cultural and linguistic 'counter insurgency' policy on the part of the schools. A variety of the ethnic language is being used as a new means to an old end. The traditional policy of 'Speak Only English' is amended to 'We Will Speak Only English--' just as soon as possible and even sooner and more completely, if we begin with a variety of the ethnic language rather than only English!

Cultural pluralists who measure the success of bilingual education programs by the extent to which they help maintain and cultivate native languages and cultures are disappointed by the development of programs which in the long run only serve to make acculturation smoother. Yet many parents and policy-makers consider themselves fortunate to have any type of bilingual education program and thus the dominant society successfully quiets dissent.

Dominant group strategies are aimed at maintaining the legitimacy of an unequal situation. Tactics include convincing ethnic minorities of their inferiority, coopting minority group members to become spokespersons for the dominant group's philosophy, and diffusing challenges to the ruling class by absorbing them into the system and assuring minority group members that their needs are being met.

5 Conclusion. In summary, the framework proposed by Giles et al. for analyzing language and ethnic group relations is useful in examining the controversy surrounding *A hunger of memory*, particularly in terms of some of the dominant and subordinate group strategies aimed at legitimizing the present language policy situation in the United States. Rodríguez's work, as well as the praise and criticism it has generated, are important in illuminating how the dominant group continues to be successful in legitimizing the English-only tradition to the detriment of the fourteen million Spanish speakers in this country. Yet despite this success, some of the reviews also indicate that Latinos continue to challenge the present system which attempts to render Latino language and culture invisible. As the number of Spanish speakers in this country continues to increase, due to increased immigration from Spanish-speaking countries, and as the status of the Spanish language continues to

improve, thanks to the growing institutional support from the Spanish language media, the dominant culture will inevitably need to create new strategies to maintain and legitimize its linguistic, political, and economic hegemony. Latinos must understand the strategies used by the dominant group in order to avoid cooptation of their interests; and an understanding of some of the subordinate group strategies employed so far by Latinos will help in the development of new strategies which will facilitate the ongoing struggle for Spanish language legitimacy within the United States.

References

Fishman, J., and W. Milán. 1983. Spanish language resources of the United States: Some preliminary findings. In: *Spanish in the U.S. setting: Beyond the Southwest.* L. Elías-Olivares, ed. Rosslyn, Va.: National Clearinghouse for Bilingual Education. 167-79.

García, O. 1982. Sociolinguistics and language planning for Hispanics in the United States. *International Journal of the Sociology of Language* 44.43-54.

Giles, H., R.Y. Bourhis, and D. Taylor. 1977. Towards a theory of language in ethnic group relations. In: *Language, ethnicity and intergroup relations.* H. Giles, ed. London: Academic Press.

Hortas, C. 1983. *Hunger of memory.* The education of Richard Rodríguez by Richard Rodríguez. Review of: *A hunger of memory. Harvard Educational Review* 53.355-59.

Kerr, L. 1983. An ethnic's journey. Review of: *A hunger of memory. Commonweal* (July 14), 110.26-27.

Kjolseth, R. 1972. Bilingual education programs in the United States: For assimilation or pluralism? In: *The language education of minority children.* B. Spolsky, ed. Rowley, Mass.: Newbury House. 307-25.

Marzán, J. 1982. Richard Rodríguez talks to himself. Review of: *A hunger of memory. The Village Voice* (April 27), 36-37.

Porter, H. 1983. Ethnic secrets. Review of: *A hunger of memory. The American Scholar* 52.278-85.

Rocco, R. 1977. Language as an expression of ideology: A critique of a neo-Marxist view. In: *Perspectivas en Chicano studies.* R.F. Macías, ed. Los Angeles, Calif.: The National Association of Chicano Social Science. 193-99.

Rodríguez, R. 1982. *A hunger of memory: The education of Richard Rodríguez.* Boston: David R. Godine.

Romero, M. 1983. Critical thinking and everyday life. Review of: *A hunger of memory. La Red/The Net* 69.3-5.

Smith, V. 1982. Controversy should not deter educators from reading this account of one man's education. Review of: *A hunger of memory. Phi Delta Kappan* 64.289-90.

Strouse, J. 1982. A victim of two cultures. Review of: *A hunger of memory. Newsweek* (March 15), 74.

Time. 1982. Taking bilingualism to task. Review of: *A hunger of memory. Time* (Apr. 19), 68.

Torres, G., and J. Morales. 1984. *Todo se paga.* Review of: *A hunger of memory. Chicano Law Review* 7.125-30.

Zweig, P. 1982. The child of two cultures. Review of: *A hunger of memory. New York Times Book Review* (Feb. 28), 87.1.

El impacto de la realidad socio-económica en las comunidades hispanoparlantes de los Estados Unidos: Reto a la teoría y metodología lingüística

Ana Celia Zentella
Hunter College

Fue sumamente apropiado que la séptima conferencia sobre el español en los Estados Unidos se celebrara en Nuevo México, por ser un estado que ha contribuido mucho al estudio del español en los Estados Unidos. El trabajo de Aurelio Espinosa (1909) se reconoce como el primer esfuerzo serio por describir el habla regional de un grupo de hispanoparlantes en este país. El estudio de San Antoñito por Bowen (1952) y más reciente, el de Martíneztown hecho por Hudson-Edwards y Bills (1983), demuestran que la Universidad de Nuevo México, donde también se celebró el séptimo Colloquium sobre la Lingüística Hispánica (Bergen y Bills 1983), sigue la tradición y la mantiene viva. Los estudios de Nuevo México forman parte de una larga tradición de investigación del español encabezada por figuras ilustres tales como Antonio Nebrija, Menéndez Pidal y Tomás Navarro Tomás, entre muchos otros.

Al recordar que esta conferencia continúa en los pasos de tantos que nos proceden a través de cinco siglos, nos parece útil plantearnos qué se ha logrado con nuestros estudios del español en los Estados Unidos, y cómo se distinguen de los de antes. Afortunadamente, hace poco más de una década, tres colegas de los que representan la nueva generación de la tradición del suroeste nos hicieron el gran favor de recopilar todos los estudios que se habían escrito hasta la fecha sobre el español de los Estados Unidos. Es decir, la bibliografía de Teschner, Bills y Craddock (1975) es indispensable, no sólo porque reúne los esfuerzos dispersos, sino porque el prólogo de Bills describe el enfoque de la mayoría de los estudios, y señala las limitaciones. Para el 1975 sólo se había estudiado el español de los mexicanos y los boricuas, y no se apartaban de lo hispanista, lo educativo y lo sociológico. Los investigadores se preocupaban mayormente por averiguar hasta qué punto los hispanos en los Estados Unidos se desviaban de la norma aceptada de la madre patria. La bibliografía nos sirvió de guía a muchos que pretendíamos llenar las lagunas; la verdad es que hace falta una revisión para ver hasta qué punto ha cambiado el panorama descrito por Bills en los últimos diez años.

Aunque no existe una bibliografía anotada al día, sí se han publicado cinco volúmenes que recogen algunos de los últimos esfuerzos en este campo. Tres de ellos existen gracias al trabajo editorial de Elías-Olivares: uno con Amastae (1983), y los otros que recopilan las ponencias de los colaboradores y organizadores de estas conferencias en años pasados (Elías-Olivares 1983 y Elías-Olivares, Leone, Cisneros y Gutiérrez 1985). También existe otra colección de ponencias editada por Ricardo Durán (1981). El quinto volumen es el de Fishman y Keller (1982). Al leer todo esto nos damos cuenta que los estudios sobre el español en los Estados Unidos todavía sufren de las mismas limitaciones señaladas por Bills a pesar de algunos cambios, es decir: entre los temas predominan lo educativo y lo sociológico, aunque también aparecen lo psicológico y lo legal. Además se puede ver que la orientación lingüística es menos filológica y más estructural. En cuanto a las variedades del español que se han estudiado, todavía predominan la mexicana y la puertorriqueña, lógicamente porque siguen siendo los dos grupos más grandes de hispanoparlantes, ya que constituyen el 74% de esta población en total. Sin embargo, también contamos con trabajos sobre el español de los sefarditas de Nueva York, el de los centroamericanos de Houston, el de los cubanos de Miami y Nueva Jersey, y el de distintos grupos en Wáshington, D.C., Minnesota, Indiana, Louisiana y Iowa, entre otros estados.

A pesar de las limitaciones de tema, enfoque y variedades que puedan persistir, creo que hemos empezado a elaborar distintas teorías y métodos que constituyen una contribución importante al estudio del español en general, y a la política lingüística y el porvenir de los hispanoparlantes en específico.

Quizá la mayor aportación que hemos hecho, aunque nos falta refinar la metodología, es la de subrayar la necesidad de ubicar el estudio del idioma en su marco socio-económico. Puede parecernos demasiado obvio e innecesario el insistir en que los idiomas son una creación humana que reflejan las culturas de los grupos. Como consecuencia, cada vez que dos personas hablan se enfrentan dos mundos distintos, i.e., diferencias culturales además de clase, sexo, región, estilo, edad y raza se reflejan en el habla de cada uno. Sin embargo, algunos departamentos de idioma siguen ignorando estas verdades, y siguen enseñando y analizando el habla y la literatura de una élite minoritaria. De esta manera barren con toda la variedad aún en ese grupo, y con la de todos los grupos diversos que hablan el mismo idioma. Cada día más y más estudiantes de idiomas y estudiantes de la lingüística se dan cuenta que la preparación académica que recibieron no los preparó para la variedad con la cual topan en el habla diaria. Desgraciadamente, algunos aceptan la tradición prescriptiva y denuncian todo lo que no concuerda con el patrón limitado del llamado *ideal speaker* de Chomsky (1956) o del supuesto *ideal bilingual* de Weinreich (1953). Se da el ridículo de estudiantes del español que apenas logran dar los buenos días pero quienes critican ásperamente el habla de los nativos. Afortunadamente, otros se dan cuenta que no existe tal cosa o tal persona como el *ideal* en ningún idioma.

No quiero dar la impresión que los que estudiamos el español en los Estados Unidos fuimos los primeros en señalar el nexus entre los patrones del habla y la realidad socio-económica del que habla. El transcurso de todo el siglo veinte representa la reintegración de todo el contexto lingüístico y social en el estudio del habla; por ejemplo, Gumperz y Hymes (1964, 1972), Labov (1966), Trudgill (1974) y Milroy (1987). Los estudios clásicos de los siglos pasados que trazaban la historia filológica de cada palabra desde sus orígenes en el proto-indoeuropeo u otra familia lingüística pre-histórica fueron ampliados por los estudios dialectales de las primeras décadas del siglo veinte. Estas le dieron énfasis al origen regional de las palabras, y a las variaciones regionales en la pronunciación de los viejos y de los jóvenes. A partir de los años '60, los estudios etnolingüísticos de Gumperz y Hymes (1964, 1972) y los sociolingüísticos de Labov (1966, 1972) contribuyen otras dimensiones no captadas por la dialectología regional. Labov incluye la clase social, el género sexual, los estilos formales e informales, y añade la verificación estadística de una metodología cuantitativa. Gumperz y Hymes van más allá del individuo que habla y definen la comunidad del habla. Demuestran que los que pertenecen a una comunidad del habla no sólo comparten el mismo sistema fonológico, sintáctico y semántico de un código lingüístico--lo cual constituye su competencia lingüística--sino que también comparten las formas apropiadas del hablar, por ejemplo, el uso de la palabra y del silencio, como se acostumbra en esa comunidad. Esto constituye la competencia comunicativa de cada uno, y se tiene que tomar en cuenta en cualquier estudio completo del habla de una comunidad.

Los estudios del español en los Estados Unidos se han beneficiado de los avances en la lingüística y de las teorías y metodologías de estas figuras ilustres, y contribuyen a su transformación. Aunque hace poco tiempo que podemos contar con un núcleo de investigadores adiestrados en la materia, ya se puede notar el impacto de nuestras investigaciones. Quisiera señalar en particular aquellos retos que le presentamos a algunas teorías y métodos comúnmente aceptados. Es decir, cuando las teorías y la metodología de la lingüística moderna se aplican a las realidades socio-económicas de nuestras comunidades, llegamos a cuestionar lo universal de las teorías y la eficacia de la metodología. Entre las teorías que llegamos a cuestionar están las que tienen que ver con tres áreas importantes: (1) la comunidad del habla y las normas lingüísticas, (2) el cambio lingüístico, inclusive el mantenimiento de los idiomas y el contacto entre los dialectos, y (3) el aprendizaje y la adquisición de idiomas.

1 La comunidad del habla y las normas lingüísticas. En cuanto a la comunidad del habla y las normas lingüísticas, un reto que presentan las comunidades hispanas en este país tiene que ver con el lazo que se supone que existe entre la cultura y el idioma. Indudablemente, para la mayoría de los hispanos el ser hispano necesariamente implica el tener que saber el español. No pueden concebir a un puertorriqueño, o a un mexicano, o a un cubano, etc. que no sepa el español, pero en algunas de nuestras comunidades ya hay pruebas contundentes que la mayoría sí acepta una identidad cultural hispana *sin* el español. Este es el caso con más de 90% de los entrevistados en el Barrio de Nueva York por el Centro de Estudios Puertorriqueños (Language Policy Task Force 1980) y más de 90% de unos adolescentes llamados *nuyoricans,* entrevistados en Puerto Rico (Zentella 1990). Esta actitud va completamente en contra del grano de toda persona que lucha por la supervivencia del español como parte íntegra de la cultura hispana en este país, pero es una realidad que sólo podemos entender si entendemos la realidad socio-económica de nuestros grupos. La gran mayoría son pobres, y toda la propaganda inculca la creencia que el inglés y el progreso económico van mano en mano. Si la única alternativa que tiene un pueblo para darle de comer a sus hijos es la de abandonar el idioma que se les ha convencido es un estorbo para su progreso--*pero a la vez rehusan entregar su identidad*--se entiende por qué optan por una identidad hispana sin el requisito del idioma. Un análisis de los datos presentados en los estudios ya citados, y en los de Attinasi (1985) en Indiana y Solé (1982) en Miami, revelan que las diferencias socio-económicas en los grupos tienen mucho que ver con su autodefinición de hispano con o sin el español. En Miami, la cantidad de trabajos bien remunerados que requieren el uso del español ha facilitado el mantenimiento entre los jóvenes cubanos de una identidad cubana ligada al español. Por razones parecidas los maestros puertorriqueños entrevistados por el Centro (LPTF 1980) se distinguen de las masas al darle más énfasis al lazo entre idioma y cultura. Es decir, el 62% de los maestros se pueden dar el lujo de insistir que el español es necesario para la identidad puertorriqueña porque tienen un nivel de vida que no sólo no está en peligro si saben español, sino que en muchos casos *depende* del idioma si son maestros bilingües. Sin embargo, con frecuencia ocurre que los maestros que llevamos la bandera del español en alto estamos más norteamericanizados que el pueblo, y usamos el español menos que ellos en la vida diaria. ¿Quiénes son los verdaderos hispanos? ¿Los que reclamamos el idioma pero no lo usamos, o los que no se identifican con él, pero lo usan? Quizás responderán que existe otro problema más serio--el grupo que ni lo reclama ni lo habla, i.e., los jóvenes de las últimas generaciones. Debemos recordar que una comunidad del habla no se define sólo por el compartir un código lingüístico, sino que también comparte los usos del habla y del silencio. Estos jóvenes estarán hablando sólo inglés, pero podrán estar empleando el inglés según los patrones del uso del español en su comunidad. Falta mucha investigación para verificar si este proceso ocurre o no, y para definir la variedad de grupos que existe en cada comunidad. Por ejemplo, no sabemos si estos jóvenes forman parte de la misma comunidad del habla que sus padres, o si pertenecen a otra. Aunque no tenemos los datos todavía para elucidar todos estos puntos, sólo quiero hacer hincapié en la imposibilidad de usar un criterio rígido al definir la comunidad del habla sin tomar en cuenta las realidades socio-económicas de los sub-grupos, y sus actitudes lingüísticas.

Cuando le prestamos atención a esas realidades, también nos damos cuenta del fraude que se ha cometido no sólo con los hispanoparlantes sino con todos los grupos lingüísticos minoritarios, al atribuirles su falta de progreso a la falta del inglés. Es muy común que se explique el atraso de los inmigrantes como resultado de su falta de conocimiento del inglés. Por ejemplo, Mann y Salvo (1985) observan que 'The ability of inmigrant groups to learn to speak English, an assimilation issue, has been cited as an important correlate of socio-economic success.' No hay duda que el inglés *sí* es muy útil, pero no resulta ser verdad que los que hablan más inglés tienen entradas mayores. La prueba es que de todos los grupos latinos, el que más entradas tiene es el cubano, pues gana casi el doble de los mexicanos y boricuas, y es el que tiene menos tiempo en este país y el que menos inglés sabe comparado con estos otros. Otra prueba de esta contradicción aparece en los datos del último censo de Nueva York. Cuando comparamos a los puertorriqueños con los colombianos y los dominicanos, nos sorprendemos al encontrar que aunque el 55% de los colombianos y el 68% de los dominicanos hablan poco o nada del inglés, comparados con el 30% de boricuas, tienen menos desempleados y ganan más que los puertorriqueños: el *median household income* de los boricuas es $8,181 al año y el de los dominicanos es $11,000; los colombianos ganan más de $15,000 (Mann y Salvo 1985). Indudablemente muchas otras cosas contribuyen a estas diferencias. No debemos ignorar el impacto de mayor escolaridad de los colombianos y cubanos, aunque los dominicanos tienen menos escuela que los puertorriqueños. Tampoco debemos ignorar el impacto del racismo que favorece a los grupos considerados como más blancos, y el favoritismo que existe al preferir al inmigrante nuevo y más explotable. Muchos patrones corroboran lo que algunos teóricos han propuesto, i.e., que los nuevos están más abiertos a la asimilación que los grupos incorporados a la unión norteamericana forzosamente, como los americanos indígenas, los mexicanos, los afro-americanos y los puertorriqueños (Ogbu y Matute-Bianchi 1986). Lo cierto es que estos grupos más viejos hablan más inglés que muchos de los que viven mejor que ellos. Por razones obvias, estos datos no se mencionan en toda la propaganda de *US English*, organización que pretende imponer el inglés como único idioma oficial, según ellos como una ayuda para el progreso de los inmigrantes. Más abajo analizaremos cómo y por qué este grupo usa datos erróneos para fomentar estereotipos negativos de los que hablan otros idiomas.

2 La norma. Otra vaca sagrada que hemos herido con los estudios del español en los Estados Unidos es la de la norma, o el estándar. En 1985 en la ponencia principal de esta serie de simposios, Elías-Olivares cuestionó la imposición de una norma que no encaja con la realidad de la comunidad. La noción de norma siempre conlleva una idea de lo correcto que le asigna un estatus inferior a otras variedades del habla que existen a la par, y que en realidad pueden ser las más correctas según la ocasión, el tema, etc. En el este de Austin, Tejas, por ejemplo, existen cuatro variedades: el español mexicano, el popular, el mixtureado y el caló. Los mejor preparados para vivir en este barrio de Austin son los que dominan las cuatro, no los que sólo saben un estándar que sigue una norma prescriptiva, la cual se puede escribir pero no se habla allí. Además, ya que el estándar se ha descrito, muy acertadamente, como el dialecto que goza de una fuerza armada (Weinreich, citado en Baugh 1983), se puede ver que en esto de definir el estándar nunca vamos a ganar los pobres. Pensemos en el español de Nuevo México, el cual siempre se describe como una forma anticuada del español, porque se describe en referencia a la norma de otra comunidad, no la de Nuevo México--donde todavía se usan los vocablos como *Asina se hace.* Tampoco vale ser innovador con el idioma; aparentemente ni las formas de ayer se aceptan, ni las de mañana tampoco, al notar la reacción violenta en contra de *troca, lonche, taipear* y otros préstamos. Termina siendo una cuestión de poder, no de lo correcto lingüísticamente. Si la clase trabajadora tuviera el poder político y socio-económico de la clase dominante, el habla de los pobres sería el estándar, lo correcto.

3 El cambio lingüístico. El tema del cambio lingüístico incluye por lo menos dos áreas en las cuales otra vez la situación en la que se encuentran tantos hispanos en diversas comunidades ocasiona una revisión de la teoría y metodología lingüística: (1) las teorías sobre el mantenimiento del español, tanto al nivel individual como al nivel de grupo, y (2) el impacto del contacto lingüístico entre variedades distintas, e.g., entre el inglés y el español, y entre los dialectos distintos del español.

3.1 El mantenimiento del español. Una teoría nos dice que es inevitable que el español no se mantenga en los Estados Unidos una vez crezca la tercera generación, especialmente cuando no se mantienen separados los *domains* de cada idioma. El prognóstico que el bilingüismo sin diglosia no puede sobrevivir, identificado con Fishman (1967), ha sido cuestionado por la cantidad de chicanos de cuarta generación que todavía hablan el español a través del suroeste y el oeste. En otra parte de la nación, las investigaciones del Centro de Estudios Puertorriqueños han verificado el bilingüismo de una comunidad sin diglosia, el barrio puertorriqueño de Nueva York (Pedraza, Attinasi y Hoffman 1980). No cabe duda que el bilingüismo de los chicanos y los llamados *nuyoricans* sí se debe en parte a la emigración continua de hispanoparlantes, pero también se debe al que no se puede determinar nuestro futuro lingüístico basado en la experiencia de otros grupos. No podemos basarnos en la experiencia de los europeos que emigraron durante otra época, con distintas destrezas y características distintas, y por distintas razones. Aquellos grupos perdieron el idioma porque, entre otras razones, no podían o no anhelaban regresar al país, y porque fueron integrados social y económicamente en su tercera generación. En nuestras comunidades la marginación mantiene el español; por ejemplo, se ha probado que la comunidad hispana del Barrio de Nueva York es más segregada que cualquier otra en el país, y que nuestra tercera generación todavía no participa de la buena vida lograda por otros (Mann y Salvo 1985). Debido a estos factores, el modelo de pérdida del idioma a través del tiempo no funciona para esa comunidad. Además, veremos que la metodología influye mucho y afecta el análisis y sus resultados: en este caso oscurece la realidad de otro patrón de mantenimiento del idioma.

Las entrevistas y los cuestionarios pueden revelar algunas actitudes formales y proveen datos demográficos, pero no captan el proceso dinámico del uso del habla en la comunidad y su desarrollo a través del tiempo. Si nos hubiéramos limitado a sólo una encuesta en Nueva York, es posible que los resultados hubieran sido parecidos a los de Martíneztown (Hudson-Edwards y Bills 1983) y otros lugares que aseveran que no se mantiene el español en la segunda y/o tercera generación. El estudio etnográfico que llevé a cabo en el Barrio puertorriqueño de Nueva York por 18 meses (Zentella 1981) corrobora los resultados de los aún más largos estudios del Centro (LPTF 1983, 1984); los tres revelan que aunque los niños sí van perdiendo el español a través de los años escolares, cuando se quedan en la comunidad al casarse y al criar sus hijos logran reintegrarse al uso del español. Al asumir los roles de adulto vuelven a hablar el español porque esos roles se desempeñan en ese idioma en nuestro barrio, particularmente en el caso de la mujer (Zentella 1987). Si siguen los problemas económicos como van, se espera que muchos jóvenes no tengan la oportunidad de salir del barrio, y no seguirán el patrón transgeneracional de los europeos, sino uno de madurez, en el cual la niña/el niño recobra el español al llegar a ser adulto. No pretendo insinuar que este proceso continuará así; si las realidades socio-económicas cambian, también cambian las realidades lingüísticas. Hace falta un sinnúmero de estudios que incorporen estas diferencias, y que se aparten de modelos inadecuados que resultaron de la experiencia de otros grupos cuya asimilación fue basada en otra realidad racial, económica y política.

3.2 **Los dialectos en contacto.** Además de no cumplir con el prognóstico de la pérdida del idioma, tanto al nivel individual como al nivel de grupo, los hispanos tampoco cumplimos con lo esperado en cuanto a algunos efectos del contacto entre los dialectos. Esto lo averiguamos cuando estudiamos la nivelación del léxico español que ocurre en Nueva York, donde puertorriqueños, dominicanos, cubanos, colombianos, y otros están en comunicación diaria (Zentella 1986). Muchos factores señalados por la lingüística tradicional sí juegan un papel en la aceptación y divulgación de un vocablo particular entre todos los hispanos, e.g., el tamaño de los grupos, la necesidad semántica y cuestiones estructurales, pero también es necesario señalar una vez más el impacto de las diferencias socio-económicas sobre los factores tradicionales. Por ejemplo, aunque los puertorriqueños constituyen el 62% de los hispanos en la ciudad, lo cual haría esperar que la forma de hablar puertorriqueña se extendiera a los demás, el estigma que sufren como los más pobres y más desaventajados se extiende a la variedad del español que hablan, la cual se critica mucho. Necesariamente este estigma funciona como una barrera hacia la aceptación de palabras o estructuras gramaticales que provienen del dialecto puertorriqueño. Hay quienes explicarían este rechazo como una repercusión esperada cuando los dialectos conservadores y los radicales (refiriéndose a una fonología conservadora o radical) se encuentran. Los dialectos radicales son los que fueron llevados de Andalucía a las islas del caribe y las costas de Latinoamérica. Los radicales se reconocen por la aspiración o pérdida de la /s/ al final de sílaba, la caída de la /d/ intervocálica y otros procesos de síncope/ácope. En cambio, los dialectos que llegaron a las tierras altas seguían el patrón conservador de Castilla. Según la teoría lingüística expresada por Guitart (1982), los que hablan dialectos radicales tienden a imitar a los conservadores, y no viceversa, lo cual nos haría esperar que los del caribe imitaran a los colombianos y centroamericanos, y que éstos rechazaran la adopción de la pronunciación radical. Sin duda esto ocurre y contribuye al sentido de inferioridad lingüística que sufrimos los puertorriqueños y los dominicanos. Sin embargo, también ocurre lo contrario, i.e., hay conservadores quienes imitan a los radicales debido a circunstancias personales, por ejemplo, si comparten nuestros barrios por mucho tiempo y llegan a identificarse con nuestro grupo, sea por amores o amistades. También conocemos casos de ilegales a quienes les conviene imitar el habla puertorriqueña para evitar expulsión por *la migra* (emigración), dado que los boricuas son ciudadanos americanos. Algo similar fue captado en la película *El Norte* cuando los guatemaltecos ilegales tratan de hablar como mexicanos al fugarse a este país. Es otra prueba que nuestras experiencias como pobres o ilegales o miembros de grupos colonizados y estigmatizados, afectan los procesos lingüísticos de manera inesperada.

Para subrayar el impacto del factor racial, es necesario cuestionar la preferencia que muchos le dan al español cubano entre todos los dialectos caribeños en Nueva York, a pesar de que todos son dialectos radicales que aspiran o pierden la /s/, *se comen* la /d/ intervocálica, etc. Quizás el español de los cubanos goza de mayor estatus porque tienen más educación y más dinero, pero indudablemente estas características son difíciles de desligar del hecho que la ola de inmigración cubana de los '60 también se caracterizaba por ser más blanca que las otras inmigraciones caribeñas. Falta ver si las actitudes cambian con la mayor presencia de mulatos y negros entre los cubanos que salieron por Mariel, i.e., los marielitos de los '80. El impacto lingüístico de estos factores varía de época en época, de comunidad en comunidad y de persona a persona; por eso nos urge estudiar el habla natural de todos los grupos y subgrupos bajo un marco etnográfico y con una metodología que toma en cuenta la dinámica de la conversación además de agregar los resultados por grupos--sea de un análisis de variantes lingüísticas o de las respuestas a un cuestionario. Sólo así podremos entender cómo los miembros de los grupos evalúan y responden a los factores lingüísticos y a los sociales--tales como clase, raza y género sexual--y cómo ayudan a mantener, cambiar y desarrollar los patrones del habla de su grupo.

4 Adquisición y aprendizaje de idioma. Hacemos hincapié en la necesidad de reconocer y resolver los retos que la experiencia hispana representa para la teoría y metodología lingüística porque acarrean repercusiones muy serias no sólo para el progreso de la lingüística, sino para el progreso del pueblo hispano. Las teorías inadecuadas contribuyen a la propagación de unos mitos dañinos.

Entre los mitos más obvios que nuestra experiencia en este país desmienta están los que permean la filosofía educativa de la adquisición y aprendizaje de idiomas. Me refiero en particular a las teorías que mantienen que la submersión de estudiantes en clases donde sólo se les habla inglés es mejor que la educación bilingüe, que la presencia de papeletas electorales y otros documentos bilingües retrasan el conocimiento del inglés, que un bilingüe capaz no mezcla los dos idiomas, que la mezcla es dañina para la estructura de los dos idiomas, que el crecer bilingüe confunde y causa desventajas cognitivas. Una vez más vemos cómo nuestra condición de pobres explica por qué el sistema dominante insiste en imponer estas ideas; aparentemente cuando se nos compara con otros grupos más privilegiados, no respondemos como ellos responden, y en vez de cuestionar cuán apropiadas son las teorías para nosotros, se cuestionan nuestra habilidad y hasta nuestras ganas de progresar.

4.1 La metodología monolingüe versus la bilingüe. La preferencia del gobierno de Reagan por la *educación de submersión* donde sólo se les habla en el idioma que pretenden aprender, en vez de la educación bilingüe, se basa en la experiencia de estudiantes de clase media, i.e., ingleses en Quebec y norteamericanos en Redwood City, quienes sobresalieron en aprender un segundo idioma en clases de submersión. Sin embargo, la experiencia de los niños que aprenden un idioma de menos prestigio porque ya tienen el orgullo de dominar el de más prestigio como nativos que son, no se puede comparar con los que se someten a un proceso de subtracción vía la submersión. Al tratar de reemplazar el idioma nativo y estigmatizado de los niños de grupos minoritarios y sustituirlo con el de mayor poder, los resultados son más negativos que positivos porque el proceso no enriquece, debilita (Lambert 1984). La submersión funciona bien cuando forma parte de una experiencia educativa que pretende expandir el repertorio lingüístico y cultural de los estudiantes del grupo mayoritario, no cuando intenta eliminar el idioma y la cultura del grupo minoritario.

4.2 Los efectos cognitivos. La necesidad de distinguir las diferencias de clase además de los otros factores sociales se verifica a través de la historia de la investigación de los efectos psicológicos del bilingüísmo. La gran mayoría de los estudios hechos antes del 1962 encontraron que el bilingüismo era una desventaja, hasta que los estudiosos de los últimos veinte años probaron que los previos ignoraban la clase social de los niños y otros factores muy relevantes, como el número de años en el país, edad, etc. Recientemente el estudio de Hakuta (1986) representa un repudio completo de las primeras investigaciones, pues prueba que los niños pobres bilingües tienen una capacidad cognitiva superior a la de los monolingües, aunque dominen un idioma más que el otro, y que los beneficios crecen si aumenta el bilingüismo.

4.3 El rol del primer idioma. Otra repercusión negativa de las teorías inadecuadas es el menosprecio de la contribución lingüística que hacen los padres, aunque no sepan inglés. Es común oír a los maestros insistir con los padres que deben tratar de hablarles inglés a los niños a cuanto más sea posible. Se entiende que el niño necesita practicar su inglés, pero los maestros no entienden que sería más valioso que los padres les hablaran el idioma que saben mejor. Al hablarles más español en vez de menos, los padres ayudarían al niño a desarrollar las variedades del uso del idioma oral y escrito, tales como argumentos lógicos, indagaciones, planteamientos y cuestionamientos formales e informales, etc. El trabajo de Heath (1986) explica cómo estas formas verbales y escritas, las cuales son indispensables para el éxito académico, no sólo son transferibles de un idioma a otro, sino que ayudan a acelerar el aprendizaje del segundo idioma.

4.4 La deficiencia verbal. Desgraciadamente, en muchos casos no se aprecia ni se estimula la contribución de los padres porque se juzga el habla de los padres como inferior. Dos décadas después de la refutación devastadora de la teoría de *deficiencia verbal* hecha por Labov (1972), la misma evaluación negativa que se hizo del dialecto afroamericano se extiende a los distintos dialectos del español de la clase trabajadora. Se comete el error de evaluar lo diferente como inferior, pues la lingüística ha comprobado que todo dialecto sigue unas reglas gramaticales que permiten expresar todas las necesidades del grupo cuya historia reflejan. Son diferentes porque la historia de cada grupo es diferente, y llegan a ser juzgadas como inferiores sin ninguna base lingüística.

4.5 La alternancia de idiomas. Los críticos de nuestra habla no se limitan a criticar la variedad del español que hablamos, sino que se sienten muy confiados al menospreciar la alternancia de idiomas que practicamos. Proviene en parte de la definición del *ideal bilingual* como uno que nunca cambia de idiomas cuando habla con la misma persona (Weinreich 1953). En aquellas comunidades donde hay una separación estricta entre los grupos que hablan dos idiomas, como en algunas partes de Europa que Weinreich estudió, es lógico esperar que los bilingües mantendrán los dos idiomas separados. En nuestras comunidades, donde hay un contacto largo, intensivo y conflictivo entre el español y el inglés y las culturas que éstos representan, es de esperarse que los que se sienten parte de estos dos mundos mezclen los dos idiomas entre ellos, en parte como señal de los lazos que los unen. También lo facilita el hecho que las estructuras del inglés y el español son similares y permiten la alternancia. Los lingüistas que hemos analizado esta mezcla encontramos que en su gran mayoría no rompe las leyes gramaticales de ninguno de los dos idiomas, y que provee la oportunidad de lograr unos propósitos comunicativos muy importantes, como lo son el de enfatizar, intercalar, cambiar de roles y facilitar la comprensión, entre muchos más (Poplack 1979; Valdés 1981; y Zentella 1981, 1982). Es más: resulta que los mejores bilingües son los que saben alternar los dos idiomas porque dominan dos estructuras gramaticales. Pero es difícil convencer a los que nos siguen comparando con un ideal estático basado en otra realidad; desafortunadamente terminan convenciendo a los hispanos mismos que sufrimos de una terrible desventaja, en vez de hacernos conscientes del poder comunicativo de esta destreza lingüística.

5 La amenaza del movimiento 'English only.' Nos debemos preguntar por qué no hemos tenido más éxito al tratar de rechazar los mitos que prevalecen sobre nuestra habla. Se debe en parte a lo recién de las investigaciones sociolingüísticas en general, y de la aplicación apropiada de las teorías en relación a la experiencia de los hispanos en este país en específico. También es verdad que los portavoces somos pocos y con pocos recursos para hacernos llegar a las estructuras del poder académico o educativo. De más peso aún es el hecho que la propagación de los mitos de la inferioridad del habla de los hispanos en los Estados Unidos encaja con unas metas nacionales e internacionales de suma importancia. La exaltación de la homogeneidad y la desconfianza de lo diferente surge de una visión muy limitada del futuro de los Estados Unidos. Nada representa esta visión limitada más claramente que los esfuerzos para imponer el inglés como el único idioma oficial.

Los respaldadores para las enmiendas constitucionales tanto al nivel estatal como al federal tienen más fuerza cada día--hay más de 500,000 miembros en *US English* y *English First*--porque tienen acceso a los medios comunicativos. Aparecen en los periódicos, emisoras, canales de televisión y revistas a diario; han podido convencer a miles de norteamericanos que los inmigrantes no quieren aprender el inglés y que las enmiendas asegurarán que lo aprendan. Pretenden ignorar las listas de espera que existen para las clases de inglés--hay más de 30,000 esperando en Los Angeles y aún más en Nueva York--como ignoran todos los estudios que prueban que el 99% de hispanos le dan mucha importancia al poder hablar inglés. Todos respetan y apoyan el inglés como el idioma común del país, pero defienden el derecho de mantener su idioma nativo. También desean contar con unos servicios básicos como la educación, las papeletas electorales y los servicios de emergencia, para los que todavía no saben inglés. Si los respaldadores de *English Only* quieren ayudar, deben expandir los cursos de inglés y entrenamiento para trabajos; ésas son las maneras más efectivas de aprender inglés. Las enmiendas constitucionales no enseñarán inglés pero sí fomentarán actitudes anti-inmigrantes y anti-bilingües.

English Only se aprovecha del miedo que le tienen unos americanos a la presencia creciente en este país y en el hemisferio de otros grupos culturales-- en particular los que hablan español--para atacar la educación bilingüe y las naciones bilingües. Utilizan datos erróneos y hacen prognósticos cataclísmicos. Por ejemplo, mantienen que la educación bilingüe no enseña inglés: 'Research findings on the effectiveness of bilingual education are inconclusive' (*US English* 1987:2); pero los análisis más sistemáticos de estos programas revelan que 'the better the methodology used in the studies, the greater the effect in favor of bilingual programs' (Hakuta y Snow 1986:18). En cuanto a las naciones bilingües, acostumbran decir que la discordia nacional es inevitable; por ejemplo, nos preguntan: 'In order to avoid the political upheavals over language that have torn apart Canada, Belgium, Sri Lanka (Ceylon), India and other nations, would you favor legislation making English the official language of the United States?' (*US English*, sin fecha.) Ni es cierto que los países monolingües evitan la discordia nacional, ni que el bilingüismo la causa en otros países. Las discordias nacionales tienen sus raíces en las inigualdades económicas y políticas, las cuales pueden reflejarse en diferencias lingüísticas, pero no son causadas por éstas. Es más, un estudio amplio de 200 países revela que la discordia se evita precisamente en los países que respetan y reconocen sus diferencias lingüísticas, y que se precipita cuando esas diferencias se ignoran o se repudian (Fishman 1986).

6 La investigación comprometida. Hemos tratado de demostrar cómo los análisis del español en los Estados Unidos, cuando parten de la realidad socio-económica de la comunidad que se estudia, rompen con las definiciones y teorías que son basadas en las experiencias de otros grupos. Exigen que la lingüística defina de nuevo conceptos como la norma, la comunidad del habla y el bilingüe ideal. También contribuimos un enfoque nuevo a las teorías del bilingüismo sin diglosia, el contacto entre los dialectos radicales y conservadores, el proceso de adquisición de idiomas, y los efectos psicológicos de ser bilingüe. En poco tiempo y con pocos recursos hemos logrado bastante, aunque nos falta mucho más. Además de la expansión necesaria de los datos lingüísticos sobre la fonología, morfología, sintaxis y formas de hablar de todos los grupos hispanoparlantes, nos debe preocupar el porqué de nuestro trabajo científico.

No cabe duda que existen visiones distintas de las metas, o lo que debe ser el propósito de la investigación. Algunos creemos que los estudios lingüísticos del habla de un pueblo deberían contribuir no sólo a la mayor comprensión y aceptación de las formas verbales empleadas por el grupo, sino también a la mayor comprensión y aceptación del *grupo*. Eso es esperar mucho más de nuestros esfuerzos que los que se conforman con el expandir la base de nuestro conocimiento con más datos, o la renovación de unas teorías lingüísticas. En los últimos siete años de estos simposios hemos discutido estos distintos puntos de vista, y algunos nos hemos identificado con la primera meta, la *investigación comprometida,* o sea, una investigación que aspira a contribuir al progreso del pueblo a través de los estudios del habla. Según este punto de vista, no nos podemos conformar con investigaciones que sólo acumulan datos, esclarecen algunos puntos, y cambian unas teorías. Debemos utilizar los resultados para mejorar la situación precaria de los hispanos en los Estados Unidos.

¿Cómo se puede lograr un propósito tan difícil a través de unos estudios lingüísticos? Hemos señalado algunas áreas en las cuales la refutación de unos mitos erróneos podría eliminar algunas actitudes dañinas en las escuelas y en las comunidades. Los educadores a quienes se les puede ayudar a apreciar las destrezas de los niños bilingües pueden adaptar una metodología basada en ellas para acelerar su dominio del inglés tanto como el del español. Los legisladores que llegan a entender las diferencias--tanto lingüísticas como históricas y socio-económicas--entre las distintas comunidades hispanas, pueden presentar proyectos de ley que responden a las necesidades de estas comunidades. Un pueblo que pueda aceptar el gran valor de la riqueza multi-cultural y lingüística que los hispanos y otros grupos minoritarios representan para el país, rechazaría todo intento de atacar y eliminar esa variedad, tal como *English Only*. A los estudiosos de la lengua nos toca un rol importantísimo en todo esto, y nos esperan beneficios múltiples. Si ponemos a un lado las actitudes puristas y los marcos inadecuados, no cabe duda que contribuiríamos a una teoría y metodología lingüística más científica. A la vez, podríamos gozar de los frutos de la creatividad lingüística de todos los grupos que son atacados por su forma de hablar, y elaborar una política lingüística que reconociera esa creatividad y la ayudara a florecer para el bienestar de los hispanos y toda la nación.

Referencias

Amastae, J., y L. Elías-Olivares, eds. 1982. *Spanish in the United States: Sociolinguistic aspects.* Nueva York: Cambridge University Press.
Attinasi, J. 1983. Hispanic attitudes in northwest Indiana and Nueva York. En: L. Elías-Olivares et al., eds. (1983).
Baugh, J. 1983. *Black street speech.* Austin: University of Texas Press.
Bergen, J.J., y G.D. Bills, eds. 1983. *Spanish and Portuguese in social context.* Wáshington, D.C.: Georgetown University Press.
Bowen, J.D. 1952. The Spanish of San Antoñito, New Mexico. Tesis doctoral, University of New Mexico.
Chomsky, N. 1965. *Aspects of the theory of syntax.* Cambridge, Mass.: MIT Press.
Durán, R., ed. 1981. *Latino language and communicative behavior.* Norwood, N.J.: Ablex Press.
Elías-Olivares, L., ed. 1983. *Spanish in the U.S. setting: Beyond the Southwest.* Riverside, Calif.: National Clearinghouse for Bilingual Education.

_____. 1986. El español chicano y el problema de la norma lingüística. Keynote address, VI simposio anual sobre el español en los Estados Unidos. University of Texas at Austin.

_____, E. Leone, R. Cisneros y J. Gutiérrez, eds. 1983. *Spanish language use and public life in the United States.* Berlín: Mouton.

Espinosa, A. 1909. Studies in New Mexican Spanish. Part I: Phonology. Tesis doctoral, University of Chicago.

Ferguson, C. 1964. Diglossia. En: *Language in culture and society.* D. Hymes, ed. Nueva York: Harper and Row.

_____, y S.B. Heath, eds. 1983. *Language in the U.S.A.* Nueva York: Cambridge University Press.

Fishman, J. 1967. Bilingualism with and without diglossia. *Journal of Social Issues* 23.29-38.

_____. 1986. Bilingualism and separatism. *Annals of the American Academy of Political and Social Sciences* 487.169-80.

_____, y G. Keller, eds. 1982. *Bilingual education for Hispanic students in the U.S.* Nueva York: Teachers College, Columbia University.

Guitart, J. 1982. Conservative versus radical dialects in Spanish: Implications for language instruction. En: J. Fishman y G. Keller (1982:167-77).

Gumperz, J., y D. Hymes, eds. 1964. The ethnography of communication. Special publication, *American Anthropologist* 66.1-34. Wáshington, D.C.: American Anthropological Association.

_____, eds. 1972. Directions in sociolinguistics. Nueva York: Holt, Rinehart and Winston.

Hakuta, K. 1986. *The mirror of language.* Nueva York: Basic Books.

_____, y C. Snow. 1986. The role of research in policy decisions about bilingual education. *NABE News IX* 3:1.18-21.

Heath, S.B. 1986. Sociocultural contexts of language development. En: *Beyond language: Social and cultural factors in schooling language minority students.* Bilingual Education Office, California State Department of Education, editores. Evaluation, Dissemination and Assessment Center, California State University at Los Angeles.

Hudson-Edwards, A., y G.D. Bills. 1982. Intergenerational language shift in an Albuquerque barrio. En: J. Amastae y L. Elías-Olivares, eds. (1982:135-53).

Hymes, D. 1974. *Foundations in sociolinguistics: An ethnographic approach.* Filadelfia: University of Pennsylvania Press.

Labov, W. 1966. The social stratification of English in New York City. Wáshington, D.C.: Center for Applied Linguistics.

_____. 1972. The logic of non-standard English. En: *Language in the inner city: Studies in the Black English vernacular.* W. Labov, ed. Filadelfia: University of Pennsylvania Press.

Lambert, W. 1984. An overview of issues in immersion education. En: *Studies on immersion education: A collection for United States educators.* Office of Bilingual Education, eds. Los Angeles: California State Department of Education.

Language Policy Task Force (LPTF). 1980. *Social dimensions of language use in East Harlem.* Nueva York: Centro de Estudios Puertorriqueños.

_____. 1983. *Intergenerational perspectives on bilingualism.* Nueva York: Centro de Estudios Puertorriqueños.

_____. 1984. *Speech and ways of speaking in a bilingual Puerto Rican community.* Final report to the National Institute of Education, G 81-0054. Nueva York: Research Foundation of City University of New York.

Mann, E., y J. Salvo. 1985. Characteristics of new Hispanic immigrants to New York City: A comparison of Puerto Rican and non-Puerto Rican Hispanics. *Research Bulletin of the Hispanic Research Center* 8.1-2:1-8.

Milroy, L. 1987. *Language and social networks.* 2a ed. Oxford: Basil Blackwell.

Ogbu, J., y M.E. Matute-Bianchi. 1986. Understanding sociocultural factors: Knowledge, identity, and school adjustment. En: *Beyond language: Social and cultural factors in schooling language minority students.* 73-142.

Pedraza, P., J. Attinasi y G. Hoffman. 1980. Rethinking diglossia. *Working Paper No. 9*. Nueva York: Centro de Estudios Puertorriqueños, City University of New York.

Poplack, S. 1979. Sometimes I'll start a sentence in English Y TERMINO EN ESPAÑOL. *Working Paper No. 5*. Nueva York: Centro de Estudios Puertorriqueños, City University of New York.

Solé, C. 1982. Language loyalty and language attitudes among Cuban Americans. En: J. Fishman y G. Keller (1982:254-69).

Teschner, R., G.D. Bills y J. Craddock, eds. 1975. *Spanish and English of United States Hispanos: A critical, annotated, linguistic bibliography*. Arlington, Va.: Center for Applied Linguistics.

Trudgill, P. 1974. *Sociolinguistics: An introduction*. Nueva York: Penguin.

U.S. English. Sin fecha. *National opinion survey on language use in the United States*.

_____. 1987. *Fact sheet: Bilingual education*.

Valdés, G. 1981. Code switching as a deliberate verbal strategy: A microanalysis of direct and indirect requests among Chicano bilingual speakers. En: Durán (1981).

Weinreich, U. 1953. *Languages in contact*. Nueva York: Linguistic Circle of New York.

Zentella, A.C. 1981. Hablamos los dos. We speak both: Growing up bilingual en el barrio. Tesis doctoral, University of Pennsylvania.

_____. 1982. Spanish and English in contact in the U.S.: The Puerto Rican experience. En: *Spanish in the Western Hemisphere*. Special issue of *Word* 33:1-2.41-57.

_____. 1986. Dialect levelling in New York City Spanish. Trabajo presentado en el Northeast regional meeting of the American Association of Teachers of Spanish and Portuguese, University of Massachusetts, Amherst.

_____. 1987. Language and female identity in the Puerto Rican community. En: *Women and language in transition*. J. Penfield, ed. Albany, N.Y.: SUNY Press.

_____. 1990. Returned migration, language, and identity: Puerto Rican bilinguals in *dos worlds/two mundos*. En: *Spanish in the USA: New quandaries and prospects*. F. Coulmas, ed. *International Journal of the Sociology of Language* 8.